Ensemble Methods

Foundations and Algorithms

Chapman & Hall/CRC
Machine Learning & Pattern Recognition Series

SERIES EDITORS

Ralf Herbrich and Thore Graepel
Microsoft Research Ltd.
Cambridge, UK

AIMS AND SCOPE

This series reflects the latest advances and applications in machine learning and pattern recognition through the publication of a broad range of reference works, textbooks, and handbooks. The inclusion of concrete examples, applications, and methods is highly encouraged. The scope of the series includes, but is not limited to, titles in the areas of machine learning, pattern recognition, computational intelligence, robotics, computational/statistical learning theory, natural language processing, computer vision, game AI, game theory, neural networks, computational neuroscience, and other relevant topics, such as machine learning applied to bioinformatics or cognitive science, which might be proposed by potential contributors.

PUBLISHED TITLES

MACHINE LEARNING: An Algorithmic Perspective
Stephen Marsland

HANDBOOK OF NATURAL LANGUAGE PROCESSING,
Second Edition
Nitin Indurkhya and Fred J. Damerau

UTILITY-BASED LEARNING FROM DATA
Craig Friedman and Sven Sandow

A FIRST COURSE IN MACHINE LEARNING
Simon Rogers and Mark Girolami

COST-SENSITIVE MACHINE LEARNING
Balaji Krishnapuram, Shipeng Yu, and Bharat Rao

ENSEMBLE METHODS: FOUNDATIONS AND ALGORITHMS
Zhi-Hua Zhou

Chapman & Hall/CRC
Machine Learning & Pattern Recognition Series

Ensemble Methods

Foundations and Algorithms

Zhi-Hua Zhou

CRC Press
Taylor & Francis Group
Boca Raton   London   New York

CRC Press is an imprint of the
Taylor & Francis Group, an **informa** business

A CHAPMAN & HALL BOOK

CRC Press
Taylor & Francis Group
6000 Broken Sound Parkway NW, Suite 300
Boca Raton, FL 33487-2742

International Standard Book Number: 978-1-4398-3003-1 (Hardback)

Library of Congress Cataloging-in-Publication Data

Zhou, Zhi-Hua, Ph. D.
    Ensemble methods : foundations and algorithms / Zhi-Hua Zhou.
        p. cm. -- (Chapman & Hall/CRC machine learning & pattern recognition series)
    Summary: "This comprehensive book presents an in-depth and systematic introduction to ensemble methods for researchers in machine learning, data mining, and related areas. It helps readers solve modern problems in machine learning using these methods. The author covers the spectrum of research in ensemble methods, including such famous methods as boosting, bagging, and rainforest, along with current directions and methods not sufficiently addressed in other books. Chapters explore cutting-edge topics, such as semi-supervised ensembles, cluster ensembles, and comprehensibility, as well as successful applications"-- Provided by publisher.
    Includes bibliographical references and index.
    ISBN 978-1-4398-3003-1 (hardback)
    1. Multiple comparisons (Statistics) 2. Set theory. 3. Mathematical analysis. I. Title.

QA278.4.Z47 2012
006.3'1--dc23   2012014555

Visit the Taylor & Francis Web site at
http://www.taylorandfrancis.com

and the CRC Press Web site at
http://www.crcpress.com

To my parents, wife and son.

Z.-H. Zhou

Preface

Ensemble methods that train multiple learners and then combine them for use, with Boosting and Bagging as representatives, are a kind of state-of-the-art learning approach. It is well known that an ensemble is usually significantly more accurate than a single learner, and ensemble methods have already achieved great success in many real-world tasks.

It is difficult to trace the starting point of the history of ensemble methods since the basic idea of deploying multiple models has been in use in human society for a long time; however, it is clear that ensemble methods have become a hot topic since the 1990s, and researchers from various fields such as machine learning, pattern recognition, data mining, neural networks and statistics have explored ensemble methods from different aspects.

This book provides researchers, students and practitioners with an introduction to ensemble methods. The book consists of eight chapters which naturally constitute three parts.

Part I is composed of Chapter 1. Though this book is mainly written for readers with a basic knowledge of machine learning and pattern recognition, to enable readers who are unfamiliar with these fields to access the main contents, Chapter 1 presents some "background knowledge" of ensemble methods. It is impossible to provide a detailed introduction to all backgrounds in one chapter, and therefore this chapter serves mainly as a guide to further study. This chapter also serves to explain the terminology used in this book, to avoid confusion caused by other terminologies used in different but relevant fields.

Part II is composed of Chapters 2 to 5 and presents "core knowledge" of ensemble methods. Chapters 2 and 3 introduce Boosting and Bagging, respectively. In addition to algorithms and theories, Chapter 2 introduces multi-class extension and noise tolerance, since classic Boosting algorithms are designed for binary classification, and are usually hurt seriously by noise. Bagging is naturally a multi-class method and less sensitive to noise, and therefore, Chapter 3 does not discuss these issues; instead, Chapter 3 devotes a section to Random Forest and some other random tree ensembles that can be viewed as variants of Bagging. Chapter 4 introduces combination methods. In addition to various averaging and voting schemes, the Stacking method and some other combination methods as well as relevant methods such as mixture of experts are introduced. Chapter 5 focuses on ensemble diversity. After introducing the error-ambiguity and bias-variance decompositions, many diversity measures are presented, followed by recent advances in information theoretic diversity and diversity generation methods.

Part III is composed of Chapters 6 to 8, and presents "advanced knowledge" of ensemble methods. Chapter 6 introduces ensemble pruning, which tries to prune a trained ensemble to get a better performance. Chapter 7 introduces clustering ensembles, which try to generate better clustering results by combining multiple clusterings. Chapter 8 presents some developments of ensemble methods in semi-supervised learning, active learning, cost-sensitive learning and class-imbalance learning, as well as comprehensibility enhancement.

It is not the goal of the book to cover all relevant knowledge of ensemble methods. Ambitious readers may be interested in *Further Reading* sections for further information.

Two other books [Kuncheva, 2004, Rokach, 2010] on ensemble methods have been published before this one. To reflect the fast development of this field, I have attempted to present an updated and in-depth overview. However, when writing this book, I found this task more challenging than expected. Despite abundant research on ensemble methods, a thorough understanding of many essentials is still needed, and there is a lack of thorough empirical comparisons of many technical developments. As a consequence, several chapters of the book simply introduce a number of algorithms, while even for chapters with discussions on theoretical issues, there are still important yet unclear problems. On one hand, this reflects the still developing situation of the ensemble methods field; on the other hand, such a situation provides a good opportunity for further research.

The book could not have been written, at least not in its current form, without the help of many people. I am grateful to Tom Dietterich who has carefully read the whole book and given very detailed and insightful comments and suggestions. I want to thank Songcan Chen, Nan Li, Xu-Ying Liu, Fabio Roli, Jianxin Wu, Yang Yu and Min-Ling Zhang for helpful comments. I also want to thank Randi Cohen and her colleagues at Chapman & Hall/CRC Press for cooperation.

Last, but definitely not least, I am indebted to my family, friends and students for their patience, support and encouragement.

Zhi-Hua Zhou
Nanjing, China

Notations

x	variable
$\boldsymbol{x}$	vector
$\mathbf{A}$	matrix
$\mathbf{I}$	identity matrix
$\mathcal{X}, \mathcal{Y}$	input and output spaces
$\mathcal{D}$	probability distribution
D	data sample (data set)
$\mathcal{N}$	normal distribution
$\mathcal{U}$	uniform distribution
$\mathcal{H}$	hypothesis space
H	set of hypotheses
$h(\cdot)$	hypothesis (learner)
$\mathfrak{L}$	learning algorithm
$p(\cdot)$	probability density function
$p(\cdot \mid \cdot)$	conditional probability density function
$P(\cdot)$	probability mass function
$P(\cdot \mid \cdot)$	conditional probability mass function
$\mathbb{E}_{.\sim\mathcal{D}}[f(\cdot)]$	mathematical expectation of function $f(\cdot)$ to $\cdot$ under distribution $\mathcal{D}$. $\mathcal{D}$ and/or $\cdot$ is ignored when the meaning is clear
$var._{.\sim\mathcal{D}}[f(\cdot)]$	variance of function $f(\cdot)$ to $\cdot$ under distribution $\mathcal{D}$
$\mathbb{I}(\cdot)$	indicator function which takes 1 if $\cdot$ is true, and 0 otherwise
$\text{sign}(\cdot)$	sign function which takes -1,1 and 0 when $\cdot < 0$, $\cdot > 0$ and $\cdot = 0$, respectively
$err(\cdot)$	error function
$\{\dots\}$	set
$(\dots)$	row vector

$(\ldots)^{\top}$	column vector
$\lvert \cdot \rvert$	size of data set
$\lVert \cdot \rVert$	L_2-norm

Contents

Contents

1
Introduction

1.1 Basic Concepts

One major task of machine learning, pattern recognition and data mining is to construct *good* **models** from **data sets**.

A "data set" generally consists of **feature vectors**, where each feature vector is a description of an object by using a set of **features**. For example, take a look at the synthetic *three-Gaussians* data set as shown in Figure 1.1. Here, each object is a data point described by the features x-coordinate, y-coordinate and shape, and a feature vector looks like (.5, .8, cross) or (.4, .5, circle). The number of features of a data set is called **dimension** or **dimensionality**; for example, the dimensionality of the above data set is three. Features are also called **attributes**, a feature vector is also called an **instance**, and sometimes a data set is called a **sample**.

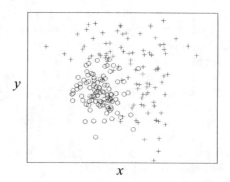

FIGURE 1.1: The synthetic *three-Gaussians* data set.

A "model" is usually a predictive model or a model of the structure of the data that we want to construct or discover from the data set, such as a decision tree, a neural network, a support vector machine, etc. The process of generating models from data is called **learning** or **training**, which is accomplished by a **learning algorithm**. The learned model can be called a **hypothesis**, and in this book it is also called a **learner**. There are different learning settings, among which the most common ones are **supervised learning** and **unsupervised learning**. In supervised learning, the goal is to predict the value of a target feature on unseen instances, and the learned model is also called a **predictor**. For example, if we want to predict the shape of the *three-Gaussians* data points, we call "cross" and "circle" **labels**, and the predictor should be able to predict the label of an instance for which the label information is unknown, e.g., (.2, .3). If the label is *categorical*, such as shape, the task is also called **classification** and the learner is also called **classifier**; if the label is *numerical*, such as x-coordinate, the task is also called **regression** and the learner is also called **fitted regression model**. For both cases, the training process is conducted on data sets containing label information, and an instance with known label is also called an **example**. In **binary classification**, generally we use "positive" and "negative" to denote the two class labels. Unsupervised learning does not rely on label information, the goal of which is to discover some inherent distribution information in the data. A typical task is **clustering**, aiming to discover the cluster structure of data points. In most of this book we will focus on supervised learning, especially classification. We will introduce some popular learning algorithms briefly in Section 1.2.

Basically, whether a model is "good" depends on whether it can meet the requirements of the user or not. Different users might have different expectations of the learning results, and it is difficult to know the "right expectation" before the concerned task has been tackled. A popular strategy is to evaluate and estimate the performance of the models, and then let the user to decide whether a model is acceptable, or choose the best available model from a set of candidates. Since the fundamental goal of learning is **generalization**, i.e., being capable of generalizing the "knowledge" learned from training data to unseen instances, a good learner should generalize well, i.e., have a small **generalization error**, also called the **prediction error**. It is infeasible, however, to estimate the generalization error directly, since that requires knowing the **ground-truth** label information which is unknown for unseen instances. A typical empirical process is to let the predictor make predictions on **test data** of which the ground-truth labels are known, and take the **test error** as an estimate of the generalization error. The process of applying a learned model to unseen data is called **testing**. Before testing, a learned model often needs to be configured, e.g., tuning the parameters, and this process also involves the use of data with known ground-truth labels to evaluate the learning performance; this is called **validation** and the data is **validation data**. Generally, the test data should not overlap with the training and validation data; otherwise the estimated performance can be over-optimistic. More introduction on performance evaluation will be given in Section 1.3.

A formal formulation of the learning process is as follows: Denote $\mathcal{X}$ as the instance space, $\mathcal{D}$ as a distribution over $\mathcal{X}$, and f the *ground-truth* target function. Given a training data set $D = \{(\boldsymbol{x}_1, y_1), (\boldsymbol{x}_2, y_2), \ldots, (\boldsymbol{x}_m, y_m)\}$, where the instances $\boldsymbol{x}_i$ are drawn ***i.i.d.*** (independently and identically distributed) from $\mathcal{D}$ and $y_i = f(\boldsymbol{x}_i)$, taking classification as an example, the goal is to construct a learner h which minimizes the generalization error

$$err(h) = \mathbb{E}_{\boldsymbol{x} \sim \mathcal{D}}[\mathbb{I}(h(\boldsymbol{x}) \neq f(\boldsymbol{x}))]. \tag{1.1}$$

1.2 Popular Learning Algorithms

1.2.1 Linear Discriminant Analysis

A **linear classifier** consists of a **weight vector** $\boldsymbol{w}$ and a **bias** b. Given an instance $\boldsymbol{x}$, the predicted class label y is obtained according to

$$y = \mathtt{sign}(\boldsymbol{w}^\top \boldsymbol{x} + b). \tag{1.2}$$

The classification process is accomplished by two steps. First, the instance space is mapped onto a one-dimensional space (i.e., a line) through the weight vector $\boldsymbol{w}$; then, a point on the line is identified to separate the positive instances from negative ones.

To find the best $\boldsymbol{w}$ and b for separating different classes, a classical linear learning algorithm is *Fisher's linear discriminant analysis* (LDA). Briefly, the idea of LDA is to enable instances of different classes to be far away while instances within the same class to be close; this can be accomplished by making the distance between centers of different classes large while keeping the variance within each class small.

Given a two-class training set, we consider all the positive instances, and obtain the mean $\boldsymbol{\mu}_+$ and the covariance matrix Σ_+; similarly, we consider all the negative instances, and obtain the mean $\boldsymbol{\mu}_-$ and the covariance matrix Σ_-. The distance between the projected class centers is measured as

$$S_B(\boldsymbol{w}) = (\boldsymbol{w}^\top \boldsymbol{\mu}_+ - \boldsymbol{w}^\top \boldsymbol{\mu}_-)^2, \tag{1.3}$$

and the variance within classes is measured as

$$S_W(\boldsymbol{w}) = \boldsymbol{w}^\top \Sigma_+ \boldsymbol{w} + \boldsymbol{w}^\top \Sigma_- \boldsymbol{w}. \tag{1.4}$$

LDA combines these two measures by maximizing

$$J(\boldsymbol{w}) = S_B(\boldsymbol{w})/S_W(\boldsymbol{w}), \tag{1.5}$$

of which the optimal solution has a closed-form

$$\boldsymbol{w}^* = (\Sigma_+ + \Sigma_-)^{-1}(\boldsymbol{\mu}_+ - \boldsymbol{\mu}_-). \tag{1.6}$$

After obtaining $\boldsymbol{w}$, it is easy to calculate the bias b. The simplest way is to let b be the middle point between the projected centers, i.e.,

$$b^* = \boldsymbol{w}^\top (\boldsymbol{\mu}_+ + \boldsymbol{\mu}_-)/2, \tag{1.7}$$

which is optimal when the two classes are from normal distributions sharing the same variance.

Figure 1.2 illustrates the decision boundary of an LDA classifier.

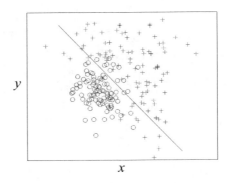

FIGURE 1.2: Decision boundary of LDA on the *three-Gaussians* data set.

1.2.2   Decision Trees

A decision tree consists of a set of tree-structured decision tests working in a *divide-and-conquer* way. Each non-leaf node is associated with a **feature test** also called a **split**; data falling into the node will be split into different subsets according to their different values on the feature test. Each leaf node is associated with a label, which will be assigned to instances falling into this node. In prediction, a series of feature tests is conducted starting from the root node, and the result is obtained when a leaf node is reached. Take Figure 1.3 as an example. The classification process starts by testing whether the value of the feature y-coordinate is larger than 0.73; if so, the instance is classified as "cross", and otherwise the tree tests whether the feature value of x-coordinate is larger than 0.64; if so, the instance is classified as "cross" and otherwise is classified as "circle".

Decision tree learning algorithms are generally recursive processes. In each step, a data set is given and a split is selected, then this split is used to divide the data set into subsets, and each subset is considered as the given data set for the next step. The key of a decision tree algorithm is how to select the splits.

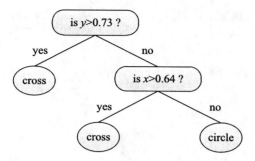

FIGURE 1.3: An example of a decision tree.

In the ID3 algorithm [Quinlan, 1998], the **information gain** criterion is employed for split selection. Given a training set D, the **entropy** of D is defined as

$$Ent(D) = -\sum_{y \in \mathcal{Y}} P(y|D) \log P(y|D). \qquad (1.8)$$

If the training set D is divided into subsets $D_1, \ldots, D_k$, the entropy may be reduced, and the amount of the reduction is the information gain, i.e.,

$$G(D; D_1, \ldots, D_k) = Ent(D) - \sum_{i=1}^{k} \frac{|D_k|}{|D|} Ent(D_k). \qquad (1.9)$$

Thus, the feature-value pair which will cause the largest information gain is selected for the split.

One problem with the information gain criterion is that features with a lot of possible values will be favored, disregarding their relevance to classification. For example, suppose we are dealing with binary classification and each instance has a unique "*id*", and if the "*id*" is considered as a feature, the information gain of taking this feature as split would be quite large since this split will classify every training instance correctly; however, it cannot generalize and thus will be useless for making prediction on unseen instances.

This deficiency of the information gain criterion is addressed in C4.5 [Quinlan, 1993], the most famous decision tree algorithm. C4.5 employs the **gain ratio**

$$P(D; D_1, \ldots, D_k) = G(D; D_1, \ldots, D_k) \cdot \left(-\sum_{i=1}^{k} \frac{|D_k|}{|D|} \log \frac{|D_k|}{|D|} \right)^{-1}, \qquad (1.10)$$

which is a variant of the information gain criterion, taking **normalization** on the number of feature values. In practice, the feature with the highest gain ratio, among features with better-than-average information gains, is selected as the split.

CART [Breiman et al., 1984] is another famous decision tree algorithm, which uses **Gini index** for selecting the split maximizing the Gini

$$G_{gini}(D; D_1, \ldots, D_k) = I(D) - \sum_{i=1}^{k} \frac{|D_k|}{|D|} I(D_k), \qquad (1.11)$$

where

$$I(D) = 1 - \sum_{y \in \mathcal{Y}} P(y \mid D)^2. \qquad (1.12)$$

It is often observed that a decision tree, which is perfect on the training set, will have a worse generalization ability than a tree which is not-so-good on the training set; this is called **overfitting** which may be caused by the fact that some peculiarities of the training data, such as those caused by noise in collecting training examples, are misleadingly recognized by the learner as the underlying truth. To reduce the risk of overfitting, a general strategy is to employ **pruning** to cut off some tree branches caused by noise or peculiarities of the training set. **Pre-pruning** tries to prune branches when the tree is being grown, while **post-pruning** re-examines fully grown trees to decide which branches should be removed. When a validation set is available, the tree can be pruned according to the validation error: for pre-pruning, a branch will not be grown if the validation error will increase by growing the branch; for post-pruning, a branch will be removed if the removal will decrease the validation error.

Early decision tree algorithms, such as ID3, could only deal with categorical features. Later ones, such as C4.5 and CART, are enabled to deal with numerical features. The simplest way is to evaluate every possible split point on the numerical feature that divides the training set into two subsets, where one subset contains instances with the feature value smaller than the split point while the other subset contains the remaining instances.

When the height of a decision tree is limited to 1, i.e., it takes only one test to make every prediction, the tree is called a **decision stump**. While decision trees are nonlinear classifiers in general, decision stumps are a kind of linear classifiers.

Figure 1.4 illustrates the decision boundary of a typical decision tree.

1.2.3 Neural Networks

Neural networks, also called **artificial neural networks**, originated from simulating biological neural networks. The function of a neural network is determined by the model of **neuron**, the network structure, and the learning algorithm.

Neuron is also called **unit**, which is the basic computational component in neural networks. The most popular neuron model, i.e., the *McCulloch-Pitts* model (**M-P model**), is illustrated in Figure 1.5(a). In this model, input

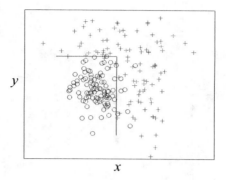

FIGURE 1.4: Decision boundary of a typical decision tree on the *three-Gaussians* data set.

signals are multiplied with corresponding **connection weights** at first, and then signals are aggregated and compared with a threshold, also called **bias** of the neuron. If the aggregated signal is larger than the bias, the neuron will be activated and the output signal is generated by an **activation function**, also called *transfer function* or *squashing function*.

Neurons are linked by weighted connections to form a network. There are many possible network structures, among which the most popular one is the **multi-layer feed-forward network**, as illustrated in Figure 1.5(b). Here the neurons are connected layer-by-layer, and there are neither in-layer connections nor cross-layer connections. There is an **input layer** which receives input feature vectors, where each neuron usually corresponds to one element of the feature vector. The activation function for input neurons is usually set as $f(x) = x$. There is an **output layer** which outputs labels, where each neuron usually corresponds to a possible label, or an element of a *label vector*. The layers between the input and output layers are called **hidden layers**. The hidden neurons and output neurons are functional units, and a popular activation function for them is the **sigmoid function**

$$f(x) = \frac{1}{1 + e^{-x}}. \tag{1.13}$$

Although one may use a network with many hidden layers, the most popular setting is to use one or two hidden layers, since it is known that a feed-forward neural network with one hidden layer is already able to approximate any continuous function, and more complicated algorithms are needed to prevent networks with many hidden layers from suffering from problems such as divergence (i.e., the networks do not converge to a stable state).

The goal of training a neural network is to determine the values of the connection weights and the biases of the neurons. Once these values are

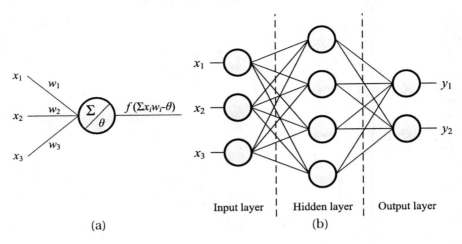

(a)   (b)

FIGURE 1.5: Illustration of (a) a neuron, and (b) a neural network.

decided, the function computed by the neural network is decided. There are many neural network learning algorithms. The most commonly applied idea for training a multi-layer feed-forward neural network is that, as long as the activation function is differentiable, the whole neural network can be regarded as a differentiable function which can be optimized by **gradient descent** method.

The most successful algorithm, **Back-Propagation (BP)** [Werbos, 1974, Rumelhart et al., 1986], works as follows. At first, the inputs are feed-forwarded from the input layer via the hidden layer to the output layer, at which the error is calculated by comparing the network output with the ground-truth. Then, the error will be back propagated to the hidden layer and the input layer, during which the connection weights and biases are adjusted to reduce the error. The process is accomplished by tuning towards the direction with the gradient. Such a process will be repeated in many rounds, until the training error is minimized or the training process is terminated to avoid overfitting.

1.2.4 Naïve Bayes Classifier

To classify a test instance x, one approach is to formulate a probabilistic model to estimate the posterior probability $P(y \mid x)$ of different y's, and predict the one with the largest posterior probability; this is the ***maximum a posterior*** (**MAP**) rule. By *Bayes Theorem*, we have

$$P(y \mid x) = \frac{P(x \mid y)P(y)}{P(x)},$$

(1.14)

where $P(y)$ can be estimated by counting the proportion of class y in the training set, and $P(x)$ can be ignored since we are comparing different y's on the same x. Thus we only need to consider $P(x \mid y)$. If we can get an accurate estimate of $P(x \mid y)$, we will get the best classifier in theory from the given training data, that is, the **Bayes optimal classifier** with the **Bayes error rate**, the smallest error rate in theory. However, estimating $P(x \mid y)$ is not straightforward, since it involves the estimation of exponential numbers of joint-probabilities of the features. To make the estimation tractable, some assumptions are needed.

The naïve Bayes classifier assumes that, given the class label, the n features are independent of each other within each class. Thus, we have

$$P(x \mid y) = \prod_{i=1}^{n} P(x_i \mid y),$$ (1.15)

which implies that we only need to estimate each feature value in each class in order to estimate the conditional probability, and therefore the calculation of joint-probabilities is avoided.

In the training stage, the naïve Bayes classifier estimates the probabilities $P(y)$ for all classes $y \in \mathcal{Y}$, and $P(x_i \mid y)$ for all features $i = 1, \ldots, n$ and all feature values x_i from the training set. In the test stage, a test instance x will be predicted with label y if y leads to the largest value of

$$P(y \mid x) \propto P(y) \prod_{i=1}^{n} P(x_i \mid y)$$ (1.16)

among all the class labels.

1.2.5 k-Nearest Neighbor

The k-nearest neighbor (kNN) algorithm relies on the principle that objects similar in the input space are also similar in the output space. It is a **lazy learning** approach since it does not have an explicit training process, but simply stores the training set instead. For a test instance, a k-nearest neighbor learner identifies the k instances from the training set that are closest to the test instance. Then, for classification, the test instance will be classified to the majority class among the k instances; while for regression, the test instance will be assigned the average value of the k instances. Figure 1.6(a) illustrates how to classify an instance by a 3-nearest neighbor classifier. Figure 1.6(b) shows the decision boundary of a 1-nearest neighbor classifier, also called the **nearest neighbor classifier**.

1.2.6 Support Vector Machines and Kernel Methods

Support vector machines (SVMs) [Cristianini and Shawe-Taylor, 2000], originally designed for binary classification, are **large margin classifiers**

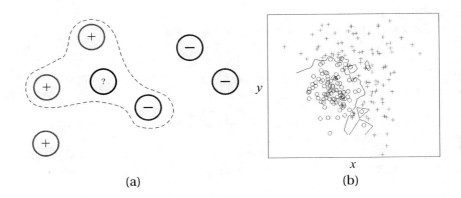

(a)   (b)

FIGURE 1.6: Illustration of (a) how a k-nearest neighbor classifier predicts on a test instance, and (b) the decision boundary of the nearest neighbor classifier on the *three-Gaussians* data set.

that try to separate instances of different classes with the maximum margin hyperplane. The **margin** is defined as the minimum distance from instances of different classes to the classification hyperplane.

Considering a linear classifier $y = \text{sign}(\boldsymbol{w}^\top \boldsymbol{x} + b)$, or abbreviated as $(\boldsymbol{w}, b)$, we can use the **hinge loss** to evaluate the fitness to the data:

$$\sum_{i=1}^{m} \max\{0, 1 - y_i(\boldsymbol{w}^\top \boldsymbol{x}_i + b)\}. \tag{1.17}$$

The Euclidean distance from an instance $\boldsymbol{x}_i$ to the hyperplane $\boldsymbol{w}^\top \boldsymbol{x} + b$ is

$$\frac{|\boldsymbol{w}^\top \boldsymbol{x}_i + b|}{\|\boldsymbol{w}\|}. \tag{1.18}$$

If we restrict $|\boldsymbol{w}^\top \boldsymbol{x}_i + b| \geq 1$ for all instances, the minimum distance to the hyperplane is $\|\boldsymbol{w}\|^{-1}$. Therefore, SVMs maximize $\|\boldsymbol{w}\|^{-1}$.

Thus, SVMs solve the optimization problem

$$(\boldsymbol{w}^*, b^*) = \underset{\boldsymbol{w}, b, \xi_i}{\arg\min} \frac{\|\boldsymbol{w}\|^2}{2} + C \sum_{i=1}^{m} \xi_i \tag{1.19}$$

$$s.t. \quad y_i(\boldsymbol{w}^\top \boldsymbol{x}_i + b) \geq 1 - \xi_i \ (\forall i = 1, \dots, m)$$

$$\xi_i \geq 0 \ (\forall i = 1, \dots, m),$$

where C is a parameter and ξ_i's are *slack variables* introduced to enable the learner to deal with data that could not be perfectly separated, such as data with noise. An illustration of an SVM is shown in Figure 1.7.

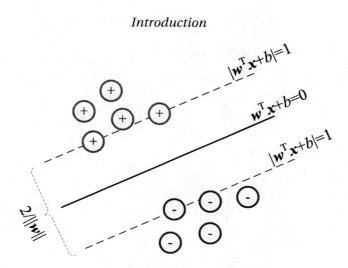

FIGURE 1.7: Illustration of SVM.

(1.19) is called the *primal* form of the optimization. The *dual* form, which gives the same optimal solution, is

$$\boldsymbol{\alpha}^* = \arg\max_{\boldsymbol{\alpha}} \sum_{i=1}^{m} \alpha_i - \frac{1}{2} \sum_{i=1}^{m} \sum_{j=1}^{m} \alpha_i \alpha_j y_i y_j \langle \boldsymbol{x}_i, \boldsymbol{x}_j \rangle \qquad (1.20)$$

$$s.t. \quad \sum_{i=1}^{m} \alpha_i y_i = 0$$

$$\alpha_i \geq 0 \; (\forall i = 1, \ldots, m) \,,$$

where $\langle \cdot, \cdot \rangle$ is the inner product. The solution $\boldsymbol{w}^*$ of the primal form is now presented as

$$\boldsymbol{w}^* = \sum_{i=1}^{m} \alpha_i^* y_i \boldsymbol{x}_i \,, \qquad (1.21)$$

and the inner product between $\boldsymbol{w}^*$ and an instance $\boldsymbol{x}$ can be calculated as

$$\langle \boldsymbol{w}^*, \boldsymbol{x} \rangle = \sum_{i=1}^{m} \alpha_i^* y_i \langle \boldsymbol{x}_i, \boldsymbol{x} \rangle \,. \qquad (1.22)$$

A limitation of the linear classifiers is that, when the data is intrinsically nonlinear, linear classifiers cannot separate the classes well. In such cases, a general approach is to map the data points onto a higher-dimensional feature space where the data linearly non-separable in the original feature space become linearly separable. However, the learning process may become very slow and even intractable since the inner product will be difficult to calculate in the high-dimensional space.

Fortunately, there is a class of functions, **kernel functions** (also called **kernels**), which can help address the problem. The feature space derived by kernel functions is called the **Reproducing Kernel Hilbert Space (RKHS)**. An inner product in the RKHS equals kernel mapping of inner product of instances in the original lower-dimensional feature space. In other words,

$$K(\boldsymbol{x}_i, \boldsymbol{x}_j) = \langle \phi(\boldsymbol{x}_i), \phi(\boldsymbol{x}_j) \rangle \tag{1.23}$$

for all $\boldsymbol{x}_i$'s, where ϕ is a mapping from the original feature space to a higher-dimensional space and K is a kernel. Thus, we can simply replace the inner products in the dual form of the optimization by the kernel.

According to *Mercer's Theorem* [Cristianini and Shawe-Taylor, 2000], every positive semi-definite symmetric function is a kernel. Popular kernels include the **linear kernel**

$$K(\boldsymbol{x}_i, \boldsymbol{x}_j) = \langle \boldsymbol{x}_i, \boldsymbol{x}_j \rangle , \tag{1.24}$$

the **polynomial kernel**

$$K(\boldsymbol{x}_i, \boldsymbol{x}_j) = \langle \boldsymbol{x}_i, \boldsymbol{x}_j \rangle^d , \tag{1.25}$$

where d is the degree of the polynomial, and the **Gaussian kernel** (or called **RBF kernel**)

$$K(\boldsymbol{x}_i, \boldsymbol{x}_j) = \exp\left(-\frac{\|\boldsymbol{x}_i - \boldsymbol{x}_j\|^2}{2\sigma^2} \right) , \tag{1.26}$$

where σ is the parameter of the Gaussian width.

The **kernel trick**, i.e., mapping the data points with a kernel and then accomplishing the learning task in the RKHS, is a general strategy that can be incorporated into any learning algorithm that considers only inner products between the input feature vectors. Once the kernel trick is used, the learning algorithms are called **kernel methods**. Indeed, SVMs are a special kind of kernel method, i.e., linear classifiers facilitated with kernel trick.

1.3 Evaluation and Comparison

Usually, we have multiple alternative learning algorithms to choose among, and a number of parameters to tune. The task of choosing the best algorithm and the settings of its parameters is known as **model selection**, and for this purpose we need to estimate the performance of the learner. By empirical ways, this involves design of experiments and statistical hypothesis tests for comparing the models.

It is unwise to estimate the generalization error of a learner by its **training error**, i.e., the error that the learner makes on the training data, since training error prefers complex learners rather than learners that generalize well. Usually, a learner with very high complexity can have zero training error, such as a fully grown decision tree; however, it is likely to perform badly on unseen data due to overfitting. A proper process is to evaluate the performance on a validation set. Note that the labels in the training set and validation set are known *a priori* to the training process, and should be used together to derive and tune the final learner once the model has been selected.

In fact, in most cases the training and validation sets are obtained by splitting a given data set into two parts. While splitting, the properties of the original data set should be kept as much as possible; otherwise the validation set may provide misleading estimates, for an extreme example, the training set might contain only positive instances while the validation set contains only negative instances. In classification, when the original data set is split randomly, the class percentage should be maintained for both training and validation sets; this is called **stratification**, or *stratified sampling*.

When there is not enough labeled data available to create a separate validation set, a commonly used validation method is **cross-validation**. In k-**fold cross-validation**, the original data set is partitioned by stratified split into k equal-size disjoint subsets, $D_1, \ldots, D_k$, and then k runs of training-tests are performed. In the ith run, D_i is used as the validation set while the union of all the other subsets, i.e., $\bigcup_{j \neq i} D_j$, is used as the training set. The average results of the k runs are taken as the results of the cross-validation. To reduce the influence of randomness introduced by data split, the k-fold cross-validation can be repeated t times, which is called t-**times k-fold cross-validation**. Usual configurations include *10-times 10-fold cross-validation*, and *5-times 2-fold cross-validation* suggested by Dietterich [1998]. Extremely, when k equals the number of instances in the original data set, there is only one instance in each validation set; this is called **leave-one-out (LOO)** validation.

After obtaining the estimated errors, we can compare different learning algorithms. A simple comparison on average errors, however, is not reliable since the winning algorithm may occasionally perform well due to the randomness in data split. **Hypothesis test** is usually employed for this purpose.

To compare learning algorithms that are efficient enough to run 10 times, the **5 × 2 cv paired t-test** is a good choice [Dietterich, 1998]. In this test, we run 5-times 2-fold cross-validation. In each run of 2-fold cross-validation, the data set D is randomly split into two subsets D_1 and D_2 of equal size. Two algorithms a and b are trained on each set and tested on the other, resulting in four error estimates: $err_a^{(1)}$ and $err_b^{(1)}$ (trained on D_1 and tested on D_2) and $err_a^{(2)}$ and $err_b^{(2)}$ (trained on D_2 and tested on D_1). We have the error differences

$$d^{(i)} = err_a^{(i)} - err_b^{(i)} \qquad (i = 1, 2) \tag{1.27}$$

with the mean and the variance, respectively:

$$\mu = \frac{d^{(1)} + d^{(2)}}{2} , \tag{1.28}$$

$$s^2 = (d^{(1)} - \mu)^2 + (d^{(2)} - \mu)^2 . \tag{1.29}$$

Let s_i^2 denote the variance in the ith time 2-fold cross-validation, and $d_1^{(1)}$ denote the error difference in the first time. Under the null hypothesis, the 5×2 cv $\tilde{t}$-statistic

$$\tilde{t} = \frac{d_1^{(1)}}{\sqrt{\frac{1}{5} \sum_{i=1}^{5} s_i^2}} \sim t_5 , \tag{1.30}$$

would be distributed according to the *Student's t-distribution* with 5 degrees of freedom. We then choose a significance level α. If $\tilde{t}$ falls into the interval $[-t_5(\alpha/2), t_5(\alpha/2)]$, the null hypothesis is accepted, suggesting that there is no significant difference between the two algorithms. Usually α is set to 0.05 or 0.1.

To compare learning algorithms that can be run only once, the **McNemar's test** can be used instead [Dietterich, 1998]. Let err_{01} denote the number of instances on which the first algorithm makes a wrong prediction while the second algorithm is correct, and err_{10} denotes the inverse. If the two algorithms have the same performance, err_{01} is close to err_{10}, and therefore, the quantity

$$\frac{(|err_{01} - err_{10}| - 1)^2}{err_{01} + err_{10}} \sim \chi_1^2 \tag{1.31}$$

would be distributed according to the χ^2-*distribution*.

Sometimes, we evaluate multiple learning algorithms on multiple data sets. In this situation, we can conduct the **Friedman test** [Demšar, 2006]. First, we sort the algorithms on each data set according to their average errors. On each data set, the best algorithm is assigned rank 1, the worse algorithms are assigned increased ranks, and average ranks are assigned in case of ties. Then, we average the ranks of each algorithm over all data sets, and use the *Nemenyi post-hoc test* [Demšar, 2006] to calculate the *critical difference* value

$$CD = q_\alpha \sqrt{\frac{k(k+1)}{6N}} , \tag{1.32}$$

where k is the number of algorithms, N is the number of data sets and q_α is the *critical value* [Demšar, 2006]. A pair of algorithms are believed to be significantly different if the difference of their average ranks is larger than the critical difference.

The Friedman test results can be visualized by plotting the **critical difference diagram**, as illustrated in Figure 1.8, where each algorithm corresponds to a bar centered at the average rank with the width of critical difference value. Figure 1.8 discloses that the algorithm A is significantly better

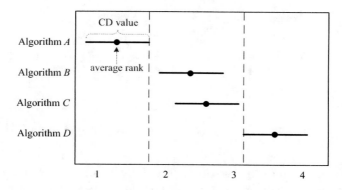

FIGURE 1.8: Illustration of critical difference diagram.

than all the other algorithms, the algorithm D is significantly worse than all the other algorithms, and the algorithms B and C are not significantly different, according to the given significance level.

1.4 Ensemble Methods

Ensemble methods train multiple learners to solve the same problem. In contrast to ordinary learning approaches which try to construct one learner from training data, ensemble methods try to construct a set of learners and combine them. Ensemble learning is also called **committee-based learning**, or learning **multiple classifier systems**.

Figure 1.9 shows a common ensemble architecture. An ensemble contains a number of learners called **base learners**. Base learners are usually generated from training data by a **base learning algorithm** which can be decision tree, neural network or other kinds of learning algorithms. Most ensemble methods use a single base learning algorithm to produce *homogeneous* base learners, i.e., learners of the same type, leading to **homogeneous ensembles**, but there are also some methods which use multiple learning algorithms to produce *heterogeneous* learners, i.e., learners of different types, leading to **heterogeneous ensembles**. In the latter case there is no single base learning algorithm and thus, some people prefer calling the learners **individual learners** or **component learners** to *base learners*.

The generalization ability of an ensemble is often much stronger than that of base learners. Actually, ensemble methods are appealing mainly because they are able to boost **weak learners** which are even just slightly better than random guess to **strong learners** which can make very accurate predictions. So, *base learners* are also referred to as *weak learners*.

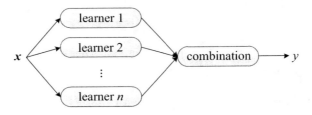

FIGURE 1.9: A common ensemble architecture.

It is difficult to trace the starting point of the history of ensemble methods since the basic idea of deploying multiple models has been in use in human society for a long time. For example, even earlier than the introduction of **Occam's razor**, the common basic assumption of scientific research which prefers simple hypotheses to complex ones when both fit empirical observations well, the Greek philosopher Epicurus (341 - 270 B.C.) introduced the **principle of multiple explanations** [Asmis, 1984] which advocated to keep all hypotheses that are consistent with empirical observations.

There are three threads of early contributions that led to the current area of ensemble methods; that is, **combining classifiers**, **ensembles of weak learners** and **mixture of experts**. *Combining classifiers* was mostly studied in the pattern recognition community. In this thread, researchers generally work on strong classifiers, and try to design powerful *combining rules* to get stronger combined classifiers. As the consequence, this thread of work has accumulated deep understanding on the design and use of different combining rules. *Ensembles of weak learners* was mostly studied in the machine learning community. In this thread, researchers often work on weak learners and try to design powerful algorithms to boost the performance from weak to strong. This thread of work has led to the birth of famous ensemble methods such as AdaBoost, Bagging, etc., and theoretical understanding on why and how weak learners can be boosted to strong ones. *Mixture of experts* was mostly studied in the neural networks community. In this thread, researchers generally consider a **divide-and-conquer** strategy, try to learn a mixture of parametric models jointly and use combining rules to get an overall solution.

Ensemble methods have become a major learning paradigm since the 1990s, with great promotion by two pieces of pioneering work. One is empirical [Hansen and Salamon, 1990], in which it was found that predictions made by the combination of a set of classifiers are often more accurate than predictions made by the best single classifier. A simplified illustration is shown in Figure 1.10. The other is theoretical [Schapire, 1990], in which it was proved that weak learners can be boosted to strong learners. Since strong learners are desirable yet difficult to get, while weak learners are easy to obtain in real practice, this result opens a promising direction of gener-

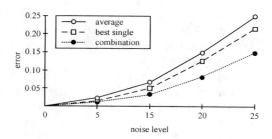

FIGURE 1.10: A simplified illustration of Hansen and Salamon [1990]'s observation: Ensemble is often better than the best single.

ating strong learners by ensemble methods.

Generally, an ensemble is constructed in two steps, i.e., generating the base learners, and then combining them. To get a good ensemble, it is generally believed that the base learners should be as *accurate* as possible, and as *diverse* as possible.

It is worth mentioning that generally, the computational cost of constructing an ensemble is not much larger than creating a single learner. This is because when we want to use a single learner, we usually need to generate multiple versions of the learner for model selection or parameter tuning; this is comparable to generating base learners in ensembles, while the computational cost for combining base learners is often small since most combination strategies are simple.

1.5 Applications of Ensemble Methods

The *KDD-Cup* [1] is the most famous data mining competition. Since 1997, it is held every year and attracts the interests of data mining teams all over the world. The competition problems cover a large variety of practical tasks, such as network intrusion detection (1999), molecular bioactivity & protein locale prediction (2001), pulmonary embolisms detection (2006), customer relationship management (2009), educational data mining (2010), music recommendation (2011), etc. In the past KDD-Cup competitions, among various techniques utilized in the solutions, ensemble methods have drawn the most attention and won the competitions for the most times. For example, in KDD-Cups of the last three years (2009-2011), all the first-place and second-place winners used ensemble methods.

---

[1] http://www.sigkdd.org/kddcup/.

Another famous competition, the *Netflix Prize*,[2] is held by the online DVD-rental service Netflix and seeks to improve the accuracy of predictions about how much someone is going to enjoy a movie based on their preferences; if one participating team improves Netflix's own algorithm by 10% accuracy, they would win the grand prize of $1,000,000. On September 21, 2009, Nexflix awarded the $1M grand prize to the team *BellKor's Pragmatic Chaos*, whose solution was based on combining various classifiers including asymmetric factor models, regression models, restricted Boltzmann machines, matrix factorization, k-nearest neighbor, etc. Another team, which achieved the winning performance but was defeated because the result was submitted 20 minutes later, even used *The Ensemble* as the team name.

In addition to the impressive results in competitions, ensemble methods have been successfully applied to diverse real-world tasks. Indeed, they have been found useful in almost all places where learning techniques are exploited. For example, computer vision has benefited much from ensemble methods in almost all branches such as object detection, recognition and tracking.

Viola and Jones [2001, 2004] proposed a general object detection framework by combining AdaBoost with a cascade architecture. Viola and Jones [2004] reported that, on a 466MHz machine, the face detector spent only 0.067 seconds for a 384×288 image; this is almost 15 times faster than state-of-the-art face detectors, while the detection accuracy is comparable. This framework was recognized as one of the most exciting breakthroughs in computer vision (especially, face detection) during the past decade.

Huang et al. [2000] designed an ensemble architecture for pose-invariant face recognition, particularly for recognizing faces with in-depth rotations. The basic idea is to combine a number of view-specific neural networks with a specially designed combination module. In contrast to conventional techniques which require pose information as input, this framework does not need pose information and it can even output pose estimation in addition to the recognition result. Huang et al. [2000] reported that this framework even outperformed conventional techniques facilitated with perfect pose information. A similar method was later applied to multi-view face detection [Li et al., 2001].

Object tracking aims to assign consistent labels to the target objects in consecutive frames of a video. By considering tracking as a binary classification problem, Avidan [2007] proposed *ensemble tracking*, which trains an ensemble online to distinguish between the object and the background. This framework constantly updates a set of weak classifiers, which can be added or removed at any time to incorporate new information about changes in object appearance and the background. Avidan [2007] showed

---

[2]http://www.netflixprize.com/.

that the ensemble tracking framework could work in a large variety of videos with various object size, and it runs very efficiently, at a few frames per second without optimization, hence can be used in online applications.

Ensemble methods have been found very appropriate to characterize computer security problems because each activity performed on computer systems can be observed at *multiple abstraction levels*, and the relevant information may be collected from *multiple information sources* [Corona et al., 2009].

Giacinto et al. [2003] applied ensemble methods to intrusion detection. Considering that there are different types of features characterizing the connection, they constructed an ensemble from each type of features independently, and then combined the outputs from these ensembles to produce the final decision. Giacinto et al. [2003] reported that, when detecting known attacks, ensemble methods lead to the best performance. Later, Giacinto et al. [2008] proposed an ensemble method for anomaly-based intrusion detection which is able to detect intrusions never seen before.

Malicious executables are programs designed to perform a malicious function without the owner's permission, and they generally fall into three categories, i.e., viruses, worms, and Trojan horses. Schultz et al. [2001] proposed an ensemble method to detect previously unseen malicious executables automatically, based on representing the programs using binary profiling, string sequences and hex dumps. Kolter and Maloof [2006] represented programs using n-grams of byte codes, and reported that boosted decision trees achieved the best performance; they also suggested that this method could be used as the basis for an operational system for detecting new malicious executables never seen before.

Ensemble methods have been found very useful in diverse tasks of computer aided medical diagnosis, particularly for increasing the diagnosis reliability.

Zhou et al. [2002a] designed a two-layered ensemble architecture for lung cancer cell identification, where the first layer predicts benign cases if and only if all component learners agree, and otherwise the case will be passed to the second layer to make a further decision among benign and different cancer types. Zhou et al. [2002a] reported that the two-layered ensemble results in a high identification rate with a low false-negative identification rate.

For early diagnosis of Alzheimer's disease, previous methods generally considered single channel data from the EEG (electroencephalogram). To make use of multiple data channels, Polikar et al. [2008] proposed an ensemble method where the component learners are trained on different data sources obtained from different electrodes in response to different stimuli and in different frequency bands, and their outputs are combined for the final diagnosis.

In addition to computer vision, computer security and computer aided medical diagnosis, ensemble methods have also been applied to many other domains and tasks such as credit card fraud detection [Chan et al., 1999, Panigrahi et al., 2009], bankruptcy prediction [West et al., 2005], protein structure classification [Tan et al., 2003, Shen and Chou, 2006], species distributions forecasting [Araújo and New, 2007], weather forecasting [Maqsood et al., 2004, Gneiting and Raftery, 2005], electric load forecasting [Taylor and Buizza, 2002], aircraft engine fault diagnosis [Goebel et al., 2000, Yan and Xue, 2008], musical genre and artist classification [Bergstra et al., 2006], etc.

1.6 Further Readings

There are good textbooks on machine learning [Mitchell, 1997, Alpaydin, 2010, Bishop, 2006, Hastie et al., 2001], pattern recognition [Duda et al., 2000, Theodoridis and Koutroumbas, 2009, Ripley, 1996, Bishop, 1995] and data mining [Han and Kamber, 2006, Tan et al., 2006, Hand et al., 2001]. More introductory materials can be found in these books.

Linear discriminant analysis is closely related to **principal component analysis** (PCA) [Jolliffe, 2002], both looking for linear combination of features to represent the data. LDA is a supervised approach focusing on distinguishing between different classes, while PCA is an unsupervised approach generally used to identify the largest variability. Decision trees can be mapped to a set of "if-then" rules [Quinlan, 1993]. Most decision trees use splits like "$x \geq 1$" or "$y \geq 2$", leading to axis-parallel partitions of instance space. There are also exceptions, e.g., **oblique decision trees** [Murthy et al., 1994] which use splits like "$x+y \geq 3$", leading to non-axis-parallel partitions. The BP algorithm is the most popular and most successful neural network learning algorithm. It has many variants, and can also be used to train neural networks whose structures are different from feed-forward networks, such as **recurrent neural networks** where there are cross-layer connections. Haykin [1998] provides a good introduction to neural networks. Though the nearest neighbor algorithm is very simple, it works well in most cases. The error of the nearest neighbor classifier is guaranteed to be no worse than twice of the Bayes error rate on infinite data [Cover and Hart, 1967], and kNN approaches the Bayes error rate for some k value which is related to the amount of data. The distances between instances are not constrained to be calculated by the Euclidean distance, and the contributions from different neighbors can be weighted. More information on kNN can be found in [Dasarathy, 1991]. The naïve Bayes classifier based on the conditional independence assumption works well in most cases [Domingos and Pazzani, 1997]; however, it is believed that the performance can be improved further by relaxing the assumption, and therefore many **semi-naïve Bayes classifiers** such as TAN [Friedman et al., 1997] and LBR [Zheng and Webb, 2000] have been developed. A particularly successful one is the AODE [Webb et al., 2005], which has incorporated ensemble mechanism and often beats TAN and LBR, especially on intermediate-size data sets. SVMs are rooted in the **statistical learning theory** [Vapnik, 1998]. More introductory materials on SVMs and kernel methods can be found in [Cristianini and Shawe-Taylor, 2000, Schölkopf et al., 1999].

Introductory materials on hypothesis tests can be found in [Fleiss, 1981]. Different hypothesis tests are usually based on different assumptions, and should be applied in different situations. The 10-fold cross-validation t-test was popularly used; however, Dietterich [1998] discloses that such a test underestimates the variability and it is likely to incorrectly detect a difference when no difference exists (i.e., the type I error), while the 5×2cv paired t-test is recommended instead.

The **No Free Lunch Theorem** [Wolpert, 1996, Wolpert and Macready, 1997] implies that it is hopeless to dream for a learning algorithm which is consistently better than other learning algorithms. It is important to notice, however, that the No Free Lunch Theorem considers the whole problem space, that is, all the possible learning tasks; while in real practice, we are usually only interested in a give task, and in such a situation, the effort of trying to find the best algorithm is valid. From the experience of the author of this book, for lots of tasks, the best off-the-shelf learning technique at present is ensemble methods such as Random Forest facilitated with **feature engineering** which constructs/generates usually an overly large number of new features rather than simply working on the original features.

[Kuncheva, 2004] and [Rokach, 2010] are books on ensemble methods. Xu and Amari [2009] discuss the relation between *combining classifiers* and *mixture of experts*. The *MCS* workshop (*International Workshop on Multiple Classifier Systems*) is the major forum in this area. Abundant literature on ensemble methods can also be found in various journals and conferences on machine learning, pattern recognition and data mining.

2

Boosting

2.1 A General Boosting Procedure

The term **boosting** refers to a family of algorithms that are able to convert weak learners to strong learners. Intuitively, a weak learner is just slightly better than random guess, while a strong learner is very close to perfect performance. The birth of boosting algorithms originated from the answer to an interesting theoretical question posed by Kearns and Valiant [1989]. That is, whether two complexity classes, *weakly learnable* and *strongly learnable* problems, are equal. This question is of fundamental importance, since if the answer is positive, any weak learner is potentially able to be boosted to a strong learner, particularly if we note that in real practice it is generally very easy to obtain weak learners but difficult to get strong learners. Schapire [1990] proved that the answer is positive, and the proof is a construction, i.e., boosting.

The general boosting procedure is quite simple. Suppose the weak learner will work on any data distribution it is given, and take the binary classification task as an example; that is, we are trying to classify instances as *positive* and *negative*. The training instances in space $\mathcal{X}$ are drawn *i.i.d.* from distribution $\mathcal{D}$, and the ground-truth function is f. Suppose the space $\mathcal{X}$ is composed of three parts $\mathcal{X}_1, \mathcal{X}_2$ and $\mathcal{X}_3$, each takes $1/3$ amount of the distribution, and a learner working by random guess has 50% classification error on this problem. We want to get an accurate (e.g., zero error) classifier on the problem, but we are unlucky and only have a weak classifier at hand, which only has correct classifications in spaces $\mathcal{X}_1$ and $\mathcal{X}_2$ and has wrong classifications in $\mathcal{X}_3$, thus has $1/3$ classification error. Let's denote this weak classifier as h_1. It is obvious that h_1 is not desired.

The idea of boosting is to correct the mistakes made by h_1. We can try to derive a new distribution $\mathcal{D}'$ from $\mathcal{D}$, which makes the mistakes of h_1 more evident, e.g., it focuses more on the instances in $\mathcal{X}_3$. Then, we can train a classifier h_2 from $\mathcal{D}'$. Again, suppose we are unlucky and h_2 is also a weak classifier, which has correct classifications in $\mathcal{X}_1$ and $\mathcal{X}_3$ and has wrong classifications in $\mathcal{X}_2$. By combining h_1 and h_2 in an appropriate way (we will explain how to combine them in the next section), the combined classifier will have correct classifications in $\mathcal{X}_1$, and maybe some errors in $\mathcal{X}_2$ and $\mathcal{X}_3$.

Input: Sample distribution $\mathcal{D}$;
   Base learning algorithm $\mathfrak{L}$;
   Number of learning rounds T.

Process:
1. $\mathcal{D}_1 = \mathcal{D}$.   % Initialize distribution
2.   **for** $t = 1, \ldots, T$:
3. $h_t = \mathfrak{L}(\mathcal{D}_t)$;   % Train a weak learner from distribution $\mathcal{D}_t$
4. $\epsilon_t = P_{\boldsymbol{x} \sim D_t}(h_t(\boldsymbol{x}) \neq f(\boldsymbol{x}))$;   % Evaluate the error of h_t
5. $\mathcal{D}_{t+1} = Adjust\_Distribution(\mathcal{D}_t, \epsilon_t)$
6.   **end**

Output: $H(\boldsymbol{x}) = Combine\_Outputs(\{h_1(\boldsymbol{x}), \ldots, h_t(\boldsymbol{x})\})$

FIGURE 2.1: A general boosting procedure

Again, we derive a new distribution $\mathcal{D}''$ to make the mistakes of the combined classifier more evident, and train a classifier h_3 from the distribution, so that h_3 has correct classifications in $\mathcal{X}_2$ and $\mathcal{X}_3$. Then, by combining h_1, h_2 and h_3, we have a perfect classifier, since in each space of $\mathcal{X}_1$, $\mathcal{X}_2$ and $\mathcal{X}_3$, at least two classifiers make correct classifications.

Briefly, boosting works by training a set of learners sequentially and combining them for prediction, where the later learners focus more on the mistakes of the earlier learners. Figure 2.1 summarizes the general boosting procedure.

2.2 The AdaBoost Algorithm

The general boosting procedure described in Figure 2.1 is not a real algorithm since there are some unspecified parts such as *Adjust_Distribution* and *Combine_Outputs*. The AdaBoost algorithm [Freund and Schapire, 1997], which is the most influential boosting algorithm, can be viewed as an instantiation of these parts as shown in Figure 2.2.

Consider binary classification on classes $\{-1, +1\}$. One version of derivation of AdaBoost [Friedman et al., 2000] is achieved by minimizing the **exponential loss** function

$$\ell_{\exp}(h \mid \mathcal{D}) = \mathbb{E}_{\boldsymbol{x} \sim \mathcal{D}}[e^{-f(\boldsymbol{x})h(\boldsymbol{x})}] \tag{2.1}$$

Input: Data set $D = \{(\boldsymbol{x}_1, y_1), (\boldsymbol{x}_2, y_2), \ldots, (\boldsymbol{x}_m, y_m)\}$;
      Base learning algorithm $\mathfrak{L}$;
      Number of learning rounds T.

Process:
1. $\mathcal{D}_1(\boldsymbol{x}) = 1/m.$ % Initialize the weight distribution
2. **for** $t = 1, \ldots, T$:
3. $h_t = \mathfrak{L}(D, \mathcal{D}_t);$ % Train a classifier h_t from D under distribution $\mathcal{D}_t$
4. $\epsilon_t = P_{\boldsymbol{x} \sim \mathcal{D}_t}(h_t(\boldsymbol{x}) \neq f(\boldsymbol{x}));$ % Evaluate the error of h_t
5.   **if** $\epsilon_t > 0.5$ **then break**
6. $\alpha_t = \frac{1}{2} \ln \left(\frac{1 - \epsilon_t}{\epsilon_t} \right);$ % Determine the weight of h_t
7. $\mathcal{D}_{t+1}(\boldsymbol{x}) = \frac{\mathcal{D}_t(\boldsymbol{x})}{Z_t} \times \begin{cases} \exp(-\alpha_t) & \text{if } h_t(\boldsymbol{x}) = f(\boldsymbol{x}) \\ \exp(\alpha_t) & \text{if } h_t(\boldsymbol{x}) \neq f(\boldsymbol{x}) \end{cases}$

          $= \frac{\mathcal{D}_t(\boldsymbol{x}) \exp(-\alpha_t f(\boldsymbol{x}) h_t(\boldsymbol{x}))}{Z_t}$ % Update the distribution, where
                                     % Z_t is a normalization factor which
                                     % enables $\mathcal{D}_{t+1}$ to be a distribution

8. **end**

Output: $H(\boldsymbol{x}) = \text{sign} \left(\sum_{t=1}^{T} \alpha_t h_t(\boldsymbol{x}) \right)$

FIGURE 2.2: The AdaBoost algorithm

using *additive* weighted combination of weak learners as

$$H(\boldsymbol{x}) = \sum_{t=1}^{T} \alpha_t h_t(\boldsymbol{x}) . \tag{2.2}$$

The exponential loss is used since it gives an elegant and simple update formula, and it is consistent with the goal of minimizing classification error and can be justified by its relationship to the standard log likelihood. When the exponential loss is minimized by H, the partial derivative of the exponential loss for every $\boldsymbol{x}$ is zero, i.e.,

$$\frac{\partial e^{-f(\boldsymbol{x})H(\boldsymbol{x})}}{\partial H(\boldsymbol{x})} = -f(\boldsymbol{x})e^{-f(\boldsymbol{x})H(\boldsymbol{x})} \tag{2.3}$$

$$= -e^{-H(\boldsymbol{x})}P(f(\boldsymbol{x}) = 1 \mid \boldsymbol{x}) + e^{H(\boldsymbol{x})}P(f(\boldsymbol{x}) = -1 \mid \boldsymbol{x})$$

$$= 0 .$$

Then, by solving (2.3), we have

$$H(\boldsymbol{x}) = \frac{1}{2} \ln \frac{P(f(x) = 1 \mid \boldsymbol{x})}{P(f(x) = -1 \mid \boldsymbol{x})} , \tag{2.4}$$

and hence,

$$\texttt{sign}(H(\boldsymbol{x})) = \texttt{sign}\left(\frac{1}{2}\ln\frac{P(f(x)=1\mid\boldsymbol{x})}{P(f(x)=-1\mid\boldsymbol{x})}\right)$$

$$= \begin{cases} 1, & P(f(x)=1\mid\boldsymbol{x}) > P(f(x)=-1\mid\boldsymbol{x}) \\ -1, & P(f(x)=1\mid\boldsymbol{x}) < P(f(x)=-1\mid\boldsymbol{x}) \end{cases}$$

$$= \underset{y\in\{-1,1\}}{\arg\max} P(f(x)=y\mid\boldsymbol{x}), \tag{2.5}$$

which implies that $\texttt{sign}(H(\boldsymbol{x}))$ achieves the Bayes error rate. Note that we ignore the case $P(f(x)=1\mid\boldsymbol{x}) = P(f(x)=-1\mid\boldsymbol{x})$. The above derivation shows that when the exponential loss is minimized, the classification error is also minimized, and thus the exponential loss is a proper optimization target for replacing the non-differentiable classification error.

The H is produced by iteratively generating h_t and α_t. The first weak classifier h_1 is generated by invoking the weak learning algorithm on the original distribution. When a classifier h_t is generated under the distribution $\mathcal{D}_t$, its weight α_t is to be determined such that $\alpha_t h_t$ minimizes the exponential loss

$$\begin{aligned} \ell_{\exp}(\alpha_t h_t \mid \mathcal{D}_t) &= \mathbb{E}_{\boldsymbol{x}\sim\mathcal{D}_t}[e^{-f(\boldsymbol{x})\alpha_t h_t(\boldsymbol{x})}] \tag{2.6} \\ &= \mathbb{E}_{\boldsymbol{x}\sim\mathcal{D}_t}\left[e^{-\alpha_t}\mathbb{I}(f(\boldsymbol{x})=h_t(\boldsymbol{x})) + e^{\alpha_t}\mathbb{I}(f(\boldsymbol{x})\neq h_t(\boldsymbol{x}))\right] \\ &= e^{-\alpha_t}P_{\boldsymbol{x}\sim\mathcal{D}_t}(f(\boldsymbol{x})=h_t(\boldsymbol{x})) + e^{\alpha_t}P_{\boldsymbol{x}\sim\mathcal{D}_t}(f(\boldsymbol{x})\neq h_t(\boldsymbol{x})) \\ &= e^{-\alpha_t}(1-\epsilon_t) + e^{\alpha_t}\epsilon_t\,, \end{aligned}$$

where $\epsilon_t = P_{\boldsymbol{x}\sim\mathcal{D}_t}(h_t(\boldsymbol{x})\neq f(\boldsymbol{x}))$. To get the optimal α_t, let the derivative of the exponential loss equal zero, that is,

$$\frac{\partial\ell_{\exp}(\alpha_t h_t \mid \mathcal{D}_t)}{\partial\alpha_t} = -e^{-\alpha_t}(1-\epsilon_t) + e^{\alpha_t}\epsilon_t = 0\,, \tag{2.7}$$

then the solution is

$$\alpha_t = \frac{1}{2}\ln\left(\frac{1-\epsilon_t}{\epsilon_t}\right)\,, \tag{2.8}$$

as in line 6 of Figure 2.2.

Once a sequence of weak classifiers and their corresponding weights have been generated, these classifiers are combined as H_{t-1}. Then, AdaBoost adjusts the sample distribution such that in the next round, the base learning algorithm will output a weak classifier h_t that corrects some mistakes of H_{t-1}. Considering the exponential loss again, the ideal classifier h_t that corrects all mistakes of H_{t-1} should minimize the exponential loss

$$\begin{aligned} \ell_{\exp}(H_{t-1} + h_t \mid \mathcal{D}) &= \mathbb{E}_{\boldsymbol{x}\sim\mathcal{D}}[e^{-f(\boldsymbol{x})(H_{t-1}(\boldsymbol{x})+h_t(\boldsymbol{x}))}] \tag{2.9} \\ &= \mathbb{E}_{\boldsymbol{x}\sim\mathcal{D}}[e^{-f(\boldsymbol{x})H_{t-1}(\boldsymbol{x})}e^{-f(\boldsymbol{x})h_t(\boldsymbol{x})}]\,. \end{aligned}$$

Using Taylor expansion of $e^{-f(\boldsymbol{x})h_t(\boldsymbol{x})}$, the exponential loss is approximated by

$$\ell_{\exp}(H_{t-1} + h_t \mid \mathcal{D}) \approx \mathbb{E}_{\boldsymbol{x} \sim \mathcal{D}} \left[e^{-f(\boldsymbol{x})H_{t-1}(\boldsymbol{x})} \left(1 - f(\boldsymbol{x})h_t(\boldsymbol{x}) + \frac{f(\boldsymbol{x})^2 h_t(\boldsymbol{x})^2}{2} \right) \right]$$

$$= \mathbb{E}_{\boldsymbol{x} \sim \mathcal{D}} \left[e^{-f(\boldsymbol{x})H_{t-1}(\boldsymbol{x})} \left(1 - f(\boldsymbol{x})h_t(\boldsymbol{x}) + \frac{1}{2} \right) \right] , \quad (2.10)$$

by noticing that $f(\boldsymbol{x})^2 = 1$ and $h_t(\boldsymbol{x})^2 = 1$.

Thus, the ideal classifier h_t is

$$h_t(\boldsymbol{x}) = \arg\min_h \ell_{\exp}(H_{t-1} + h \mid \mathcal{D}) \quad (2.11)$$

$$= \arg\min_h \mathbb{E}_{\boldsymbol{x} \sim \mathcal{D}} \left[e^{-f(\boldsymbol{x})H_{t-1}(\boldsymbol{x})} \left(1 - f(\boldsymbol{x})h(\boldsymbol{x}) + \frac{1}{2} \right) \right]$$

$$= \arg\max_h \mathbb{E}_{\boldsymbol{x} \sim \mathcal{D}} \left[e^{-f(\boldsymbol{x})H_{t-1}(\boldsymbol{x})} f(\boldsymbol{x})h(\boldsymbol{x}) \right]$$

$$= \arg\max_h \mathbb{E}_{\boldsymbol{x} \sim \mathcal{D}} \left[\frac{e^{-f(\boldsymbol{x})H_{t-1}(\boldsymbol{x})}}{\mathbb{E}_{\boldsymbol{x} \sim \mathcal{D}} [e^{-f(\boldsymbol{x})H_{t-1}(\boldsymbol{x})}]} f(\boldsymbol{x})h(\boldsymbol{x}) \right] ,$$

by noticing that $\mathbb{E}_{\boldsymbol{x} \sim \mathcal{D}}[e^{-f(\boldsymbol{x})H_{t-1}(\boldsymbol{x})}]$ is a constant.

Denote a distribution $\mathcal{D}_t$ as

$$\mathcal{D}_t(x) = \frac{\mathcal{D}(x)e^{-f(\boldsymbol{x})H_{t-1}(\boldsymbol{x})}}{\mathbb{E}_{\boldsymbol{x} \sim \mathcal{D}}[e^{-f(\boldsymbol{x})H_{t-1}(\boldsymbol{x})}]} . \quad (2.12)$$

Then, by the definition of mathematical expectation, it is equivalent to write that

$$h_t(\boldsymbol{x}) = \arg\max_h \mathbb{E}_{\boldsymbol{x} \sim \mathcal{D}} \left[\frac{e^{-f(\boldsymbol{x})H_{t-1}(\boldsymbol{x})}}{\mathbb{E}_{\boldsymbol{x} \sim \mathcal{D}}[e^{-f(\boldsymbol{x})H_{t-1}(\boldsymbol{x})}]} f(\boldsymbol{x})h(\boldsymbol{x}) \right] \quad (2.13)$$

$$= \arg\max_h \mathbb{E}_{\boldsymbol{x} \sim \mathcal{D}_t} [f(\boldsymbol{x})h(\boldsymbol{x})] .$$

Further noticing that $f(\boldsymbol{x})h_t(\boldsymbol{x}) = 1 - 2\mathbb{I}(f(\boldsymbol{x}) \neq h_t(\boldsymbol{x}))$, the ideal classifier is

$$h_t(\boldsymbol{x}) = \arg\min_h \mathbb{E}_{\boldsymbol{x} \sim \mathcal{D}_t} [\mathbb{I}(f(\boldsymbol{x}) \neq h(\boldsymbol{x}))] . \quad (2.14)$$

As can be seen, the ideal h_t minimizes the classification error under the distribution $\mathcal{D}_t$. Therefore, the weak learner is to be trained under $\mathcal{D}_t$, and has less than 0.5 classification error according to $\mathcal{D}_t$. Considering the relation between $\mathcal{D}_t$ and $\mathcal{D}_{t+1}$, we have

$$
\begin{aligned}
\mathcal{D}_{t+1}(\boldsymbol{x}) &= \frac{\mathcal{D}(\boldsymbol{x})e^{-f(\boldsymbol{x})H_t(\boldsymbol{x})}}{\mathbb{E}_{\boldsymbol{x}\sim\mathcal{D}}[e^{-f(\boldsymbol{x})H_t(\boldsymbol{x})}]} \\
&= \frac{\mathcal{D}(\boldsymbol{x})e^{-f(\boldsymbol{x})H_{t-1}(\boldsymbol{x})}e^{-f(\boldsymbol{x})\alpha_t h_t(\boldsymbol{x})}}{\mathbb{E}_{\boldsymbol{x}\sim\mathcal{D}}[e^{-f(\boldsymbol{x})H_t(\boldsymbol{x})}]} \\
&= \mathcal{D}_t(\boldsymbol{x}) \cdot e^{-f(\boldsymbol{x})\alpha_t h_t(\boldsymbol{x})}\frac{\mathbb{E}_{\boldsymbol{x}\sim\mathcal{D}}[e^{-f(\boldsymbol{x})H_{t-1}(\boldsymbol{x})}]}{\mathbb{E}_{\boldsymbol{x}\sim\mathcal{D}}[e^{-f(\boldsymbol{x})H_t(\boldsymbol{x})}]} \, ,
\end{aligned}
\tag{2.15}
$$

which is the way AdaBoost updates the sample distribution as in line 7 of Figure 2.2.

It is noteworthy that the AdaBoost algorithm described in Figure 2.2 requires the base learning algorithm being able to learn with specified distributions. This is often accomplished by **re-weighting**, that is, weighting training examples in each round according to the sample distribution. For base learning algorithms that cannot handle weighted training examples, **re-sampling**, that is, sampling training examples in each round according to the desired distribution, can be applied.

For base learning algorithms which can be used with both re-weighting and re-sampling, generally there is no clear performance difference between these two implementations. However, re-sampling provides an option for **Boosting with restart** [Kohavi and Wolpert, 1996]. In each round of AdaBoost, there is a *sanity check* to ensure that the current base learner is better than random guess (see line 5 of Figure 2.2). This sanity check might be violated on some tasks when there are only a few weak learners and the AdaBoost procedure will be early-terminated far before the specified number of rounds T. This occurs particularly often on multiclass tasks. When re-sampling is used, the base learner that cannot pass the sanity check can be removed, and a new data sample can be generated, on which a new base learner will be trained; in this way, the AdaBoost procedure can avoid the early-termination problem.

2.3   Illustrative Examples

It is helpful to gain intuitive understanding of AdaBoost by observing its behavior. Consider an artificial data set in a two-dimensional space, plotted in Figure 2.3(a). There are only four instances, i.e.,

$$
\left\{
\begin{array}{l}
(\boldsymbol{z}_1 = (+1, 0), y_1 = +1) \\
(\boldsymbol{z}_2 = (-1, 0), y_2 = +1) \\
(\boldsymbol{z}_3 = (0, +1), y_3 = -1) \\
(\boldsymbol{z}_4 = (0, -1), y_4 = -1)
\end{array}
\right\} ,
$$

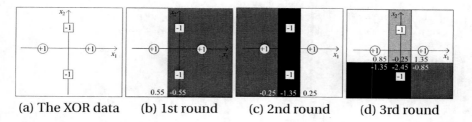

(a) The XOR data   (b) 1st round   (c) 2nd round   (d) 3rd round

FIGURE 2.3: AdaBoost on the XOR problem.

where $y_i = f(z_i)$ is the label of each instance. This is the XOR problem. As can be seen, there is no straight line that is able to separate positive instances (i.e., z_1 and z_2) from negative instances (i.e., z_3 and z_4); in other words, the two classes cannot be separated by a linear classifier.

Suppose we have a base learning algorithm which works as follows. It evaluates eight basis functions h_1 to h_8 described in Figure 2.4 on the training data under a given distribution, and then outputs the one with the smallest error. If there is more than one basis function with the smallest error, it selects one randomly. Notice that none of these eight basis functions can separate the two classes.

Now we track how AdaBoost works:

1. The first step is to invoke the base learning algorithm on the original data. Since h_2, h_3, h_5 and h_8 all have the smallest classification errors 0.25, suppose the base learning algorithm outputs h_2 as the classifier. After that, one instance, z_1, is incorrectly classified, so the error

$$h_1(x) = \begin{cases} +1, \text{ if } (x_1 > -0.5) \\ -1, \quad \text{otherwise} \end{cases} \quad h_2(x) = \begin{cases} -1, \text{ if } (x_1 > -0.5) \\ +1, \quad \text{otherwise} \end{cases}$$

$$h_3(x) = \begin{cases} +1, \text{ if } (x_1 > +0.5) \\ -1, \quad \text{otherwise} \end{cases} \quad h_4(x) = \begin{cases} -1, \text{ if } (x_1 > +0.5) \\ +1, \quad \text{otherwise} \end{cases}$$

$$h_5(x) = \begin{cases} +1, \text{ if } (x_2 > -0.5) \\ -1, \quad \text{otherwise} \end{cases} \quad h_6(x) = \begin{cases} -1, \text{ if } (x_2 > -0.5) \\ +1, \quad \text{otherwise} \end{cases}$$

$$h_7(x) = \begin{cases} +1, \text{ if } (x_2 > +0.5) \\ -1, \quad \text{otherwise} \end{cases} \quad h_8(x) = \begin{cases} -1, \text{ if } (x_2 > +0.5) \\ +1, \quad \text{otherwise} \end{cases}$$

where x_1 and x_2 are the values of x at the first and the second dimension, respectively.

FIGURE 2.4: The eight basis functions considered by the base learning algorithm.

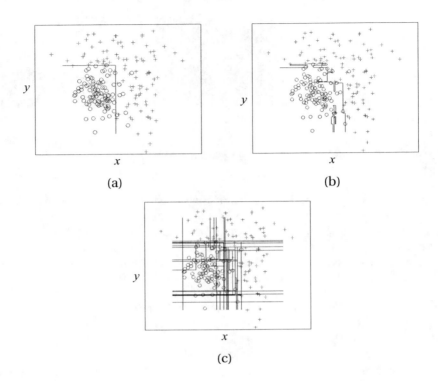

(a)   (b)

(c)

FIGURE 2.5: Decision boundaries of (a) a single decision tree, (b) AdaBoost and (c) the 10 decision trees used by AdaBoost, on the *three-Gaussians* data set.

is $1/4 = 0.25$. The weight of h_2 is $0.5 \ln 3 \approx 0.55$. Figure 2.3(b) visualizes the classification, where the shadow area is classified as negative (-1) and the weights of the classification, 0.55 and -0.55, are displayed.

2. The weight of z_1 is increased, and the base learning algorithm is invoked again. This time h_3, h_5 and h_8 have the smallest error, and suppose h_3 is picked, of which the weight is 0.80. Figure 2.3(c) shows the combined classification of h_2 and h_3 with their weights, where different gray levels are used for distinguishing the negative areas according to the combination weights.

3. The weight of z_2 is increased. This time only h_5 and h_8 equally have the smallest errors, and suppose h_5 is picked, of which the weight is 1.10. Figure 2.3(d) shows the combined classification of h_2, h_3 and h_5.

After the three steps, let us consider the sign of classification weights in each area in Figure 2.3(d). It can be observed that the sign of classification weights of z_1 and z_2 is "+", while that of z_3 and z_4 is "−". This means all the

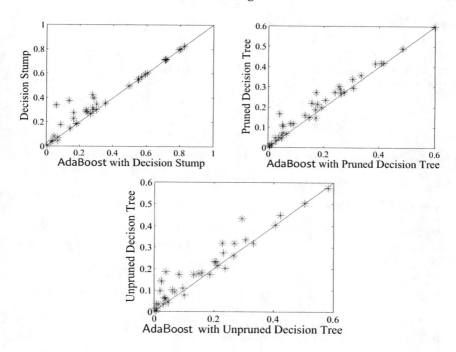

FIGURE 2.6: Comparison of predictive errors of AdaBoost against single base learners on 40 UCI data sets. Each point represents a data set and locates according to the predictive error of the two compared algorithms. The diagonal line indicates where the two compared algorithms have identical errors.

instances are correctly classified; thus, by combining the imperfect linear classifiers, AdaBoost has produced a non-linear classifier with zero error.

For a further understanding of AdaBoost, we visualize the decision boundaries of a single decision tree, AdaBoost and its component decision trees on the *three-Gaussians* data set, as shown in Figure 2.5. It can be observed that the decision boundary of AdaBoost is more flexible than that of a single decision tree, and this helps to reduce the error from 9.4% of the single decision tree to 8.3% of the boosted ensemble.

We also evaluate the AdaBoost algorithm on 40 data sets from the UCI Machine Learning Repository,[1] which covers a broad range of real-world tasks. The Weka[2] implementation of AdaBoost.M1 using re-weighting with 50 weak learners is evaluated. Almost all kinds of learning algorithms can be

---

[1]http://www.ics.uci.edu/~mlearn/MLRepository.html

[2]http://www.cs.waikato.ac.nz/ml/weka/

taken as base learning algorithms, such as decision trees, neural networks, etc. Here, we have tried three base learning algorithms: decision stumps, and pruned and unpruned J48 decision trees (Weka implementation of C4.5 decision trees). We plot the comparison results in Figure 2.6, from which it can be observed that AdaBoost usually outperforms its base learning algorithm, with only a few exceptions on which it hurts performance.

2.4   Theoretical Issues

2.4.1   Initial Analysis

Freund and Schapire [1997] proved that, if the base learners of AdaBoost have errors $\epsilon_1, \epsilon_2, \ldots, \epsilon_T$, the error of the final combined learner, ϵ, is upper bounded by

$$\epsilon = \mathbb{E}_{\boldsymbol{x} \sim \mathcal{D}} \mathbb{I}[H(\boldsymbol{x}) \neq f(\boldsymbol{x})] \leq 2^T \prod_{t=1}^{T} \sqrt{\epsilon_t(1 - \epsilon_t)} \leq e^{-2\sum_{t=1}^{T} \gamma_t^2} , \qquad (2.16)$$

where $\gamma_t = 0.5 - \epsilon_t$ is called the **edge** of h_t. It can be seen that AdaBoost reduces the error exponentially fast. Also, it can be derived that, to achieve an error less than ϵ, the number of learning rounds T is upper bounded by

$$T \leq \lceil \frac{1}{2\gamma^2} \ln \frac{1}{\epsilon} \rceil , \qquad (2.17)$$

where it is assumed that $\gamma \geq \gamma_1 \geq \ldots \geq \gamma_T$.

In practice, however, all the estimates can only be carried out on training data D, i.e., $\epsilon_D = \mathbb{E}_{\boldsymbol{x} \sim D} \mathbb{I}[H(\boldsymbol{x}) \neq f(\boldsymbol{x})]$, and thus the errors are training errors, while the generalization error $\epsilon_{\mathcal{D}}$ is of more interest. Freund and Schapire [1997] showed that the generalization error of AdaBoost is upper bounded by

$$\epsilon_{\mathcal{D}} \leq \epsilon_D + \tilde{O}\left(\sqrt{\frac{dT}{m}}\right) \qquad (2.18)$$

with probability at least $1 - \delta$, where d is the **VC-dimension** of base learners, m is the number of training instances, T is the number of learning rounds and $\tilde{O}(\cdot)$ is used instead of $O(\cdot)$ to hide logarithmic terms and constant factors.

2.4.2   Margin Explanation

The generalization bound (2.18) suggests that, in order to achieve a good generalization, it is necessary to constrain the complexity of base learners

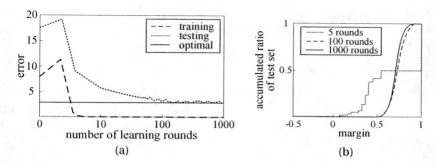

FIGURE 2.7: (a) Training and test error, and (b) margin distribution of Ada-Boost on the UCI *letter* data set. (Plot based on a similar figure in [Schapire et al., 1998])

as well as the number of learning rounds, and otherwise AdaBoost will over-fit.

Empirical studies, however, show that AdaBoost often does not overfit; that is, the test error often tends to decrease even after the training error reaches zero, even after a large number of rounds such as 1,000. For example, Schapire et al. [1998] plotted the typical performance of AdaBoost as shown in Figure 2.7(a). It can be observed that AdaBoost achieves zero training error in less than 10 rounds but after that, the generalization error keeps reducing. This phenomenon seems to contradict with the Occam's Razor which prefers simple hypotheses to complex ones when both fit empirical observations well. So, it is not strange that explaining why AdaBoost seems resistant to overfitting becomes one of the central theoretical issues and has attracted much attention.

Schapire et al. [1998] introduced the margin-based explanation to Ada-Boost. Formally, in the context of binary classification, i.e., $f(\boldsymbol{x}) \in \{-1, +1\}$, the **margin** of the classifier h on the instance $\boldsymbol{x}$, or in other words, the distance of $\boldsymbol{x}$ to the classification hyperplane of h, is defined as $f(\boldsymbol{x})h(\boldsymbol{x})$, and similarly, the margin of the ensemble $H(\boldsymbol{x}) = \sum_{t=1}^{T} \alpha_t h_t(\boldsymbol{x})$ is $f(\boldsymbol{x})H(\boldsymbol{x}) = \sum_{t=1}^{T} \alpha_t f(\boldsymbol{x})h_t(\boldsymbol{x})$, while the **normalized margin** of the ensemble is

$$f(\boldsymbol{x})H(\boldsymbol{x}) = \frac{\sum_{t=1}^{T} \alpha_t f(\boldsymbol{x})h_t(\boldsymbol{x})}{\sum_{t=1}^{T} \alpha_t} , \qquad (2.19)$$

where α_t's are the weights of base learners.

Based on the concept of margin, Schapire et al. [1998] proved that, given any threshold $\theta > 0$ of margin over the training sample D, with probability at least $1 - \delta$, the generalization error of the ensemble $\epsilon_{\mathcal{D}} = P_{\boldsymbol{x} \sim \mathcal{D}}(f(\boldsymbol{x}) \neq$

$H(\boldsymbol{x})$) can be bounded by

$$\epsilon_{\mathcal{D}} \leq P_{\boldsymbol{x} \sim D}(f(\boldsymbol{x})H(\boldsymbol{x}) \leq \theta) + \tilde{O}\left(\sqrt{\frac{d}{m\theta^2} + \ln\frac{1}{\delta}}\right) \qquad (2.20)$$

$$\leq 2^T \prod_{t=1}^{T} \sqrt{\epsilon_t^{1-\theta}(1-\epsilon_t)^{1+\theta}} + \tilde{O}\left(\sqrt{\frac{d}{m\theta^2} + \ln\frac{1}{\delta}}\right),$$

where d, m, T and $\tilde{O}(\cdot)$ are the same as those in (2.18), and ϵ_t is the training error of the base learner h_t. The bound (2.20) discloses that when other variables are fixed, the larger the margin over the training set, the smaller the generalization error. Thus, Schapire et al. [1998] argued that AdaBoost tends to be resistant to overfitting since it is able to increase the ensemble margin even after the training error reaches zero. Figure 2.7(b) illustrates the margin distribution of AdaBoost at different numbers of learning rounds.

Notice that the bound (2.20) depends heavily on the smallest margin, since the probability $P_{\boldsymbol{x} \sim D}(f(\boldsymbol{x})H(\boldsymbol{x}) \leq \theta)$ will be small if the smallest margin is large. Based on this recognition, Breiman [1999] developed the arc-gv algorithm, which is a variant of AdaBoost but directly maximizes the **minimum margin**

$$\varrho = \min_{\boldsymbol{x} \in D} f(\boldsymbol{x})H(\boldsymbol{x}). \qquad (2.21)$$

In each round, arc-gv updates α_t according to

$$\alpha_t = \frac{1}{2}\ln\left(\frac{1+\gamma_t}{1-\gamma_t}\right) - \frac{1}{2}\ln\left(\frac{1+\varrho_t}{1-\varrho_t}\right), \qquad (2.22)$$

where γ_t is the edge of h_t, and ϱ_t is the minimum margin of the combined classifier up to the current round.

Based on the minimum margin, Breiman [1999] proved a generalization error bound tighter than (2.20). Since the minimum margin of arc-gv converges to the largest possible minimum margin, the margin theory would appear to predict that arc-gv should perform better than AdaBoost. However, Breiman [1999] found in experiments that, though arc-gv does produce uniformly larger minimum margin than AdaBoost, the test error of arc-gv increases drastically in almost every case. Hence, Breiman [1999] convincingly concluded that the margin-based explanation for AdaBoost was in serious doubt and a new understanding is needed. This almost sentenced the margin theory to death.

Seven years later, Reyzin and Schapire [2006] reported an interesting finding. The bound of generalization error (2.20) is relevant to the margin, the number of learning rounds and the complexity of base learners. To study the influence of margin, the other factors should be fixed. When comparing arc-gv and AdaBoost, Breiman [1999] tried to control the complexity

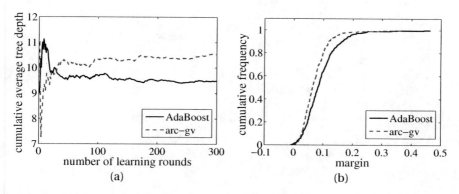

FIGURE 2.8: (a) Tree depth and (b) margin distribution of AdaBoost against arc-gv on the UCI *clean1* data set.

of base learners by using decision trees with a fixed number of leaves. However, Reyzin and Schapire [2006] found that these trees have very different shapes. The trees generated by arc-gv tend to have larger depth, while those generated by AdaBoost tend to have larger width. Figure 2.8(a) depicts the difference of the depth of typical trees generated by the two algorithms. Though the trees have the same number of leaves, it seems that a deeper tree makes more attribute tests than a wider tree, and therefore they are unlikely to have equal complexity. So, Reyzin and Schapire [2006] repeated Breiman's experiments by using decision stumps which have only two leaves and therefore have a fixed complexity, and found that the **margin distribution** of AdaBoost is better than that of arc-gv, as illustrated in Figure 2.8(b).

Thus, the margin distribution is believed crucial to the generalization performance of AdaBoost, and Reyzin and Schapire [2006] suggested to consider *average margin* or *median margin* as measures to compare margin distributions.

2.4.3 Statistical View

Though the margin-based explanation to AdaBoost has a nice geometrical intuition and is attractive to the learning community, it is not that attractive to the statistics community, and statisticians have tried to understand AdaBoost from the perspective of statistical methods. A breakthrough in this direction was made by Friedman et al. [2000] who showed that the AdaBoost algorithm can be interpreted as a stagewise estimation procedure for fitting an additive logistic regression model, which is exactly how we derive the AdaBoost in Section 2.2.

Notice that (2.2) is a form of **additive model**. The exponential loss func-

---

Input: Data set $D = \{(\boldsymbol{x}_1, y_1), (\boldsymbol{x}_2, y_2), \ldots, (\boldsymbol{x}_m, y_m)\}$;
Least square base learning algorithm $\mathfrak{L}$;
Number of learning rounds T.

Process:
1. $y_0(\boldsymbol{x}) = f(\boldsymbol{x})$.   % Initialize target
2. $H_0(\boldsymbol{x}) = 0$.   % Initialize function
3. **for** $t = 1, \ldots, T$:
4. $p_t(\boldsymbol{x}) = \frac{1}{1 + e^{-2H_{t-1}(\boldsymbol{x})}}$;   %Calculate probability
5. $y_t(\boldsymbol{x}) = \frac{y_{t-1}(\boldsymbol{x}) - p_t(\boldsymbol{x})}{p_t(\boldsymbol{x})(1 - p_t(\boldsymbol{x}))}$; % Update target
6. $\mathcal{D}_t(\boldsymbol{x}) = p_t(\boldsymbol{x})(1 - p_t(\boldsymbol{x}))$; % Update weight
7. $h_t = \mathfrak{L}(D, y_t, \mathcal{D}_t)$;   % Train a least square classifier h_t to fit y_t
                    in data set D under distribution $\mathcal{D}_t$
8. $H_t(\boldsymbol{x}) = H_{t-1}(\boldsymbol{x}) + \frac{1}{2}h_t(\boldsymbol{x})$;   %Update combined classifier
9. **end**

Output: $H(\boldsymbol{x}) = \mathrm{sign}\left(\sum_{t=1}^{T} h_t(\boldsymbol{x})\right)$

FIGURE 2.9: The LogitBoost algorithm

tion (2.1) adopted by AdaBoost is a differentiable upper bound of the 0/1-loss function that is typically used for measuring misclassification error [Schapire and Singer, 1999]. If we take a logistic function and estimate probability via

$$P(f(\boldsymbol{x}) = 1 \mid \boldsymbol{x}) = \frac{e^{H(\boldsymbol{x})}}{e^{H(\boldsymbol{x})} + e^{-H(\boldsymbol{x})}} , \tag{2.23}$$

we can find that the exponential loss function and the *log loss* function (negative log-likelihood)

$$\ell_{log}(h \mid \mathcal{D}) = \mathbb{E}_{\boldsymbol{x} \sim \mathcal{D}}\left[\ln\left(1 + e^{-2f(\boldsymbol{x})h(\boldsymbol{x})}\right)\right] \tag{2.24}$$

are minimized by the same function (2.4). So, instead of taking the Newton-like updates in AdaBoost, Friedman et al. [2000] suggested to fit the additive logistic regression model by optimizing the log loss function via gradient decent with the base regression models, leading to the LogitBoost algorithm shown in Figure 2.9.

According to the explanation of Friedman et al. [2000], AdaBoost is just an optimization process that tries to fit an additive model based on a **surrogate loss function**. Ideally, a surrogate loss function should be *consistent*, i.e., optimizing the surrogate loss will yield ultimately an optimal function with the Bayes error rate for true loss function, while the optimization of the surrogate loss is computationally more efficient. Many variants of AdaBoost have been developed by considering different surrogate loss functions, e.g., the LogitBoost which considers the log loss, the L2Boost which considers the l_2 *loss* [Bühlmann and Yu, 2003], etc.

On the other hand, if we just regard a boosting procedure as an optimization of a loss function, an alternative way for this purpose is to use mathematical programming [Demiriz et al., 2002, Warmuth et al., 2008] to solve the weights of weak learners. Consider an additive model $\sum_{h\in\mathcal{H}}\alpha_h h$ of a pool $\mathcal{H}$ of weak learners, and let ξ_i be the loss of the model on instance $\boldsymbol{x}_i$. Demiriz et al. [2002] derived that, if the sum of coefficients and losses is bounded such that

$$\sum_{h\in\mathcal{H}}\alpha_h + C\sum_{i=1}^{m}\xi_i \leq B , \tag{2.25}$$

which actually bounds the complexity (or **covering number**) of the model [Zhang, 1999], the generalization error is therefore bounded as

$$\epsilon_{\mathcal{D}} \leq \tilde{O}\left(\frac{\ln m}{m}B^2\ln(Bm) + \frac{1}{m}\ln\frac{1}{\delta}\right) , \tag{2.26}$$

where $C \geq 1$ and $\alpha_h \geq 0$, and $\tilde{O}$ hides other variables. It is evident that minimizing B also minimizes this upper bound. Thus, considering T weak learners, letting $y_i = f(\boldsymbol{x}_i)$ be the label of training instance $\boldsymbol{x}_i$ and $H_{i,j} = h_j(\boldsymbol{x}_i)$ be the output of weak learner h_j on $\boldsymbol{x}_i$, we have the optimization task

$$\min_{\alpha_j,\xi_i} \sum_{j=1}^{T}\alpha_j + C\sum_{i=1}^{m}\xi_i \tag{2.27}$$

$$\text{s.t.} \quad y_i\sum_{j=1}^{T}H_{i,j}\alpha_j + \xi_i \geq 1 \ (\forall i = 1,\ldots,m)$$

$$\xi_i \geq 0 \ (\forall i = 1,\ldots,m)$$

$$\alpha_j \geq 0 \ (\forall j = 1,\ldots,T) ,$$

or equivalently,

$$\max_{\alpha_j,\xi_i,\rho} \rho - C'\sum_{i=1}^{m}\xi_i \tag{2.28}$$

$$\text{s.t.} \quad y_i\sum_{j=1}^{T}H_{i,j}\alpha_j + \xi_i \geq \rho \ (\forall i = 1,\ldots,m)$$

$$\sum_{j=1}^{T}\alpha_j = 1$$

$$\xi_i \geq 0 \ (\forall i = 1,\ldots,m)$$

$$\alpha_j \geq 0 \ (\forall j = 1,\ldots,T) ,$$

of which the dual form is

$$\min_{w_i, \beta} \beta \qquad (2.29)$$

$$s.t. \qquad \sum_{i=1}^{m} w_i y_i H_{i,j} \leq \beta \ (\forall j = 1, \ldots, T)$$

$$\sum_{i=1}^{m} w_i = 1$$

$$w_i \in [0, C'] \ (\forall i = 1, \ldots, m).$$

A difficulty for the optimization task is that T can be very large. Considering the final solution of the first linear programming, some α will be zero. One way to handle this problem is to find the smallest subset of all the columns; this can be done by *column generation* [Nash and Sofer, 1996]. Using the dual form, set $w_i = 1/m$ for the first column, and then find the jth column that violates the constraint

$$\sum_{i=1}^{m} w_i y_i H_{i,j} \leq \beta \qquad (2.30)$$

to the most. This is equivalent to maximizing $\sum_{i=1}^{m} w_i y_i H_{i,j}$; in other words, finding the weak learner h_j with the smallest error under the weight distribution w. When the solved h_j does not violate any constraint, optimality is reached and the column generation process terminates. The whole procedure forms the LPBoost algorithm [Demiriz et al., 2002] summarized in Figure 2.10. The performance advantage of LPBoost against AdaBoost is not apparent [Demiriz et al., 2002], while it is observed that an improved version, entropy regularized LPBoost, often beats AdaBoost [Warmuth et al., 2008].

It is noteworthy that though the statistical view of boosting is well accepted by the statistics community, it does not answer the question why AdaBoost seems resistant to overfitting. Moreover, the AdaBoost algorithm was designed as a classification algorithm for minimizing the misclassification error, while the statistical view focuses on the minimization of the surrogate loss function (or equivalently, probability estimation); these two problems are often very different. As indicated by Mease and Wyner [2008], in addition to the optimization aspect, a more comprehensive view should also consider the stagewise nature of the algorithm as well as the empirical variance reduction effect.

2.5 Multiclass Extension

In the previous sections we focused on AdaBoost for binary classification, i.e., $\mathcal{Y} = \{+1, -1\}$. In many classification tasks, however, an instance be-

---

Input: Data set $D = \{(\boldsymbol{x}_1, y_1), (\boldsymbol{x}_2, y_2), \ldots, (\boldsymbol{x}_m, y_m)\}$;
 Base learning algorithm $\mathfrak{L}$;
 Parameter ν.
 Number of learning rounds T.

Process:
1. $w_{1,i} = 1/m \ (\forall i = 1, \ldots, m)$.
2. $\beta_1 = 0$.
3. **for** $t = 1, \ldots$, T:
4. $h_t = \mathfrak{L}(D, \boldsymbol{w})$; % Train a learner h_t from D under $\boldsymbol{w}$
5.   **if** $\sum_{i=1}^{m} w_{t,i} y_i h_t(\boldsymbol{x}_i) \leq \beta_t$ **then** $T = t - 1$; **break**; % Check optimality
6. $H_{i,t} = h_t(\boldsymbol{x}_i) \ (i = 1, \ldots, m)$; % Fill a column
7. $(\boldsymbol{w}_{t+1}, \beta_{t+1}) = \arg\min_{\boldsymbol{w}, \beta} \beta$
   $s.t. \quad \sum_{i=1}^{m} w_i y_i h_j(\boldsymbol{x}_i) \leq \beta \ (\forall j \leq t)$
   $$\sum_{i=1}^{m} w_i = 1$$
   $$w_i \in [0, \frac{1}{m\nu}] \ (\forall i = 1, \ldots, m)$$

8. **end**
9. solve α from the dual solution $(\boldsymbol{w}_{T+1}, \beta_{T+1})$;
Output: $H(\boldsymbol{x}) = \text{sign}\left(\sum_{t=1}^{T} \alpha_t h_t(\boldsymbol{x})\right)$

FIGURE 2.10: The LPBoost algorithm

longs to one of many instead of two classes. For example, a handwritten digit belongs to one of the 10 classes, i.e., $\mathcal{Y} = \{0, \ldots, 9\}$. There are many alternative ways to extend AdaBoost for multiclass classification.

AdaBoost.M1 [Freund and Schapire, 1997] is a very straightforward extension, which is the same as the algorithm shown in Figure 2.2 except that the base learners now are multiclass learners instead of binary classifiers. This algorithm could not use binary classifiers, and has an overly strong constraint that every base learner has less than $1/2$ multiclass $0/1$-loss.

SAMME [Zhu et al., 2006] is an improvement over AdaBoost.M1, which replaces line 6 of AdaBoost.M1 in Figure 2.2 by

$$\alpha_t = \frac{1}{2} \ln\left(\frac{1 - \epsilon_t}{\epsilon_t}\right) + \ln(|\mathcal{Y}| - 1). \qquad (2.31)$$

This modification is derived from the minimization of multiclass exponential loss, and it was proved that, similar to the case of binary classification, optimizing the multiclass exponential loss approaches to the Bayes error rate, i.e.,

$$\text{sign}(h^*(\boldsymbol{x})) = \arg\max_{y \in \mathcal{Y}} P(y|\boldsymbol{x}), \qquad (2.32)$$

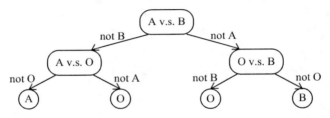

FIGURE 2.11: A directed acyclic graph that aggregates one-versus-one de-composition for classes of A, B and O.

where h^* is the optimal solution to the multiclass exponential loss.

A commonly used solution to the multiclass classification problem is to decompose the task into multiple binary classification problems. Popular decomposition schemes include **one-versus-rest** and **one-versus-one**. One-versus-rest decomposes a multiclass task of $|\mathcal{Y}|$ classes into $|\mathcal{Y}|$ binary classification tasks, where the ith task is to classify whether an instance belongs to the ith class or not. One-versus-one decomposes a multiclass task of $|\mathcal{Y}|$ classes into $\frac{|\mathcal{Y}|(|\mathcal{Y}|-1)}{2}$ binary classification tasks, where each task is to classify whether an instance belongs to, say, the ith class or the jth class.

AdaBoost.MH [Schapire and Singer, 1999] follows the one-versus-rest strategy. After training $|\mathcal{Y}|$ number of binary AdaBoost classifiers, the real-value output $H(\boldsymbol{x}) = \sum_{t=1}^{T} \alpha_t h_t(\boldsymbol{x})$ rather than the crisp classification of each AdaBoost classifier is used to identify the most probable class, that is,

$$H(\boldsymbol{x}) = \arg\max_{y \in \mathcal{Y}} H_y(\boldsymbol{x}) , \qquad (2.33)$$

where H_y is the binary AdaBoost classifier that classifies the yth class from the rest.

AdaBoost.M2 [Freund and Schapire, 1997] follows the one-versus-one strategy, which minimizes a *pseudo-loss*. This algorithm is later generalized as AdaBoost.MR [Schapire and Singer, 1999] which minimizes a *ranking loss* motivated by the fact that the highest ranked class is more likely to be the correct class. Binary classifiers obtained by one-versus-one decomposition can also be aggregated by voting, pairwise coupling, directed acyclic graph, etc. [Hsu and Lin, 2002, Hastie and Tibshirani, 1998]. Voting and pairwise coupling are well known, while Figure 2.11 illustrates the use of a directed acyclic graph.

2.6 Noise Tolerance

Real-world data are often noisy. The AdaBoost algorithm, however, was originally designed for clean data and has been observed to be very sensitive to noise. The noise sensitivity of AdaBoost is generally attributed to the exponential loss function (2.1) which specifies that if an instance were not classified as the same as its given label, the weight of the instance will increase drastically. Consequently, when a training instance is associated with a wrong label, AdaBoost still tries to make the prediction resemble the given label, and thus degenerates the performance.

MadaBoost [Domingo and Watanabe, 2000] improves AdaBoost by depressing large instance weights. It is almost the same as AdaBoost except for the weight updating rule. Recall the weight updating rule of AdaBoost, i.e.,

$$
\begin{aligned}
\mathcal{D}_{t+1}(\boldsymbol{x}) &= \frac{\mathcal{D}_t(\boldsymbol{x})}{Z_t} \times \begin{cases} e^{-\alpha_t}, & \text{if } h_t(\boldsymbol{x}) = f(\boldsymbol{x}) \\ e^{\alpha_t}, & \text{if } h_t(\boldsymbol{x}) \neq f(\boldsymbol{x}) \end{cases} \\
&= \frac{\mathcal{D}_t(\boldsymbol{x})}{Z_t} \times e^{-\alpha_t \cdot h_t(\boldsymbol{x}) \cdot f(\boldsymbol{x})} \\
&= \frac{\mathcal{D}_1(\boldsymbol{x})}{Z_t'} \times \prod_{i=1}^{t} e^{-\alpha_i \cdot h_i(\boldsymbol{x}) \cdot f(\boldsymbol{x})} \,,
\end{aligned}
\tag{2.34}
$$

where Z_t and Z_t' are the normalization terms. It can be seen that, if the prediction on an instance is different from its given label for a number of rounds, the term $\prod_{i=1}^{t} e^{-\alpha_i \cdot h_i(\boldsymbol{x}) \cdot f(\boldsymbol{x})}$ will grow very large, pushing the instance to be classified according to the given label in the next round. To reduce the undesired dramatic increase of instance weights caused by noise, MadaBoost sets an upper limit on the weights:

$$
\mathcal{D}_{t+1}(\boldsymbol{x}) = \frac{\mathcal{D}_1(\boldsymbol{x})}{Z_t'} \times \min \left\{ 1, \prod_{i=1}^{t} e^{-\alpha_i \cdot h_i(\boldsymbol{x}) \cdot f(\boldsymbol{x})} \right\} \,,
\tag{2.35}
$$

where Z_t' is the normalization term. By using this weight updating rule, the instance weights will not grow without bound.

FilterBoost [Bradley and Schapire, 2008] does not employ the exponential loss function used in AdaBoost, but adopts the log loss function (2.24). Similar to the derivation of AdaBoost in Section 2.2, we consider fitting an additive model to minimize the log loss function. At round t, denote the combined learner as H_{t-1} and the classifier to be trained as h_t. Using the

Taylor expansion of the loss function, we have

$$\ell_{log}(H_{t-1} + h_t \mid \mathcal{D}) = \mathbb{E}_{\boldsymbol{x} \sim \mathcal{D}}\left[-\ln \frac{1}{1 + e^{-f(\boldsymbol{x})(H_{t-1}(\boldsymbol{x}) + h_t(\boldsymbol{x}))}}\right] \tag{2.36}$$

$$\approx \mathbb{E}_{\boldsymbol{x} \sim \mathcal{D}}\left[\ln(1 + e^{-f(\boldsymbol{x})H_{t-1}(\boldsymbol{x})}) - \frac{f(\boldsymbol{x})h_t(\boldsymbol{x})}{1 + e^{f(\boldsymbol{x})H_{t-1}(\boldsymbol{x})}} + \frac{e^{f(\boldsymbol{x})H_{t-1}(\boldsymbol{x})}}{2(1 + e^{f(\boldsymbol{x})H_{t-1}(\boldsymbol{x})})^2}\right]$$

$$\approx \mathbb{E}_{\boldsymbol{x} \sim \mathcal{D}}\left[-\frac{f(\boldsymbol{x})h_t(\boldsymbol{x})}{1 + e^{f(\boldsymbol{x})H_{t-1}(\boldsymbol{x})}}\right] ,$$

by noticing that $f(\boldsymbol{x})^2 = 1$ and $h_t(\boldsymbol{x})^2 = 1$. To minimize the loss function, h_t needs to satisfy

$$h_t = \arg\min_h \ell_{log}(H_{t-1} + h \mid \mathcal{D}) \tag{2.37}$$

$$= \arg\max_h \mathbb{E}_{\boldsymbol{x} \sim \mathcal{D}}\left[\frac{f(\boldsymbol{x})h(\boldsymbol{x})}{1 + e^{f(\boldsymbol{x})H_{t-1}(\boldsymbol{x})}}\right]$$

$$= \arg\max_h \mathbb{E}_{\boldsymbol{x} \sim \mathcal{D}}\left[\frac{f(\boldsymbol{x})h(\boldsymbol{x})}{Z_t(1 + e^{f(\boldsymbol{x})H_{t-1}(\boldsymbol{x})})}\right]$$

$$= \arg\max_h \mathbb{E}_{\boldsymbol{x} \sim \mathcal{D}_t}\left[f(\boldsymbol{x})h(\boldsymbol{x})\right] ,$$

where $Z_t = \mathbb{E}_{\boldsymbol{x} \sim \mathcal{D}}\left[\frac{1}{1 + e^{f(\boldsymbol{x})H_{t-1}(\boldsymbol{x})}}\right]$ is the normalization factor, and the weight updating rule is

$$\mathcal{D}_t(\boldsymbol{x}) = \frac{\mathcal{D}(\boldsymbol{x})}{Z_t} \frac{1}{1 + e^{f(\boldsymbol{x})H_{t-1}(\boldsymbol{x})}} . \tag{2.38}$$

It is evident that with this updating rule, the increase of the instance weights is upper bounded by 1, similar to the weight depressing in MadaBoost, but smoother.

The BBM (Boosting-By-Majority) [Freund, 1995] algorithm was the first iterative boosting algorithm. Though it is noise tolerant [Aslam and Decatur, 1993], it requires the user to specify mysterious parameters in advance; excluding the requirement on unknown parameters motivated the development of AdaBoost. BrownBoost [Freund, 2001] is another adaptive version of BBM, which inherits BBM's noise tolerance property. Derived from the loss function of BBM, which is an accumulated binomial distribution, the loss function of BrownBoost is corresponding to the *Brownian motion process* [Gardiner, 2004], i.e.,

$$\ell_{bmp}(H_{t-1} + h_t \mid \mathcal{D}) = \mathbb{E}_{\boldsymbol{x} \sim \mathcal{D}}\left[1 - erf\left(\frac{f(\boldsymbol{x})H_{t-1}(\boldsymbol{x}) + f(\boldsymbol{x})h_t(\boldsymbol{x}) + c - t}{\sqrt{c}}\right)\right], \tag{2.39}$$

where the parameter c specifies the total *time* for the boosting procedure, t is the current time which starts from zero and increases in each round, and

$erf(\cdot)$ is the error function

$$erf(a) = \frac{1}{\pi} \int_{-\infty}^{a} e^{-x^2} dx \ . \tag{2.40}$$

The loss function (2.39) can be expanded as

$$\ell_{bmp}(H_{t-1} + h_t \mid \mathcal{D}) \approx \mathbb{E}_{\boldsymbol{x} \sim \mathcal{D}} \left[\begin{array}{l} 1 - erf(\frac{1}{\sqrt{c}}(f(\boldsymbol{x})H_{t-1}(\boldsymbol{x}) + c - t) \\ - \frac{2}{c\pi} e^{-(f(\boldsymbol{x})H_{t-1}(\boldsymbol{x})+c-t)^2/c} f(\boldsymbol{x})h_t(\boldsymbol{x}) \\ - \frac{4}{c^2\pi} e^{-(f(\boldsymbol{x})H_{t-1}(\boldsymbol{x})+c-t)^2/c} f(\boldsymbol{x})^2 h_t(\boldsymbol{x})^2 \end{array} \right]$$

$$\approx -\mathbb{E}_{\boldsymbol{x} \sim \mathcal{D}} \left[e^{-(f(\boldsymbol{x})H_{t-1}(\boldsymbol{x})+c-t)^2/c} f(\boldsymbol{x})h_t(\boldsymbol{x}) \right] , \tag{2.41}$$

and thus, the learner which minimizes the loss function is

$$h_t = \arg\min_h \ell_{bmp}(H_{t-1} + h \mid \mathcal{D}) \tag{2.42}$$

$$= \arg\max_h \mathbb{E}_{\boldsymbol{x} \sim \mathcal{D}} \left[e^{-(f(\boldsymbol{x})H_{t-1}(\boldsymbol{x})+c-t)^2/c} f(\boldsymbol{x})h(\boldsymbol{x}) \right]$$

$$= \arg\max_h \mathbb{E}_{\boldsymbol{x} \sim \mathcal{D}_t} \left[f(\boldsymbol{x})h(\boldsymbol{x}) \right] ,$$

where the weight updating rule is

$$\mathcal{D}_t(\boldsymbol{x}) = \frac{\mathcal{D}(\boldsymbol{x})}{Z_t} e^{-(f(\boldsymbol{x})H_{t-1}(\boldsymbol{x})+c-t)^2/c} , \tag{2.43}$$

and Z_t is the normalization term. Notice that the weighting function $e^{-(f(\boldsymbol{x})H_{t-1}(\boldsymbol{x})+c-t)^2/c}$ at here is quite different from that used in the boosting algorithms introduced above. When the classification margin $f(\boldsymbol{x})H_{t-1}(\boldsymbol{x})$ equals the negative remaining time $-(c-t)$, the weight is set to the largest and will reduce as the margin goes either larger or smaller. This implies that BrownBoost/BBM "gives up" on some very hard training instances. With more learning rounds, $-(c-t)$ approaches 0. This implies that BrownBoost/BBM pushes the margin on most instances to be positive, while leaving alone the remaining hard instances that could be noise.

RobustBoost [Freund, 2009] is an improvement of BrownBoost, aiming at improving the noise tolerance ability by boosting the normalized classification margin, which is believed to be related to the generalization error (see Section 2.4.2). In other words, instead of minimizing the classification error, RobustBoost tries to minimize

$$\mathbb{E}_{\boldsymbol{x} \sim \mathcal{D}} \left[\mathbb{I} \left(\frac{\sum_{t=1}^{T} \alpha_t f(\boldsymbol{x})h_t(\boldsymbol{x})}{\sum_{t=1}^{T} \alpha_t} \leq \theta \right) \right] , \tag{2.44}$$

where θ is the goal margin. For this purpose, the Brownian motion process in BrownBoost is changed to the mean-reverting *Ornstein-Uhlenbeck process* [Gardiner, 2004], with the loss function

$$\ell_{oup}(H_{t-1} + h_t \mid \mathcal{D}) = \mathbb{E}_{\boldsymbol{x} \sim \mathcal{D}} \left[1 - erf \left(\frac{\tilde{m}(H_{t-1}(\boldsymbol{x}) + h_t(\boldsymbol{x})) - \mu(\frac{t}{c})}{\sigma(\frac{t}{c})} \right) \right],$$

(2.45)

where $\tilde{m}(H)$ is the normalized margin of H, $0 \le \frac{t}{c} \le 1$, $\mu(\frac{t}{c}) = (\theta - 2\rho)e^{1 - \frac{t}{c}} + 2\rho$ and $\sigma(\frac{t}{c})^2 = (\sigma_f^2 + 1)e^{2(1 - \frac{t}{c})} - 1$ are respectively the mean and variance of the process, ρ, σ_f as well as θ are parameters of the algorithm. By a similar derivation as that of BrownBoost, the weight updating rule of RobustBoost is

$$\mathcal{D}_t(\boldsymbol{x}) = \frac{\mathcal{D}(\boldsymbol{x})}{Z_t} e^{-(f(\boldsymbol{x})H_{t-1}(\boldsymbol{x}) - \mu(\frac{t}{c}))^2 / (2\sigma(\frac{t}{c})^2)}.$$

(2.46)

A major difference between the weighting functions (2.46) of RobustBoost and (2.43) of BrownBoost lies in the fact that $\mu(\frac{t}{c})$ approaches θ as t approaches the total time c; thus, RobustBoost pushes the normalized classification margin to be larger than the goal margin θ, while BrownBoost just pushes the classification margin to be larger than zero.

2.7   Further Readings

Computational learning theory studies some fundamental theoretical issues of learning. First introduced by Valiant [1984], the **PAC (Probably Approximately Correct)** framework models learning algorithms in a distribution free manner. Roughly speaking, for binary classification, a problem is *learnable* or *strongly learnable* if there exists an algorithm that outputs a learner h in polynomial time such that for all $0 < \delta, \epsilon \le 0.5$, $P(\mathbb{E}_{\boldsymbol{x} \sim \mathcal{D}}[\mathbb{I}[h(\boldsymbol{x}) \ne f(\boldsymbol{x})]] < \epsilon) \ge 1 - \delta$, and a problem is *weakly learnable* if there exists an algorithm that outputs a learner with error $0.5 - 1/p$ where p is a polynomial in problem size and other parameters. Anthony and Biggs [1992], and Kearns and Vazirani [1994] provide good introductions to computational learning theory.

In 1990, Schapire [1990] proved that strongly learnable problem class equals the weakly learnable problem class, an open problem raised by Kearns and Valiant [1989]. The proof is a construction, which is the first boosting algorithm. One year later, Freund developed the more efficient BBM algorithm, which was later published in [Freund, 1995]. Both algorithms, however, suffered from the practical deficiency that the error bounds of the base learners need to be known in advance. Later in 1995,

Freund and Schapire [1995, 1997] developed the AdaBoost algorithm, which avoids the requirement on unknown parameters, thus named from *adaptive boosting*. The AdaBoost paper [Freund and Schapire, 1997] won its authors the *Gödel Prize* in 2003.

Understanding why AdaBoost seems resistant to overfitting is one of the most interesting open problems on boosting. Notice that the concern is why AdaBoost *often* does not overfit, and it does not *never* overfit, e.g., Grove and Schuurmans [1998] showed that overfitting eventually occurs after enough learning rounds. Many interesting discussions can be found in the discussion part of [Friedman et al., 2000, Mease and Wyner, 2008].

Besides Breiman [1999], Harries [1999] also constructed an algorithm to show that the minimum margin is not crucial. Wang et al. [2008] introduced the *Emargin* and proved a new generalization error bound tighter than that based on the minimum margin. Gao and Zhou [2012] showed that the minimum margin and Emargin are special cases of the kth margin; all of them are *single margins* that cannot measure the margin distribution. By considering exactly the same factors as Schapire et al. [1998], Gao and Zhou [2012] proved a new generalization error bound based on the empirical Bernstein inequality [Maurer and Pontil, 2009]; this new generalization error bound is uniformly tighter than both the bounds of Schapire et al. [1998] and Breiman [1999], and thus defends the margin-based explanation against Breiman's doubt. Furthermore, Gao and Zhou [2012] obtained an even tighter generalization error bound by considering the empirical *average margin* and *margin variance*.

In addition to the two most popular theoretical explanations, i.e., the margin explanation and the statistical view, there are also some other theoretical explanations to boosting. For example, Breiman [2004] proposed the population theory for boosting, Bickel et al. [2006] considered boosting as the Gauss-Southwell minimization of a loss function, etc. The **stability** of AdaBoost has also been studied [Kutin and Niyogi, 2002, Gao and Zhou, 2010].

There are many empirical studies involving AdaBoost, e.g., [Bauer and Kohavi, 1999, Opitz and Maclin, 1999, Dietterich, 2000b]. The famous **bias-variance decomposition** [Geman et al., 1992] has been employed to empirically study why AdaBoost achieves excellent performance. This powerful tool breaks the expected error of a learning algorithm into the sum of three non-negative quantities, i.e., the **intrinsic noise**, the bias, and the variance. The **bias** measures how closely the average estimate of the learning algorithm is able to approximate the target, and the **variance** measures how much the estimate of the learning algorithm fluctuates for the different training sets of the same size. It has been observed that AdaBoost primarily reduces the bias though it is also able to reduce the variance [Bauer and Kohavi, 1999, Breiman, 1996a, Zhou et al., 2002b].

Ideal base learners for boosting are weak learners sufficiently strong to be boostable, since it is easy to underfit if the base learners are too weak, yet easy to overfit if the base learners are too strong. For binary classification, it is well known that the exact requirement for weak learners is to be better than random guess. While for multi-class problems, it remains a mystery until the recent work by Mukherjee and Schapire [2010]. Notice that requiring base learners to be better than random guess is too weak for multi-class problems, yet requiring better than 50% accuracy is too stringent. Recently, **Conditional Random Fields (CRFs)** and **latent variable models** are also utilized as base learners for boosting [Dietterich et al., 2008, Hutchinson et al., 2011].

Error Correcting Output Codes (ECOC) [Dietterich and Bakiri, 1995] is an important way to extend binary learners to multi-class learners, which will be introduced in Section 4.6.1 of Chapter 4. Among the alternative ways of characterizing noise in data and how a learning algorithm is resistant to noise, the **statistical query model** [Kearns, 1998] is a PAC compliant theoretical model, in which a learning algorithm learns from queries of noisy expectation values of hypotheses. We call a boosting algorithm as a **SQ Boosting** if it efficiently boosts noise tolerant weak learners to strong learners. The noise tolerance of MadaBoost was proved by showing that it is a SQ Boosting, by assuming monotonic errors for the weak learners [Domingo and Watanabe, 2000]. Aslam and Decatur [1993] showed that BBM is also a SQ Boosting. In addition to algorithms introduced in Section 2.6, there are many other algorithms, such as GentleBoost [Friedman et al., 2000], trying to improve the robustness of AdaBoost. McDonald et al. [2003] reported an empirical comparison of AdaBoost, LogitBoost and BrownBoost on noisy data. A thorough comparison of robust AdaBoost variants is an important issue to be explored.

3
Bagging

3.1 Two Ensemble Paradigms

According to how the base learners are generated, roughly speaking, there are two paradigms of ensemble methods, that is, **sequential ensemble methods** where the base learners are generated sequentially, with Ada-Boost as a representative, and **parallel ensemble methods** where the base learners are generated in parallel, with Bagging [Breiman, 1996d] as a representative.

The basic motivation of sequential methods is to exploit the *dependence* between the base learners, since the overall performance can be boosted in a *residual-decreasing* way, as seen in Chapter 2. The basic motivation of parallel ensemble methods is to exploit the *independence* between the base learners, since the error can be reduced dramatically by combining independent base learners.

Take binary classification on classes $\{-1, +1\}$ as an example. Suppose the ground-truth function is f, and each base classifier has an independent generalization error ϵ, i.e., for base classifier h_i,

$$P(h_i(\boldsymbol{x}) \neq f(\boldsymbol{x})) = \epsilon . \tag{3.1}$$

After combining T number of such base classifiers according to

$$H(\boldsymbol{x}) = \texttt{sign}\left(\sum_{i=1}^{T} h_i(\boldsymbol{x})\right) , \tag{3.2}$$

the ensemble H makes an error only when at least half of its base classifiers make errors. Therefore, by **Hoeffding inequality**, the generalization error of the ensemble is

$$P(H(\boldsymbol{x}) \neq f(\boldsymbol{x})) = \sum_{k=0}^{\lfloor T/2 \rfloor} \binom{T}{k}(1-\epsilon)^k \epsilon^{T-k} \leq \exp\left(-\frac{1}{2}T(2\epsilon - 1)^2\right) . \tag{3.3}$$

(3.3) clearly shows that the generalization error reduces exponentially to the ensemble size T, and ultimately approaches to zero as T approaches to infinity. Though it is practically impossible to get really independent base learners since they are generated from the same training data set, base learners with less dependence can be obtained by introducing randomness in the learning process, and a good generalization ability can be expected by the ensemble.

Another benefit of the parallel ensemble methods is that they are inherently favorable to parallel computing, and the training speed can be easily accelerated using multi-core computing processors or parallel computers. This is attractive as multi-core processors are commonly available nowadays.

3.2   The Bagging Algorithm

The name Bagging came from the abbreviation of *Bootstrap AGGregatING* [Breiman, 1996d]. As the name implies, the two key ingredients of Bagging are bootstrap and aggregation.

We know that the combination of independent base learners will lead to a dramatic decrease of errors and therefore, we want to get base learners as independent as possible. Given a training data set, one possibility seems to be sampling a number of non-overlapped data subsets and then training a base learner from each of the subsets. However, since we do not have infinite training data, such a process will produce very small and unrepresentative samples, leading to poor performance of base learners.

Bagging adopts the bootstrap distribution for generating different base learners. In other words, it applies **bootstrap sampling** [Efron and Tibshirani, 1993] to obtain the data subsets for training the base learners. In detail, given a training data set containing m number of training examples, a sample of m training examples will be generated by *sampling with replacement*. Some original examples appear more than once, while some original examples are not present in the sample. By applying the process T times, T samples of m training examples are obtained. Then, from each sample a base learner can be trained by applying the base learning algorithm.

Bagging adopts the most popular strategies for aggregating the outputs of the base learners, that is, *voting* for classification and *averaging* for regression. To predict a test instance, taking classification for example, Bagging feeds the instance to its base classifiers and collects all of their outputs, and then votes the labels and takes the winner label as the prediction, where ties are broken arbitrarily. Notice that Bagging can deal with binary classification as well as multi-class classification. The Bagging algorithm is summarized in Figure 3.1.

It is worth mentioning that the bootstrap sampling also offers Bagging

---

Input: Data set $D = \{(\boldsymbol{x}_1, y_1), (\boldsymbol{x}_2, y_2), \ldots, (\boldsymbol{x}_m, y_m)\}$;
   Base learning algorithm $\mathfrak{L}$;
   Number of base learners T.

Process:
1. **for** $t = 1, \ldots, T$:
2. $h_t = \mathfrak{L}(D, \mathcal{D}_{bs})$ % $\mathcal{D}_{bs}$ is the bootstrap distribution
3. **end**

Output: $H(\boldsymbol{x}) = \arg\max_{y \in \mathcal{Y}} \sum_{t=1}^{T} \mathbb{I}(h_t(\boldsymbol{x}) = y)$

FIGURE 3.1: The Bagging algorithm

another advantage. As Breiman [1996d] indicated, given m training examples, the probability that the ith training example is selected $0, 1, 2, \ldots$ times is approximately Poisson distributed with $\lambda = 1$, and thus, the probability that the ith example will occur at least once is $1 - (1/e) \approx 0.632$. In other words, for each base learner in Bagging, there are about 36.8% original training examples which have not been used in its training process. The goodness of the base learner can be estimated by using these **out-of-bag** examples, and thereafter the generalization error of the bagged ensemble can be estimated [Breiman, 1996c, Tibshirani, 1996b, Wolpert and Macready, 1999].

To get the out-of-bag estimate, we need to record the training examples used for each base learner. Denote $H^{oob}(\boldsymbol{x})$ as the out-of-bag prediction on $\boldsymbol{x}$, where only the learners that have not been trained on $\boldsymbol{x}$ are involved, i.e.,

$$H^{oob}(\boldsymbol{x}) = \arg\max_{y \in \mathcal{Y}} \sum_{t=1}^{T} \mathbb{I}(h_t(\boldsymbol{x}) = y) \cdot \mathbb{I}(\boldsymbol{x} \notin D_t) . \tag{3.4}$$

Then, the out-of-bag estimate of the generalization error of Bagging is

$$err^{oob} = \frac{1}{|D|} \sum_{(\boldsymbol{x}, y) \in D} \mathbb{I}(H^{oob}(\boldsymbol{x}) \neq y) . \tag{3.5}$$

The out-of-bag examples can also be used for many other purposes. For example, when decision trees are used as base classifiers, the *posterior* probability of each node of each tree can be estimated using the out-of-bag examples. If a node does not contain out-of-bag examples, it is marked "uncounted". For a test instance, its *posterior* probability can be estimated by averaging the *posterior* probabilities of non-uncounted nodes into which it falls.

3.3 Illustrative Examples

To get an intuitive understanding of Bagging, we visualize the decision boundaries of a single decision tree, Bagging and its component decision trees on the *three-Gaussians* data set, as shown in Figure 3.2. It can be observed that the decision boundary of Bagging is more flexible than that of a single decision tree, and this helps to reduce the error from 9.4% of the single decision tree to 8.3% of the bagged ensemble.

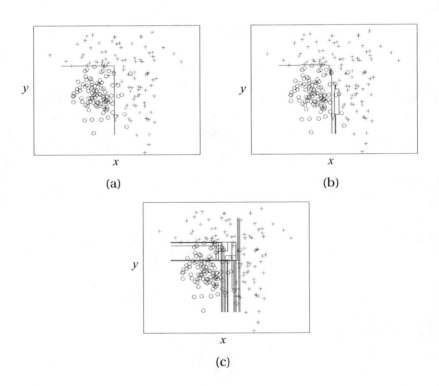

FIGURE 3.2: Decision boundaries of (a) a single decision tree, (b) Bagging and (c) the 10 decision trees used by Bagging, on the *three-Gaussians* data set.

We also evaluate the Bagging algorithm on 40 data sets from the UCI Machine Learning Repository. The Weka implementation of Bagging with 20 base classifiers is tested. We have tried three base learning algorithms: decision stumps, and pruned and unpruned J48 decision trees. We plot the

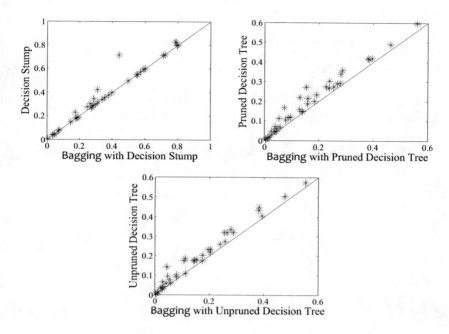

FIGURE 3.3: Comparison of predictive errors of Bagging against single base learners on 40 UCI data sets. Each point represents a data set and locates according to the predictive error of the two compared algorithms. The diagonal line indicates where the two compared algorithms have identical errors.

comparison results in Figure 3.3, and it can be observed that Bagging often outperforms its base learning algorithm, and rarely reduces performance.

With a further observation on Figure 3.3, it can be found that Bagging using decision stumps is less powerful than Bagging using decision trees. This is easier to see in Figure 3.4.

Remember that Bagging adopts bootstrap sampling to generate different data samples, while all the data samples have large overlap, say, 63.2%, with the original data set. If a base learning algorithm is insensitive to perturbation on training samples, the base learners trained from the data samples may be quite similar, and thus combining them will not help improve the generalization performance. Such learners are called **stable learners**. Decision trees are unstable learners, while decision stumps are more close to stable learners. On highly stable learners such as k-nearest neighbor classifiers, Bagging does not work. For example, Figure 3.5 shows the decision boundaries of a single 1-nearest neighbor classifier and Bagging of such classifiers. The difference between the decision boundaries is hardly visi-

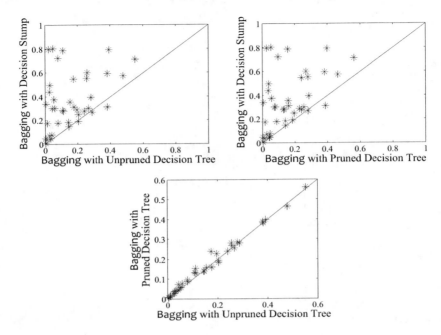

FIGURE 3.4: Comparison of predictive errors of Bagging using decision stumps, pruned decision trees and unpruned decision trees. Each point represents a data set and locates according to the predictive error of the two compared algorithms. The diagonal line indicates where the two compared algorithms have identical errors.

ble, and the predictive errors are both 9.1%.

Indeed, it is well known that Bagging should be used with unstable learners, and generally, the more unstable, the larger the performance improvement. This explains why in Figure 3.4 the performance of Bagging with unpruned decision trees is better than with pruned decision trees, since unpruned trees are more unstable than pruned ones. This provides a good implication, that is, when we use Bagging, we do not need to do the time-consuming decision tree pruning.

With independent base learners, (3.3) shows that the generalization error reduces exponentially in the ensemble size T, and ultimately approaches zero as T approaches to infinity. In practice we do not have infinite training data, and the base learners of Bagging are not independent since they are trained from bootstrap samples. However, it is worth mentioning that though the error might not drop to zero, the performance of Bagging converges as the **ensemble size**, i.e., the number of base learners, grows large, as illustrated in Figure 3.6.

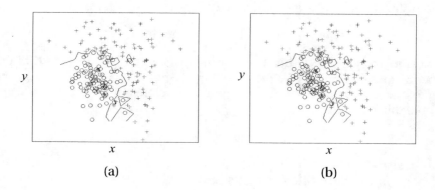

FIGURE 3.5: Decision boundaries of (a) 1-nearest neighbor classifier, and (b) Bagging of 1-nearest neighbor classifiers, on the *three-Gaussians* data set.

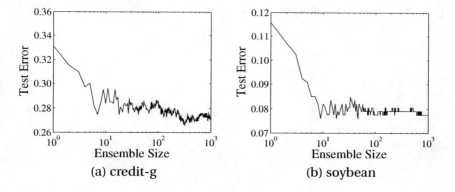

FIGURE 3.6: Impact of ensemble size on Bagging on two UCI data sets.

3.4 Theoretical Issues

Bagging has a tremendous variance reduction effect, and it is particularly effective with unstable base learners. Understanding these properties is fundamental in the theoretical studies of Bagging.

Breiman [1996d] presented an explanation when he proposed Bagging. Let's consider regression at first. Let f denote the ground-truth function and $h(x)$ denote a learner trained from the bootstrap distribution $\mathcal{D}_{bs}$. The aggregated learner generated by Bagging is

$$H(\boldsymbol{x}) = \mathbb{E}_{\mathcal{D}_{bs}}[h(\boldsymbol{x})] .\qquad (3.6)$$

With simple algebra and the inequality $(\mathbb{E}[X])^2 \leq \mathbb{E}[X^2]$, we have

$$(f(\boldsymbol{x}) - H(\boldsymbol{x}))^2 \leq \mathbb{E}_{\mathcal{D}_{bs}}\left[(f(\boldsymbol{x}) - h(\boldsymbol{x}))^2\right] . \tag{3.7}$$

Thus, by integrating both sides over the distribution, we can get that the mean-squared error of $H(\boldsymbol{x})$ is smaller than that of $h(\boldsymbol{x})$ averaged over the bootstrap sampling distribution, and the difference depends on how unequal the following inequality is:

$$(\mathbb{E}_{\mathcal{D}_{bs}}[h(\boldsymbol{x})])^2 \leq \mathbb{E}_{\mathcal{D}_{bs}}\left[h(\boldsymbol{x})^2\right] . \tag{3.8}$$

This clearly discloses the importance of *instability*. That is, if $h(\boldsymbol{x})$ does not change much with different bootstrap samples, the aggregation will not help; while if $h(\boldsymbol{x})$ changes much, the improvement provided by the aggregation will be great. This explains why Bagging is effective with **unstable learners**, and it reduces variance through the smoothing effect.

In the context of classification, suppose the classifier $h(\boldsymbol{x})$ predicts the class label $y \in \{y_1, y_2, \ldots, y_c\}$. Let $P(y \mid \boldsymbol{x})$ denote the probability of y being the ground-truth class label of $\boldsymbol{x}$. Then, the probability of h correctly classifying $\boldsymbol{x}$ is

$$\sum_y P(h(\boldsymbol{x}) = y) P(y \mid \boldsymbol{x}) , \tag{3.9}$$

and the overall correct classification probability of h is

$$\int \sum_y P(h(\boldsymbol{x}) = y) P(y \mid \boldsymbol{x}) P(\boldsymbol{x}) d\boldsymbol{x} , \tag{3.10}$$

where $P(\boldsymbol{x})$ is the input probability distribution.

If the input probability of $\boldsymbol{x}$ with class label y is larger than any other classes, while h predicts class y for $\boldsymbol{x}$ more often, i.e.,

$$\arg\max_y P(h(\boldsymbol{x}) = y) = \arg\max_y P(y \mid \boldsymbol{x}) , \tag{3.11}$$

the predictor h is called *order-correct* at the input $\boldsymbol{x}$.

The aggregated classifier of Bagging is $H(\boldsymbol{x}) = \arg\max_y P(h(\boldsymbol{x}) = y)$. Its probability of correct classification at $\boldsymbol{x}$ is

$$\sum_y \mathbb{I}\left(\arg\max_z P(h(\boldsymbol{x}) = z) = y\right) P(y \mid \boldsymbol{x}) . \tag{3.12}$$

If h is order-correct at the input $\boldsymbol{x}$, the above probability equals $\max_y P(y \mid \boldsymbol{x})$. Thus, the correct classification probability of the aggregated classifier H is

$$\int_{\boldsymbol{x} \in C} \max_y P(y \mid \boldsymbol{x}) P(\boldsymbol{x}) d\boldsymbol{x} + \int_{\boldsymbol{x} \in C'} \left[\sum_y \mathbb{I}(H(\boldsymbol{x}) = y) P(y \mid \boldsymbol{x})\right] P(\boldsymbol{x}) d\boldsymbol{x} , \tag{3.13}$$

where C is the set of all inputs x where h is order-correct, and C' is the set of inputs at which h is not order-correct. It always holds that

$$\sum_y P\left(h\left(\boldsymbol{x}\right) = y\right) P(y \mid \boldsymbol{x}) \leq \max_y P(y \mid \boldsymbol{x}) . \tag{3.14}$$

Thus, the highest achievable accuracy of Bagging is

$$\int \max_y P(y \mid \boldsymbol{x}) P(\boldsymbol{x}) d\boldsymbol{x} , \tag{3.15}$$

which equals the Bayes error rate.

Comparing (3.10) and (3.13), it can be found that if a predictor is order-correct at most instances, Bagging can transform it into a nearly optimal predictor. Notice that if the base learner is unstable, the h's generated from different samples will be quite different, and will produce different predictions on $\boldsymbol{x}$, leading to a low probability of $P(h(\boldsymbol{x}) = y)$. According to (3.9), the probability of correctly predicting $\boldsymbol{x}$ will be low. We know that, however, if h is order-correct at $\boldsymbol{x}$, Bagging will correctly classify $\boldsymbol{x}$ with high probability. This suggests that the performance improvement brought by Bagging is large when the base learner is unstable but order-correct.

Friedman and Hall [2007] studied Bagging through a decomposition of statistical predictors. They assumed that the learner $h(\boldsymbol{x}; \gamma)$ is parameterized by a parameter vector γ, which can be obtained by solving an estimation function

$$\sum_{i=1}^n g\left(\left(\boldsymbol{x}_i, y_i\right), \gamma\right) = 0 , \tag{3.16}$$

where g is a smooth multivariate function, $(\boldsymbol{x}_i, y_i)$ is the ith training example and n is the size of training set. Once γ is obtained, the learner h is decided.

Suppose γ^* is the solution of $\mathbb{E}_{\boldsymbol{x}, y}[g((\boldsymbol{x}_i, y_i), \gamma)] = 0$. Based on the Taylor expansion of $g((\boldsymbol{x}_i, y_i), \gamma)$ around γ^*, (3.16) can be rewritten as

$$\sum_{i=1}^n \left[g((\boldsymbol{x}_i, y_i), \gamma^*) + \sum_k g_k((\boldsymbol{x}_i, y_i), \gamma^*)(\gamma - \gamma^*)_k + \right. \tag{3.17}$$

$$\left. \sum_{k_1} \sum_{k_2} g_{k_1, k_2}((\boldsymbol{x}_i, y_i), \gamma^*)(\gamma - \gamma^*)_{k_1}(\gamma - \gamma^*)_{k_2} + \dots \right] = 0 ,$$

where γ_k is the kth component of γ, and g_k is the partial derivative of g with respect to γ_k. Suppose $\hat{\gamma}$ is a solution of (3.16), then from (3.17) it can be expressed as

$$\hat{\gamma} = \Gamma + \sum_{k_1} \sum_{k_2} \alpha_{k_1 k_2} (\bar{\Phi} - \phi)_{k_1} (\bar{\Phi} - \phi)_{k_2} \tag{3.18}$$

$$+ \sum_{k_1} \sum_{k_2} \sum_{k_3} \alpha_{k_1 k_2 k_3} (\bar{\Phi} - \phi)_{k_1} (\bar{\Phi} - \phi)_{k_2} (\bar{\Phi} - \phi)_{k_3} + \dots$$

with coefficients $\alpha_{k_1 k_2}$, $\alpha_{k_1 k_2 k_3}$,

$$\Gamma = \gamma^* + M^{-1} \frac{1}{n} \sum_{i=1}^{n} g((\boldsymbol{x}_i, y_i), \gamma^*) \,, \tag{3.19}$$

$$\bar{\Phi} = \frac{1}{n} \Phi_i \,, \quad \phi = \mathbb{E}[\Phi_i] \,, \tag{3.20}$$

where M is a matrix whose kth column is $\mathbb{E}_{\boldsymbol{x},y}[g_k((\boldsymbol{x}, y), \gamma^*)]$, and Φ_i is a vector of $g_k((\boldsymbol{x}_i, y_i), \gamma^*)$, $g_{k_1, k_2}((\boldsymbol{x}_i, y_i), \gamma^*)$, …… It is obvious that $\hat{\gamma}$ can be decomposed into linear and high-order parts.

Suppose the learner generated from a bootstrap sample of the training data set D is parameterized by $\hat{\gamma}'$, and the sample size is m ($m \le n$). According to (3.18), we have

$$\hat{\gamma}' = \Gamma' + \sum_{k_1} \sum_{k_2} \alpha_{k_1 k_2} (\bar{\Phi}' - \phi)_{k_1} (\bar{\Phi}' - \phi)_{k_2} \tag{3.21}$$
$$+ \sum_{k_1} \sum_{k_2} \sum_{k_3} \alpha_{k_1 k_2 k_3} (\bar{\Phi}' - \phi)_{k_1} (\bar{\Phi}' - \phi)_{k_2} (\bar{\Phi}' - \phi)_{k_3} + \dots \,.$$

The aggregated learner of Bagging is parameterized by

$$\hat{\gamma}_{bag} = \mathbb{E}[\hat{\gamma}' \mid D] \,. \tag{3.22}$$

If $\hat{\gamma}$ is linear in function of data, we have $\mathbb{E}[\Gamma' \mid D] = \Gamma$, and thus $\hat{\gamma}_{bag} = \hat{\gamma}$. This implies that Bagging does not improve linear components of $\hat{\gamma}$.

Now, let's consider higher-order components. Let

$$\rho_m = \frac{n}{m} \,, \tag{3.23}$$

$$\hat{\sigma}_{k_1 k_2} = \frac{1}{n} \sum_{i=1}^{n} (\Phi_i - \Phi)_{k_1} (\Phi_i - \Phi)_{k_2} \,, \tag{3.24}$$

$$S = \sum_{k_1} \sum_{k_2} \alpha_{k_1 k_2} \hat{\sigma}_{k_1 k_2} \,. \tag{3.25}$$

Friedman and Hall [2007] showed that if $\rho_m \to \rho$ ($1 \le \rho \le \infty$) when $n \to \infty$, $\hat{\gamma}_{bag}$ can be expressed as

$$\hat{\gamma}_{bag} = \Gamma + \frac{1}{n} \rho_m S + \delta_{bag} \,, \tag{3.26}$$

where δ_{bag} represents the terms with orders higher than quadratic. From (3.24) it is easy to see that the variance of $\hat{\sigma}_{k_1 k_2}$ will decrease if the sample size n increases, and the dependence of the variance on the sample size is in the order $O(n^{-1})$. Since S is linear in $\hat{\sigma}_{k_1 k_2}$'s, the dependence of the variance of S on the sample size is also in the order of $O(n^{-1})$. Thus, considering that

ρ_m is asymptotic to a constant and the property of variance that $var(aX) = a^2 var(X)$, the dependence of the variance of $\frac{1}{n}\rho_m S$ on the sample size is in the order of $O(n^{-3})$. If we rewrite (3.18) as $\hat{\gamma} = \Gamma + \Delta$, after a similar analysis, we can get that the dependence of the variance of Δ on the sample size is asymptotically in the order of $O(n^{-2})$. Therefore, Bagging has reduced the variance of the quadratic terms of $\hat{\gamma}$ from $O(n^{-2})$ to $O(n^{-3})$. Similar effects can be found on terms with orders higher than quadratic.

Thus, Friedman and Hall [2007] concluded that Bagging can reduce the variance of higher-order components, yet not affect the linear components. This implies that Bagging is better applied with highly nonlinear learners. Since highly nonlinear learners tend to be unstable, i.e., their performance changes much with data sample perturbation, it is understandable that Bagging is effective with unstable base learners.

It is easy to understand that Bagging converges as the ensemble size grows. Given a training set, Bagging uses bootstrap sampling to generate a set of random samples; on each a base learner is trained. This process is equivalent to picking a set of base learners from a pool of all possible learners randomly according to the distribution implied by bootstrap sampling. Thus, given a test instance, the output of a base learner on the instance can be denoted as a random variable Y drawn from the distribution. Without loss of generality, let's consider binary classification where $Y \in \{-1, +1\}$. Bagging generally employs voting to combine base classifiers, while we can consider averaging at first. Let $\bar{Y}_T = \frac{1}{T}\sum_{i=1}^T Y_i$ denote the average of the outputs of T drawn classifiers, and $\mathbb{E}[Y]$ denote the expectation. By the *law of large numbers*, we have

$$\lim_{T \to \infty} P(|\bar{Y}_T - \mathbb{E}[Y]| < \epsilon) = 1. \tag{3.27}$$

Turning to voting then, we have

$$\lim_{T \to \infty} P\left(\text{sign}\left(\bar{Y}_T\right) = \text{sign}\left(\mathbb{E}[Y]\right)\right) = 1, \tag{3.28}$$

unless $\mathbb{E}[Y] = 0$. Therefore, Bagging will converge to a steady error rate as the ensemble size grows, except for the rare case that Bagging equals random guess. Actually, this property is shared by all parallel ensemble methods.

3.5 Random Tree Ensembles

3.5.1 Random Forest

Random Forest (RF) [Breiman, 2001] is a representative of the state-of-the-art ensemble methods. It is an extension of Bagging, where the major

Input: Data set $D = \{(\boldsymbol{x}_1, y_1), (\boldsymbol{x}_2, y_2), \ldots, (\boldsymbol{x}_m, y_m)\}$;
     Feature subset size K.

Process:
1. $N \leftarrow$ create a tree node based on D;
2.   **if** *all instances in the same class* **then return** N
3. $\mathcal{F} \leftarrow$ the set of features that can be split further;
4.   **if** $\mathcal{F}$ *is empty* **then return** N
5. $\tilde{\mathcal{F}} \leftarrow$ select K features from $\mathcal{F}$ randomly;
6. $N.f \leftarrow$ the feature which has the best split point in $\tilde{\mathcal{F}}$;
7. $N.p \leftarrow$ the best split point on $N.f$;
8. $D_l \leftarrow$ subset of D with values on $N.f$ smaller than $N.p$;
9. $D_r \leftarrow$ subset of D with values on $N.f$ no smaller than $N.p$;
10. $N_l \leftarrow$ call the process with parameters (D_l, K);
11. $N_r \leftarrow$ call the process with parameters (D_r, K);
12. **return** N

Output: A random decision tree

FIGURE 3.7: The random tree algorithm in RF.

difference with Bagging is the incorporation of randomized feature selection. During the construction of a component decision tree, at each step of split selection, RF first randomly selects a subset of features, and then carries out the conventional split selection procedure within the selected feature subset.

Figure 3.7 shows the random decision tree algorithm used in RF. The parameter K controls the incorporation of randomness. When K equals the total number of features, the constructed decision tree is identical to the traditional deterministic decision tree; when $K = 1$, a feature will be selected randomly. The suggested value of K is the logarithm of the number of features [Breiman, 2001]. Notice that randomness is only introduced into the feature selection process, not into the choice of split points on the selected feature.

Figure 3.8 compares the decision boundaries of RF and Bagging as well as their base classifiers. It can be observed that decision boundaries of RF and its base classifiers are more flexible, leading to a better generalization ability. On the *three-Gaussians* data set, the test error of RF is 7.85% while that of Bagging is 8.3%. Figure 3.9 compares the test errors of RF and Bagging on 40 UCI data sets. It is clear that RF is more preferable no matter whether pruned or unpruned decision trees are used.

The convergence property of RF is similar to that of Bagging. As illustrated in Figure 3.10, RF usually has a worse starting point, particularly when the ensemble size is one, owing to the performance degeneration of single base learners by the incorporation of randomized feature selection; however, it

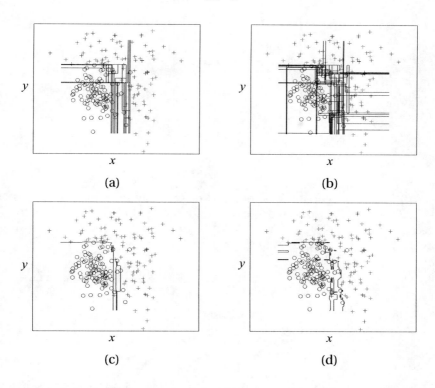

FIGURE 3.8: Decision boundaries on the *three-Gaussians* data set: (a) the 10 base classifiers of Bagging; (b) the 10 base classifiers of RF; (c) Bagging; (d) RF.

usually converges to lower test errors. It is worth mentioning that the training stage of RF is generally more efficient than Bagging. This is because in the tree construction process, Bagging uses deterministic decision trees which need to evaluate all features for split selection, while RF uses random decision trees which only need to evaluate a subset of features.

3.5.2 Spectrum of Randomization

RF generates random decision trees by selecting a feature subset randomly at each node, while the split selection within the selected feature subset is still deterministic. Liu et al. [2008a] described the VR-Tree ensemble method, which generates random decision trees by randomizing both the feature selection and split selection processes.

The base learners of VR-Tree ensembles are VR-Trees. At each node of the tree, a coin is tossed with α probability head-up. If a head is obtained, a de-

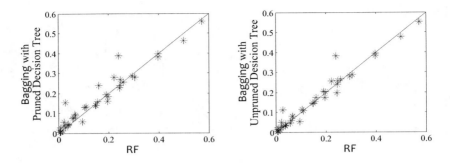

FIGURE 3.9: Comparison of predictive errors of RF against Bagging on 40 UCI data sets. Each point represents a data set and locates according to the predictive error of the two compared algorithms. The diagonal line indicates where the two compared algorithms have identical errors.

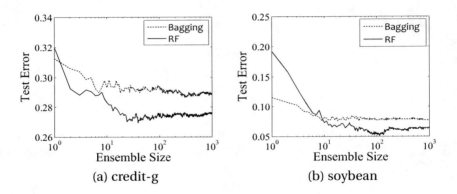

FIGURE 3.10: Impact of ensemble size on RF and Bagging on two UCI data sets.

terministic node is constructed, that is, the best split point among all possible split points is selected in the same way as traditional decision trees; otherwise, a random node is constructed, that is, a feature is selected randomly and a split point is selected on the feature randomly. Figure 3.11 shows the VR-Tree algorithm.

The parameter α controls the degree of randomness. When $\alpha = 1$, the produced VR-trees are identical to deterministic decision trees, while when $\alpha = 0$, the produced VR-trees are completely random trees. By adjusting the parameter value, we can observe a spectrum of randomization [Liu et al., 2008a], as illustrated in Figure 3.12. This provides a way to study the influence of randomness on the ensemble performance. The spectrum has

---

Input: Data set $D = \{(x_1, y_1), (x_2, y_2), \ldots, (x_m, y_m)\}$;
　　　Probability of using deterministic split selection α.

Process:
1.　$N \leftarrow$ create a tree node based on D;
2.　**if** *all instances in the same class* **then return** N
3.　$\mathcal{F} \leftarrow$ the set of features that can be split further;
4.　**if** $\mathcal{F}$ *is empty* **then return** N
5.　$r \leftarrow$ a random number in interval $[0, 1]$;
6.　**if** $r < \alpha$
7.　**then** $N.f \leftarrow$ a feature selected from $\mathcal{F}$ deterministically;
8.　　　　$N.p \leftarrow$ a split point selected on $N.f$ deterministically;
9.　**else** $N.f \leftarrow$ a feature selected from $\mathcal{F}$ randomly;
10.　　　$N.p \leftarrow$ a split point selected on $N.f$ randomly;
11.　$D_l \leftarrow$ subset of D with values on $N.f$ smaller than $N.p$;
12.　$D_r \leftarrow$ subset of D with values on $N.f$ no smaller than $N.p$;
13.　$N_l \leftarrow$ call the process with parameters (D_l, α);
14.　$N_r \leftarrow$ call the process with parameters (D_r, α);
15.　**return** N

Output: A VR-tree

FIGURE 3.11: The VR-Tree algorithm.

two ends, i.e., the random end (α close to 0) and the deterministic end (α close to 1). In the random end, the trees are more diverse and of larger sizes; in the deterministic end, the trees are with higher accuracy and of smaller sizes. While the two ends have different characteristics, ensembles can be improved by shifting toward the middle part of the spectrum. In practice, it is generally difficult to know which middle point is a really good choice. Liu et al. [2008a] suggested the Coalescence method which aggregates VR-trees with the parameter α being randomly chosen from $[0, 0.5]$, and it was observed in experiments that the performances of Coalescence are often superior to RF and VR-Tree ensemble with fixed α's.

3.5.3　Random Tree Ensembles for Density Estimation

Random tree ensembles can be used for **density estimation** [Fan et al., 2003, Fan, 2004, Liu et al., 2005]. Since density estimation is an unsupervised task, there is no label information for the training instances, and thus, *completely random* trees are used. A completely random tree does not test whether the instances belong to the same class; instead, it grows until every leaf node contains only one instance or indistinguishable instances. The completely random decision tree construction algorithm can be obtained by replacing the condition "*all instances in the same class*" in the 2nd step

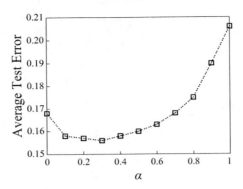

FIGURE 3.12: Illustration of the spectrum of randomization [Liu et al., 2008a]. The x-axis shows the α values, and the y-axis shows the predictive error of VR-Tree ensembles averaged over 45 UCI data sets.

of Figure 3.11 by "*only one instance*", and removing the 5th to 8th steps.

Figure 3.13 illustrates how completely random tree ensembles estimate data density. Figure 3.13(a) plots five one-dimensional data points, labeled as 1, 2, . . ., 5, respectively. The completely random tree grows until every instance falls into a sole leaf node. First, we randomly choose a split point in between points 1 and 5, to divide the data into two groups. With a dominating probability, the split point falls either in between the points 1 and 2, or in between the points 4 and 5, since the gaps between these pairs of points are large. Suppose the split point adopted is in between the points 1 and 2, and thus, the point 1 is in a sole leaf node. Then, the next split point will be picked in between the points 4 and 5 with a large probability, and this will make the point 5 be put into a sole leaf node. It is clear that the points 1 and 5 are more likely to be put into "shallow" leaf nodes, while the points 2 to 4 are more likely to be put into "deep" leaf nodes. Figure 3.13(b) plots three completely random trees generated from the data. We can count the average depth of each data point: 1.67 for the points 1 and 5, 3.33 for the point 2, 3.67 for the point 3, and 3 for the point 4. Even though there are just three trees, we can conclude that the points 1 and 5 are located in a relatively sparse area, while the points 2 to 4 are located in relatively dense areas. Figure 3.13(d) plots the density estimation result, where the density values are calculated as, e.g., $1.67/(1.67 \times 2 + 3.33 + 3.67 + 3)$ for the point 1.

The principle illustrated on one-dimensional data above also holds for higher-dimensional data and for more complex data distributions. It is also easy to extend to tasks where the ensembles are constructed incrementally, such as in online learning or on streaming data. Notice that the construction of a completely random tree is quite efficient, since all it has to do is to

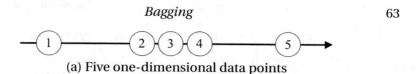

(a) Five one-dimensional data points

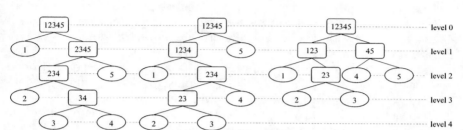

(b) Three completely random trees

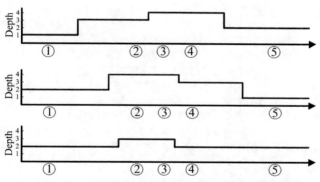

(c) The depth of leaves on the one-dimensional
data, each corresponding to a random tree in the
sub-figure (b)

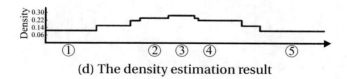

(d) The density estimation result

FIGURE 3.13: Illustration of density estimation by random tree ensemble.

pick random numbers. Overall, the data density can be estimated through generating an ensemble of completely random trees and then calculating the average depth of each data point; this provides a practical and efficient tool for density estimation.

3.5.4 Random Tree Ensembles for Anomaly Detection

Anomalies are data points which do not conform to the general or expected behavior of the majority of data, and the task of anomaly detection is to separate anomaly points from normal ones in a given data set [Chandola et al., 2009]. In general, the terms *anomalies* and **outliers** are used interchangeably, and anomalies are also referred to as *discordant observations, exceptions, peculiarities,* etc.

There are many established approaches to anomaly detection [Hodge and Austin, 2004, Chandola et al., 2009]. A typical one is to estimate the data density, and then treat the data points with very low densities as anomalies. However, as Liu et al. [2008b] disclosed, *density* is not a good indicator to anomaly, because a clustered small group of anomaly points may have a high density, while the bordering normal points may be with low density. Since the basic property of anomalies is *few and different*, **isolation** is more indicative than density [Liu et al., 2008b]. Based on this recognition, random tree ensembles can serve well for anomaly detection, since random trees are simple yet effective for measuring the difficulty of isolating data points. Figure 3.14 illustrates the idea of anomaly detection via random trees. It can be observed that a normal point x generally requires more partitions to be isolated, while an anomaly point x^* is much easier to be isolated with many fewer partitions.

Liu et al. [2008b] described the iForest (Isolation Forest) method for anomaly detection. For each random tree, the number of partitions required to isolate a data point can be measured by the path length from the

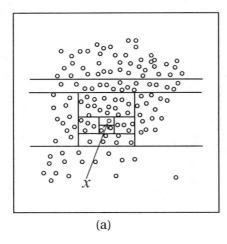
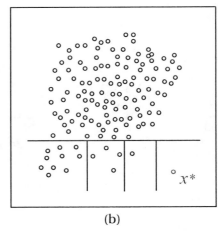

(a)   (b)

FIGURE 3.14: Illustration of anomaly detection by random trees: (a) a normal point x requires 11 random tree partitions to be isolated; (b) an anomaly point x^* requires only four random tree partitions to be isolated.

root node to the leaf node containing the data point. The fewer the required partitions, the easier the data point to be isolated. It is obvious that only the data points with short path lengths are of interest. Thus, to reduce unnecessary computation, the random trees used in iForest are set with a height limit, that is, a limit on the tree depth. This random tree construction algorithm can be obtained by replacing the condition "*all instances in the same class*" in the 2nd step of Figure 3.11 by "*only one instance or height limit is reached*", and removing the 5th to 8th steps. To improve the efficiency and scalability on large data sets, the random trees are constructed from small-sized samples instead of the original data set. Given the data sample size ψ, the height limit of iForest is set to $\lceil \log_2(\psi) \rceil$, which is approximately the average tree height with ψ leaf nodes [Knuth, 1997].

To calculate the anomaly score $s(\boldsymbol{x}_i)$ for $\boldsymbol{x}_i$, the expected path length $\mathbb{E}[h(\boldsymbol{x}_i)]$ is derived firstly by passing $\boldsymbol{x}_i$ through every random tree in the iForest ensemble. The path length obtained at each random tree is added with an adjustment term $c(n)$ to account for the ungrown branch beyond the tree height limit. For a tree with n nodes, $c(n)$ is set as the average path length [Preiss, 1999]

$$c(n) = \begin{cases} 2H(n-1) - (2(n-1)/n), & n > 1 \\ 0, & n = 1 \end{cases}, \qquad (3.29)$$

where $H(a)$ is the harmonic number that can be estimated by

$$H(a) \approx \ln(a) + 0.5772156649 \text{ (Euler's constant)}.$$

Then, the anomaly score $s(\boldsymbol{x}_i)$ is calculated according to [Liu et al., 2008b]

$$s(\boldsymbol{x}_i) = 2^{-\frac{\mathbb{E}[h(\boldsymbol{x}_i)]}{c(\psi)}}, \qquad (3.30)$$

where $c(\psi)$ serves as a normalization factor corresponding to the average path length of traversing a random tree constructed from a sub-sample with size ψ. Finally, if $s(\boldsymbol{x}_i)$ is very close to 1, $\boldsymbol{x}_i$ is definitely an anomaly; if $s(\boldsymbol{x}_i)$ is much smaller than 0.5, $\boldsymbol{x}_i$ is quite safe to be regarded as a normal data point; while if $s(\boldsymbol{x}_i) \approx 0.5$ for all $\boldsymbol{x}_i$'s, there is no distinct anomaly [Liu et al., 2008b].

Liu et al. [2010] presented the SCiForest ("SC" means "with Split selection Criterion"), a variant of iForest. In contrast to iForest which considers only axis-parallel splits of original features in the construction of random trees, SCiForest tries to get smoother decision boundaries, similar to **oblique decision trees**, by considering hyper-plane splits derived from the combination of original features. Furthermore, since the hypothesis space is more complicated by considering hyper-planes, rather than using a completely random manner, a split selection criterion is defined in SCiForest to facilitate the selection of appropriate hyper-planes at each node to reduce the risk of falling into poor sub-optimal solutions.

3.6 Further Readings

Bagging typically adopts *majority voting* for classification and *simple averaging* for regression. If the base learners are able to output confidence values, *weighted voting* or *weighted averaging* are often used. Chapter 4 will introduce combination methods.

Constructing ensembles of stable learners is difficult not only for Bagging, but also for AdaBoost and other ensemble methods relying on **data sample manipulation**. The reason is that the pure data sample perturbation could not enable the base learners to have sufficiently large diversity. Chapter 5 will introduce diversity and discuss more on ensembles of stable learners.

Bühlmann and Yu [2002] theoretically showed that Bagging tends to smooth crisp decisions, and the smoothing operation results in the variance reduction effect. Buja and Stuetzle [2000a,b, 2006] analyzed Bagging by using U-statistics, and found that the leading effect of Bagging on variance is at the second order. They also extended Bagging from statistics to statistical functional, and found that a bagged functional is also smooth.

The term *forest* was first used to refer ensembles of decision trees by Ho [1995]. There are many other random decision tree ensemble methods, in addition to the ones introduced in this chapter, e.g., Dietterich [2000b], Cutler and Zhao [2001], Robnik-Šikonja [2004], Rodriguez et al. [2006], Geurts et al. [2006].

4

Combination Methods

4.1 Benefits of Combination

After generating a set of base learners, rather than trying to find the best single learner, ensemble methods resort to combination to achieve a strong generalization ability, where the combination method plays a crucial role. Dietterich [2000a] attributed the benefit from combination to the following three fundamental reasons:

- *Statistical issue*: It is often the case that the hypothesis space is too large to explore for limited training data, and that there may be several different hypotheses giving the same accuracy on the training data. If the learning algorithm chooses one of these hypotheses, there is a risk that a mistakenly chosen hypothesis could not predict the future data well. As shown in Figure 4.1(a), by combining the hypotheses, the risk of choosing a wrong hypothesis can be reduced.

- *Computational issue*: Many learning algorithms perform some kind of local search that may get stuck in local optima. Even if there are enough training data, it may still be very difficult to find the best hypothesis. By running the local search from many different starting points, the combination may provide a better approximation to the true unknown hypothesis. As shown in Figure 4.1(b), by combining the hypotheses, the risk of choosing a wrong local minimum can be reduced.

- *Representational issue*: In many machine learning tasks, the true unknown hypothesis could not be represented by any hypothesis in the hypothesis space. As shown in Figure 4.1(c), by combing the hypotheses, it may be possible to expand the space of representable functions, and thus the learning algorithm may be able to form a more accurate approximation to the true unknown hypothesis.

These three issues are among the most important factors for which the traditional learning approaches fail. A learning algorithm that suffers from the statistical issue is generally said to have a high "*variance*", a learning algorithm that suffers from the computational issue can be described as

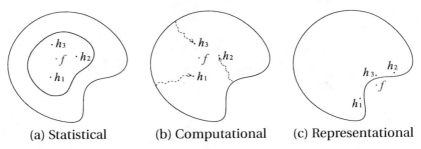

(a) Statistical   (b) Computational   (c) Representational

FIGURE 4.1: Three fundamental reasons for combination: (a) the statistical issue, (b) the computational issue, and (c) the representational issue. The outer curve represents the hypothesis space, and the inner curve in (a) represents the hypotheses with the same accuracy on the training data. The point label f is the true hypothesis, and h_i's are the individual hypotheses. (Plot based on a similar figure in [Dietterich, 2000a].)

having a high "*computational variance*", and a learning algorithm that suffers from the representational issue is generally said to have a high "*bias*". Therefore, through combination, the variance as well as the bias of learning algorithms may be reduced; this has been confirmed by many empirical studies [Xu et al., 1992, Bauer and Kohavi, 1999, Opitz and Maclin, 1999].

4.2   Averaging

Averaging is the most popular and fundamental combination method for numeric outputs. In this section we take regression as an example to explain how averaging works. Suppose we are given a set of T individual learners $\{h_1, \ldots, h_T\}$ and the output of h_i for the instance $\boldsymbol{x}$ is $h_i(\boldsymbol{x}) \in \mathbb{R}$, our task is to combine h_i's to attain the final prediction on the real-valued variable.

4.2.1   Simple Averaging

Simple averaging obtains the combined output by averaging the outputs of individual learners directly. Specifically, simple averaging gives the combined output $H(\boldsymbol{x})$ as

$$H(\boldsymbol{x}) = \frac{1}{T} \sum_{i=1}^{T} h_i(\boldsymbol{x}). \tag{4.1}$$

Suppose the underlying true function we try to learn is $f(\boldsymbol{x})$, and $\boldsymbol{x}$ is sampled according to a distribution $p(\boldsymbol{x})$. The output of each learner can be written as the true value plus an error item, i.e.,

$$h_i(\boldsymbol{x}) = f(\boldsymbol{x}) + \epsilon_i(\boldsymbol{x}), \quad i = 1, \dots, T. \tag{4.2}$$

Then, the mean squared error of h_i can be written as

$$\int \left(h_i(\boldsymbol{x}) - f(\boldsymbol{x})\right)^2 p(\boldsymbol{x})d\boldsymbol{x} = \int \epsilon_i(\boldsymbol{x})^2 p(\boldsymbol{x})d\boldsymbol{x}, \tag{4.3}$$

and the averaged error made by the individual learners is

$$\overline{err}(h) = \frac{1}{T} \sum_{i=1}^{T} \int \epsilon_i(\boldsymbol{x})^2 p(\boldsymbol{x})d\boldsymbol{x}. \tag{4.4}$$

Similarly, it is easy to derive that the expected error of the combined learner (i.e., the ensemble) is

$$err(H) = \int \left(\frac{1}{T}\sum_{i=1}^{T} h_i(\boldsymbol{x}) - f(\boldsymbol{x})\right)^2 p(\boldsymbol{x})d\boldsymbol{x} = \int \left(\frac{1}{T}\sum_{i=1}^{T} \epsilon_i(\boldsymbol{x})\right)^2 p(\boldsymbol{x})d\boldsymbol{x}. \tag{4.5}$$

It is easy to see that

$$err(H) \leq \overline{err}(h). \tag{4.6}$$

That is, the expected ensemble error will be no larger than the averaged error of the individual learners.

Moreover, if we assume that the errors ϵ_i's have zero mean and are uncorrelated, i.e.,

$$\int \epsilon_i(\boldsymbol{x})p(\boldsymbol{x})d\boldsymbol{x} = 0 \quad \text{and} \quad \int \epsilon_i(\boldsymbol{x})\epsilon_j(\boldsymbol{x})p(\boldsymbol{x})d\boldsymbol{x} = 0 \quad (\text{for } i \neq j), \tag{4.7}$$

it is not difficult to get

$$err(H) = \frac{1}{T}\overline{err}(h), \tag{4.8}$$

which suggests that the ensemble error is smaller by a factor of T than the averaged error of the individual learners.

Owing to its simplicity and effectiveness, simple averaging is among the most popularly used methods and represents the first choice in many real applications. It is worth noting, however, that the error reduction shown in (4.8) is derived based on the assumption that the errors of the individual learners are uncorrelated, while in ensemble learning the errors are typically highly correlated since the individual learners are trained on the same problem. Therefore, the error reduction shown in (4.8) is generally hard to achieve.

4.2.2   Weighted Averaging

Weighted averaging obtains the combined output by averaging the outputs of individual learners with different weights implying different importance. Specifically, weighted averaging gives the combined output $H(\boldsymbol{x})$ as

$$H(\boldsymbol{x}) = \sum_{i=1}^{T} w_i h_i(\boldsymbol{x}) , \tag{4.9}$$

where w_i is the weight for h_i, and the weights w_i's are usually assumed to be constrained by

$$w_i \geq 0 \quad \text{and} \quad \sum_{i=1}^{T} w_i = 1 . \tag{4.10}$$

Similarly as in Section 4.2.1, suppose the underlying true function we try to learn is $f(\boldsymbol{x})$, and $\boldsymbol{x}$ is sampled according to a distribution $p(\boldsymbol{x})$. The output of each learner can be written as (4.2). Then it is easy to write the ensemble error as [Perrone and Cooper, 1993]

$$err(H) = \int \left(\sum_{i=1}^{T} w_i h_i(\boldsymbol{x}) - f(\boldsymbol{x}) \right)^2 p(\boldsymbol{x}) d\boldsymbol{x}$$

$$= \int \left(\sum_{i=1}^{T} w_i h_i(\boldsymbol{x}) - f(\boldsymbol{x}) \right) \left(\sum_{j=1}^{T} w_j h_j(\boldsymbol{x}) - f(\boldsymbol{x}) \right) p(\boldsymbol{x}) d\boldsymbol{x}$$

$$= \sum_{i=1}^{T} \sum_{j=1}^{T} w_i w_j C_{ij} , \tag{4.11}$$

where

$$C_{ij} = \int \left(h_i(\boldsymbol{x}) - f(\boldsymbol{x}) \right) \left(h_j(\boldsymbol{x}) - f(\boldsymbol{x}) \right) p(\boldsymbol{x}) d\boldsymbol{x} . \tag{4.12}$$

It is evident that the optimal weights can be solved by

$$\boldsymbol{w} = \arg\min_{\boldsymbol{w}} \sum_{i=1}^{T} \sum_{j=1}^{T} w_i w_j C_{ij} . \tag{4.13}$$

By applying the famous *Lagrange multiplier* method, it can be obtained that [Perrone and Cooper, 1993]

$$w_i = \frac{\sum_{j=1}^{T} C_{ij}^{-1}}{\sum_{k=1}^{T} \sum_{j=1}^{T} C_{kj}^{-1}} . \tag{4.14}$$

(4.14) provides a closed-form solution to the optimal weights. It is worth noticing, however, that this solution requires the correlation matrix C to be invertible, yet in ensemble learning such a matrix is usually singular or ill-conditioned, since the errors of the individual learners are typically highly correlated and many individual learners may be similar since they are trained on the same problem. Therefore, the solution shown in (4.14) is generally infeasible, and moreover, it does not guarantee non-negative solutions.

It is easy to see that simple averaging, which can be regarded as taking equal weights for all individual learners, is a special case of weighted averaging. Other combination methods, such as voting, are also special cases or variants of weighted averaging. Indeed, given a set of individual learners, the weighted averaging formulation [Perrone and Cooper, 1993] provides a fundamental motivation for ensemble methods, since any ensemble method can be regarded as trying a specific way to decide the weights for combining the individual learners, and different ensemble methods can be regarded as different implementations of weighted averaging. From this aspect it is easy to know that there is no ensemble method which is consistently the best, since deciding the weights is a computationally hard problem.

Notice that though simple averaging is a special case of weighted averaging, it does not mean that weighted averaging is definitely better than simple averaging. In fact, experimental results reported in the literature do not show that weighted averaging is clearly superior to simple averaging [Xu et al., 1992, Ho et al., 1994, Kittler et al., 1998]. One important reason is that the data in real tasks are usually noisy and insufficient, and thus the estimated weights are often unreliable. In particular, with a large ensemble, there are a lot of weights to learn, and this can easily lead to overfitting; simple averaging does not have to learn any weights, and so suffers little from overfitting. In general, it is widely accepted that simple averaging is appropriate for combining learners with similar performances, whereas if the individual learners exhibit nonidentical strength, weighted averaging with unequal weights may achieve a better performance.

4.3 Voting

Voting is the most popular and fundamental combination method for nominal outputs. In this section we take classification as an example to explain how voting works. Suppose we are given a set of T individual classifiers $\{h_1, \ldots, h_T\}$ and our task is to combine h_i's to predict the class label from a set of l possible class labels $\{c_1, \ldots, c_l\}$. It is generally assumed that for an instance x, the outputs of the classifier h_i are given as an l-

dimensional label vector $(h_i^1(\boldsymbol{x}), \ldots, h_i^l(\boldsymbol{x}))^\top$, where $h_i^j(\boldsymbol{x})$ is the output of h_i for the class label c_j. The $h_i^j(\boldsymbol{x})$ can take different types of values according to the information provided by the individual classifiers, e.g.,

- *Crisp label*: $h_i^j(\boldsymbol{x}) \in \{0, 1\}$, which takes value one if h_i predicts c_j as the class label and zero otherwise.

- *Class probability*: $h_i^j(\boldsymbol{x}) \in [0, 1]$, which can be regarded as an estimate of the posterior probability $P(c_j \mid \boldsymbol{x})$.

For classifiers that produce un-normalized margins, such as SVMs, **calibration** methods such as **Platt scaling** [Platt, 2000] or **Isotonic Regression** [Zadrozny and Elkan, 2001b] can be used to convert such an output to a probability. Notice that the class probabilities estimated by most classifiers are poor; however, combination methods based on class probabilities are often highly competitive to those based on crisp labels, especially after a careful calibration.

4.3.1   Majority Voting

Majority voting is the most popular voting method. Here, every classifier votes for one class label, and the final output class label is the one that receives more than half of the votes; if none of the class labels receives more than half of the votes, a **rejection option** will be given and the combined classifier makes no prediction. That is, the output class label of the ensemble is

$$H(\boldsymbol{x}) = \begin{cases} c_j & \text{if } \sum_{i=1}^{T} h_i^j(\boldsymbol{x}) > \frac{1}{2} \sum_{k=1}^{l} \sum_{i=1}^{T} h_i^k(\boldsymbol{x}), \\ \text{rejection} & \text{otherwise}. \end{cases} \tag{4.15}$$

If there are a total of T classifiers for a binary classification problem, the ensemble decision will be correct if at least $\lfloor T/2 + 1 \rfloor$ classifiers choose the correct class label. Assume that the outputs of the classifiers are independent and each classifier has an accuracy p, implying that each classifier makes a correct classification at probability p. The probability of the ensemble for making a correct decision can be calculated using a binomial distribution; specifically, the probability of obtaining at least $\lfloor T/2 + 1 \rfloor$ correct classifiers out of T is [Hansen and Salamon, 1990]:

$$P_{mv} = \sum_{k=\lfloor T/2+1 \rfloor}^{T} \binom{T}{k} p^k (1 - p)^{T-k}. \tag{4.16}$$

The accuracy of the ensemble with different values of p and T is illustrated in Figure 4.2.

Lam and Suen [1997] showed that

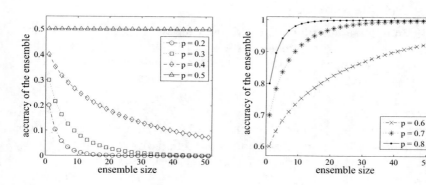

FIGURE 4.2: Ensemble accuracy of majority voting of T independent classifiers with accuracy p for binary classification.

- If $p > 0.5$, then P_{mv} is monotonically increasing in T, and

$$\lim_{T \to +\infty} P_{mv} = 1;$$

- If $p < 0.5$, then P_{mv} is monotonically decreasing in T, and

$$\lim_{T \to +\infty} P_{mv} = 0;$$

- If $p = 0.5$, then $P_{mv} = 0.5$ for any T.

Notice that this result is obtained based on the assumption that the individual classifiers are statistically independent, yet in practice the classifiers are generally highly correlated since they are trained on the same problem. Therefore, it is unpractical to expect the majority voting accuracy converges to one along with the increase of the number of individual classifiers.

4.3.2 Plurality Voting

In contrast to majority voting which requires the final winner to take at least half of votes, plurality voting takes the class label which receives the largest number of votes as the final winner. That is, the output class label of the ensemble is

$$H(\boldsymbol{x}) = c_{\arg\max_j \sum_{i=1}^{T} h_i^j(\boldsymbol{x})}, \tag{4.17}$$

and ties are broken arbitrarily. It is obvious that plurality voting does not have a reject option, since it can always find a label receiving the largest number of votes. Moreover, in the case of binary classification, plurality voting indeed coincides with majority voting.

4.3.3 Weighted Voting

If the individual classifiers are with unequal performance, intuitively, it is reasonable to give more power to the stronger classifiers in voting; this is realized by weighted voting. The output class label of the ensemble is

$$H(\boldsymbol{x}) = c_{\underset{j}{\arg\max} \sum_{i=1}^{T} w_i h_i^j(\boldsymbol{x})} \,, \qquad (4.18)$$

where w_i is the weight assigned to the classifier h_i. In practical applications, the weights are often normalized and constrained by $w_i \geq 0$ and $\sum_{i=1}^{T} w_i = 1$, similar to that in weighted averaging.

Take a simple example to compare weighted voting and majority voting. Suppose there are five independent individual classifiers with accuracies $\{0.7, 0.7, 0.7, 0.9, 0.9\}$, respectively. Thus, the accuracy of majority voting (i.e., at least three out of five classifiers are correct) is

$$P_{mv} = 0.7^3 + 2 \times 3 \times 0.7^2 \times 0.3 \times 0.9 \times 0.1 + 3 \times 0.7 \times 0.3 \times 0.9^2$$
$$\approx 0.933 \,,$$

which is better than the best individual classifier. For weighted voting, suppose that the weights given to the classifiers are $\{1/9, 1/9, 1/9, 1/3, 1/3\}$, respectively, and then the accuracy of weighted voting is

$$P_{wv} = 0.9^2 + 2 \times 3 \times 0.9 \times 0.1 \times 0.7^2 \times 0.3 + 2 \times 0.9 \times 0.1 \times 0.7^3$$
$$\approx 0.951 \,.$$

This shows that, with adequate weight assignments, weighted voting can be better than both the best individual classifier and majority voting. Similar to weighted averaging, the key is how to obtain the weights.

Let $\boldsymbol{\ell} = (\ell_1, \ldots, \ell_T)^\top$ denote the outputs of the individual classifiers, where ℓ_i is the class label predicted for the instance $\boldsymbol{x}$ by the classifier h_i, and let p_i denote the accuracy of h_i. There is a Bayesian optimal discriminant function for the combined output on class label c_j, i.e.,

$$H^j(\boldsymbol{x}) = \log\left(P\left(c_j\right) P\left(\boldsymbol{\ell} \mid c_j\right)\right) \,. \qquad (4.19)$$

Assuming that the outputs of the individual classifiers are conditionally independent, i.e., $P(\boldsymbol{\ell}|c_j) = \prod_{i=1}^{T} P(\ell_i|c_j)$, then it follows that

$$H^j(\boldsymbol{x}) = \log P(c_j) + \sum_{i=1}^{T} \log P(\ell_i \mid c_j)$$

$$= \log P(c_j) + \log \left(\prod_{i=1, \ell_i=c_j}^{T} P(\ell_i \mid c_j) \prod_{i=1, \ell_i \neq c_j}^{T} P(\ell_i \mid c_j) \right)$$

$$= \log P(c_j) + \log \left(\prod_{i=1, \ell_i=c_j}^{T} p_i \prod_{i=1, \ell_i \neq c_j}^{T} (1 - p_i) \right)$$

$$= \log P(c_j) + \sum_{i=1, \ell_i=c_j}^{T} \log \frac{p_i}{1 - p_i} + \sum_{i=1}^{T} \log(1 - p_i). \qquad (4.20)$$

Since $\sum_{i=1}^{T} \log(1 - p_i)$ does not depend on the class label c_j, and $\ell_i = c_j$ can be expressed by the result of $h_i^j(\boldsymbol{x})$, the discriminant function can be reduced to

$$H^j(\boldsymbol{x}) = \log P(c_j) + \sum_{i=1}^{T} h_i^j(\boldsymbol{x}) \log \frac{p_i}{1 - p_i}. \qquad (4.21)$$

The first term at the right-hand side of (4.21) does not rely on the individual learners, while the second term discloses that the optimal weights for weighted voting satisfy

$$w_i \propto \log \frac{p_i}{1 - p_i}, \qquad (4.22)$$

which shows that the weights should be in proportion to the performance of the individual learners.

Notice that (4.22) is obtained by assuming independence among the outputs of the individual classifiers, yet this does not hold since all the individual classifiers are trained on the same problem and they are usually highly correlated. Moreover, it requires the estimation of ground-truth accuracies of individual classifiers, and does not take the class priors into account. Therefore, in real practice, (4.22) does not always lead to a performance better than majority voting.

4.3.4   Soft Voting

For individual classifiers which produce crisp class labels, majority voting, plurality voting and weighted voting can be used, while for individual classifiers which produce class probability outputs, soft voting is generally the choice. Here, the individual classifier h_i outputs a l-dimensional vector $(h_i^1(\boldsymbol{x}), \ldots, h_i^l(\boldsymbol{x}))^\top$ for the instance $\boldsymbol{x}$, where $h_i^j(\boldsymbol{x}) \in [0, 1]$ can be regarded as an estimate of the posterior probability $P(c_j \mid \boldsymbol{x})$.

If all the individual classifiers are treated equally, the *simple soft voting* method generates the combined output by simply averaging all the individual outputs, and the final output for class c_j is given by

$$H^j(\boldsymbol{x}) = \frac{1}{T} \sum_{i=1}^{T} h_i^j(\boldsymbol{x}) . \tag{4.23}$$

If we consider combining the individual outputs with different weights, the *weighted soft voting* method can be any of the following three forms:

- A classifier-specific weight is assigned to each classifier, and the combined output for class c_j is

$$H^j(\boldsymbol{x}) = \sum_{i=1}^{T} w_i h_i^j(\boldsymbol{x}), \tag{4.24}$$

  where w_i is the weight assigned to the classifier h_i.

- A class-specific weight is assigned to each classifier per class, and the combined output for class c_j is

$$H^j(\boldsymbol{x}) = \sum_{i=1}^{T} w_i^j h_i^j(\boldsymbol{x}), \tag{4.25}$$

  where w_i^j is the weight assigned to the classifier h_i for the class c_j.

- A weight is assigned to each example of each class for each classifier, and the combined output for class c_j is

$$H^j(\boldsymbol{x}) = \sum_{i=1}^{T} \sum_{k=1}^{m} w_{ik}^j h_i^j(\boldsymbol{x}), \tag{4.26}$$

  where w_{ik}^j is the weight of the instance $\boldsymbol{x}_k$ of the class c_j for the classifier h_i.

In real practice, the third type is not often used since it may involve a large number of weight coefficients. The first type is similar with weighted averaging or weighted voting, and so, in the following we focus on the second type, i.e., class-specific weights. Since $h_i^j(\boldsymbol{x})$ can be regarded as an estimate of $P(c_j \mid \boldsymbol{x})$, it follows that

$$h_i^j(\boldsymbol{x}) = P(c_j \mid \boldsymbol{x}) + \epsilon_i^j(\boldsymbol{x}) , \tag{4.27}$$

where $\epsilon_i^j(\boldsymbol{x})$ is the approximation error. In classification, the target output is given as a class label. If the estimation is unbiased, the combined output $H^j(\boldsymbol{x}) = \sum_{i=1}^{T} w_i^j h_i^j(\boldsymbol{x})$ is also unbiased, and we can obtain a variance-minimized unbiased estimation $H^j(\boldsymbol{x})$ for $P(c_j|\boldsymbol{x})$ by setting the weights. Minimizing the variance of the combined approximation error $\sum_{i=1}^{T} w_i^j \epsilon_i^j(\boldsymbol{x})$ under the constraints $w_i^j \geq 0$ and $\sum_{i=1}^{T} w_i^j = 1$, we can get the optimization problem

$$\boldsymbol{w}^j = \arg\min_{\boldsymbol{w}^j} \sum_{k=1}^{m} \left(\sum_{i=1}^{T} w_i^j h_i^j(\boldsymbol{x}_k) - \mathbb{I}(f(x_k) = c_j) \right)^2, \quad j = 1, \ldots, l, \quad (4.28)$$

from which the weights can be solved.

Notice that soft voting is generally used for *homogeneous ensembles*. For *heterogeneous ensembles*, the class probabilities generated by different types of learners usually cannot be compared directly without a careful calibration. In such situations, the class probability outputs are often converted to class label outputs by setting $h_i^j(\boldsymbol{x})$ to 1 if $h_i^j(\boldsymbol{x}) = \max_j\{h_i^j(\boldsymbol{x})\}$ and 0 otherwise, and then the voting methods for crisp labels can be applied.

4.3.5 Theoretical Issues

4.3.5.1 Theoretical Bounds of Majority Voting

Narasimhamurthy [2003, 2005] analyzed the theoretical bounds of majority voting. In this section we focus on the introduction of this analysis.

Consider the binary classification problem, given a set of T classifiers, $h_1, \ldots, h_T$, with accuracies $p_1, \ldots, p_T$, respectively, and for simplicity, assuming that T is an odd number (similar results for an even number can be found in [Narasimhamurthy, 2005]). The joint statistics of classifiers can be represented by **Venn diagrams**, and an example of three classifiers is illustrated in Figure 4.3. Here, each classifier is represented by a bit (i.e., 1 or 0) with 1 indicating that the classifier is correct and 0 otherwise. The regions in the Venn diagram correspond to the bit combinations. For example, the region marked with x_3 corresponds to the bit combination "110", i.e., it corresponds to the event that both h_1 and h_2 are correct while h_3 is incorrect, and x_3 indicates the probability associated with this event. Now, let $\boldsymbol{x} = [x_0, \ldots, x_{2^T-1}]^{\top}$ denote the vector of joint probabilities, $bit(i, T)$ denotes the T-bit binary representation of integer i, and $\boldsymbol{f}_{mv}$ denotes a bit vector of length 2^T where the entry at the ith position is

$$\boldsymbol{f}_{mv}(i) = \begin{cases} 1 & \text{if the number of 1's in } bit(i, T) > T/2, \\ 0 & \text{otherwise.} \end{cases} \quad (4.29)$$

Then, the probability of correct classification of majority voting can be represented as $\boldsymbol{f}_{mv}^{\top}\boldsymbol{x}$. This is the objective to be maximized/minimized subject to certain constraints [Narasimhamurthy, 2003, 2005].

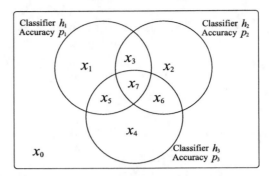

FIGURE 4.3: Venn diagram showing joint statistics of three classifiers. The regions marked with different x_i's correspond to different bit combinations, and x_i is the probability associated with the corresponding region. (Plot based on a similar figure in [Narasimhamurthy, 2003].)

Notice that the accuracy of classifier h_i is p_i, that is, the probability of h_i being correct is p_i. This can be represented as T constraints in the form of

$$\boldsymbol{b}_i^\top \boldsymbol{x} = p_i \ (1 \le i \le T), \tag{4.30}$$

and it is easy to find that

$$\boldsymbol{b}_1 = (0, 1, \ldots, 0, 1)^\top$$
$$\boldsymbol{b}_2 = (0, 0, 1, 1, \ldots, 0, 0, 1, 1)^\top$$
$$\vdots$$
$$\boldsymbol{b}_T = (\overbrace{0, 0, \ldots, 0, 0}^{2^{T-1}}, \ldots, \overbrace{1, 1, \ldots, 1, 1}^{2^{T-1}})^\top.$$

Let $B = (\boldsymbol{b}_1, \ldots, \boldsymbol{b}_T)^\top$ and $\boldsymbol{p} = (p_1, \ldots, p_T)^\top$. Considering the constraints $\sum_{i=0}^{2^T-1} x_i = 1$ and $0 \le x_i \le 1$, the lower and upper bounds of majority voting can be solved from the following linear programming problem [Narasimhamurthy, 2003, 2005]:

$$\min / \max {}_{\boldsymbol{x}} \ \boldsymbol{f}_{mv}^\top \boldsymbol{x} \tag{4.31}$$
$$\text{s.t.} \ \ B\boldsymbol{x} = \boldsymbol{p}$$
$$\boldsymbol{1}^\top \boldsymbol{x} = 1$$
$$0 \le x_i \le 1 \ \ (\forall i = 0, 1, \ldots, 2^T - 1).$$

The theoretical lower and upper bounds of majority voting for three and five classifiers are respectively illustrated in Figure 4.4 (a) and (b). For the

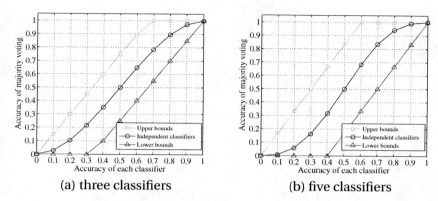

FIGURE 4.4: Theoretical lower and upper bounds of majority voting, and the accuracy of individual independent classifiers when there are (a) three classifiers, and (b) five classifiers. (Plot based on a similar figure in [Narasimhamurthy, 2003].)

purpose of illustration, all classifiers are assumed to have the same accuracy. The accuracy varies from 0 to 1 and the corresponding lower and upper bounds of majority voting are determined for each value. The accuracy of the individual classifiers is also plotted, and it is obvious that the accuracy curves locate inside the region bounded by the lower and upper bounds.

As for the role of the ensemble size T, we can find that the number of constraints is linear in T whereas the dimension of the vector x is exponential in T. In other words, the "degrees of freedom" increase exponentially as T increases. Hence, for a particular accuracy of the classifiers, increasing the ensemble size will lead to a lower theoretical minimum (lower bound) and a higher theoretical maximum (upper bound). This trend can be found by comparing Figure 4.4 (a) and (b). It is worth noting, however, that this conclusion is drawn based on the assumption that the individual classifiers are independent, while this assumption usually does not hold in real practice.

4.3.5.2 Decision Boundary Analysis

Tumer and Ghosh [1996] developed the *decision boundary analysis* framework. Later, Fumera and Roli [2005] analyzed the simple as well as weighted soft voting methods based on this framework. In this section we focus on the introduction of this framework and the main results in [Tumer and Ghosh, 1996, Fumera and Roli, 2005].

For simplicity, we consider one-dimensional feature space as in [Tumer and Ghosh, 1996, Fumera and Roli, 2005], while it is known that the same results hold for multi-dimensional feature spaces [Tumer, 1996]. According to Bayesian decision theory, an instance x should be assigned to class c_i for which the posterior probability $P(c_i \mid x)$ is the maximum. As shown in Figure 4.5, the ideal decision boundary between the classes c_i and c_j is the point x^* such that

$$P(c_i \mid x^*) = P(c_j \mid x^*) > \max_{k \neq i,j} P(c_k \mid x^*) . \tag{4.32}$$

In practice, the classifier can only provide an estimate $h^j(x)$ of the true posterior probability $P(c_j \mid x)$, that is,

$$h^j(x) = P(c_j \mid x) + \epsilon_j(x) , \tag{4.33}$$

where $\epsilon_j(x)$ denotes the error term, which is regarded as a random variable with mean β_j (named "bias") and variance σ_j^2. Thus, when Bayesian decision rule is applied, misclassification occurs if

$$\arg\max_i h^i(x) \neq \arg\max_i P(c_i \mid x) . \tag{4.34}$$

The decision boundary obtained from the estimated posteriors, denoted as x_b, is characterized by

$$h^i(x_b) = h^j(x_b) , \tag{4.35}$$

and it may differ from the ideal boundary by an offset

$$b = x_b - x^* . \tag{4.36}$$

As shown in Figure 4.5, this leads to an additional misclassification error term over Bayes error, named **added error** [Tumer and Ghosh, 1996].

In the following, we focus on the case of unbiased and uncorrelated errors (detailed analysis on other cases can be found in [Tumer and Ghosh, 1996, Fumera and Roli, 2005]). Thus, for any given x, the mean of every error item $\epsilon_j(x)$ is zero, i.e., $\beta_j = 0$, and the error items on different classes, $\epsilon_i(x)$ and $\epsilon_j(x)$, $i \neq j$, are uncorrelated.

Without loss of generality, assume $b > 0$. From Figure 4.5 it is easy to see that the added error depends on the offset b and is given by

$$\int_{x^*}^{x^*+b} [P(c_j \mid x) - P(c_i \mid x)] p(x) dx , \tag{4.37}$$

where $p(x)$ is the probability distribution of x. Assuming that the shift $b = x_b - x^*$ is small, a linear approximation can be used around x^*, that is,

$$P(c_k \mid x^* + b) = P(c_k \mid x^*) + bP'(c_k \mid x^*) . \tag{4.38}$$

Moreover, $p(x)$ is approximated by $p(x^*)$. Therefore, the added error becomes $\frac{p(x^*)t}{2}b^2$, where $t = P'(c_j \mid x^*) - P'(c_i \mid x^*)$. Based on (4.32) and (4.35), it is easy to get

$$b = \frac{\epsilon_i(x_b) - \epsilon_j(x_b)}{t} . \tag{4.39}$$

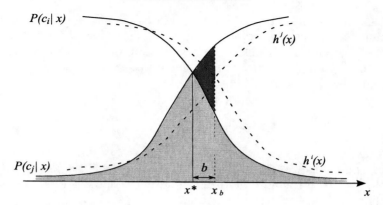

FIGURE 4.5: True posteriors $P(c_i \mid x)$ and $P(c_j \mid x)$ (solid lines) around the boundary x^*, and the estimated posteriors $h^i(x)$ and $h^j(x)$ (dashed lines) leading to the boundary x_b. Lightly and darkly shaded areas represent *Bayes error* and *added error*, respectively. (Plot based on a similar figure in [Fumera and Roli, 2005].)

Since $\epsilon_i(x)$ and $\epsilon_j(x)$ are unbiased and uncorrelated, the bias and variance of b are given by $\beta_b = 0$ and $\sigma_b^2 = \frac{\sigma_i^2 + \sigma_j^2}{t^2}$. Consequently, the expected value of the added error with respect to b, denoted by err_{add}, is then given by [Tumer and Ghosh, 1996]

$$err_{add}(h) = \frac{p(x^*)t}{2}(\beta_b^2 + \sigma_b^2) = \frac{p(x^*)}{2t}(\sigma_i^2 + \sigma_j^2). \tag{4.40}$$

Now, consider the simplest form of weighted soft voting, which assigns a non-negative weight w_i to each individual learner. Based on (4.33), the averaged estimate for the jth class is

$$h_{wsv}^j(x) = \sum_{i=1}^{T} w_i h_i^j(x) = P(c_j \mid x) + \epsilon_j^{wsv}(x), \tag{4.41}$$

where $\epsilon_j^{wsv}(x) = \sum_{i=1}^{T} w_i \epsilon_j^i(x)$ and "wsv" denotes "weighted soft voting". Analogous to that in Figure 4.5, the decision boundary $x_{b_{wsv}}$ is characterized by $h_{wsv}^i(x) = h_{wsv}^j(x)$, and it has an offset b_{wsv} from x^*. Following the same steps as above, the expected added error of weighted soft voting can be obtained as

$$err_{add}^{wsv}(H) = \frac{p(x^*)}{2t} \sum_{k=1}^{T} w_k^2 \left[(\sigma_i^k)^2 + (\sigma_j^k)^2\right] = \sum_{k=1}^{T} w_k^2 err_{add}(h_k), \tag{4.42}$$

where, from (4.40),

$$err_{add}(h_k) = \frac{p(x^*)}{2t} \left[(\sigma_i^k)^2 + (\sigma_j^k)^2\right] \tag{4.43}$$

is the expected added error of the individual classifier h_k. Thus, the performance of soft voting methods can be analyzed based on the expected added errors of individual classifiers, instead of the biases and variances.

Minimizing $err_{add}^{wsv}(H)$ under the constraints $w_k \geq 0$ and $\sum_{k=1}^{T} w_k = 1$, the optimal weights can be obtained as

$$w_k = \left(\sum_{i=1}^{T} \frac{1}{err_{add}(h_i)} \right)^{-1} \frac{1}{err_{add}(h_k)} . \tag{4.44}$$

This shows that the optimal weights are inversely proportional to the expected added error of the corresponding classifiers. This provides a theoretical support to the argument that different weights should be used for classifiers of different strengths [Tumer and Ghosh, 1996].

Substituting (4.44) into (4.42), the value of $err_{add}^{wsv}(H)$ corresponding to the optimal weights is

$$err_{add}^{wsv}(H) = \frac{1}{\frac{1}{err_{add}(h_1)} + \cdots + \frac{1}{err_{add}(h_T)}} . \tag{4.45}$$

On the other hand, if simple soft voting is used, an equal weight $w_i = 1/T$ is applied to (4.42), and the expected added error is

$$err_{add}^{ssv}(H) = \frac{1}{T^2} \sum_{k=1}^{T} err_{add}(h_k) , \tag{4.46}$$

where "ssv" denotes "simple soft voting".

When the individual classifiers exhibit identical expected added errors, i.e., $err_{add}(h_i) = err_{add}(h_j)$ $(\forall i, j)$, it follows that $err_{add}^{wsv}(H) = err_{add}^{ssv}(H)$, and the expected added error is reduced by a factor T over each individual classifier.

When the individual classifiers exhibit nonidentical added errors, it follows that $err_{add}^{wsv}(H) < err_{add}^{ssv}(H)$. Without loss of generality, denote the smallest and largest expected added errors as

$$err_{add}^{best}(H) = \min_i \{err_{add}(h_i)\} \quad \text{and} \quad err_{add}^{worst}(H) = \max_i \{err_{add}(h_i)\} , \tag{4.47}$$

and the corresponding classifiers are called the "best" and "worst" classifiers, respectively. From (4.46), the error reduction achieved by simple soft voting over the kth classifier is

$$\frac{err_{add}^{ssv}(H)}{err_{add}(h_k)} = \frac{1}{T^2} \left(1 + \sum_{i \neq k} \frac{err_{add}(h_i)}{err_{add}(h_k)} \right) . \tag{4.48}$$

It follows that the reduction factors over the best and worst classifiers are respectively in the ranges

$$\frac{err_{add}^{ssv}(H)}{err_{add}^{best}(H)} \in \left(\frac{1}{T}, +\infty \right) , \quad \frac{err_{add}^{ssv}(H)}{err_{add}^{worst}(H)} \in \left(\frac{1}{T^2}, \frac{1}{T} \right) . \tag{4.49}$$

From (4.45), the reduction factor of weighted soft voting is

$$\frac{err_{add}^{wsv}(H)}{err_{add}(h_k)} = \left(1 + \sum_{i \neq k} \frac{err_{add}(h_k)}{err_{add}(h_i)}\right)^{-1}, \tag{4.50}$$

and consequently

$$\frac{err_{add}^{wsv}(H)}{err_{add}^{best}(H)} \in \left(\frac{1}{T}, 1\right), \quad \frac{err_{add}^{wsv}(H)}{err_{add}^{worst}(H)} \in \left(0, \frac{1}{T}\right). \tag{4.51}$$

From (4.49) and (4.51) it can be seen that, if the individual classifiers have nonidentical added errors, both the simple and weighted soft voting achieve an error reduction smaller than a factor of T over the best classifier, and larger than a factor of T over the worst classifier. Moreover, weighted soft voting always performs better than the best individual classifier, while when the performances of individual classifiers are quite poor, the added error of simple soft voting may become arbitrarily larger than that of the best individual classifier. Furthermore, the reduction achieved by weighted soft voting over the worst individual classifier can be arbitrarily large, while the maximum reduction achievable by simple soft voting over the worst individual classifier is $1/T^2$. It is worth noting that all these conclusions are obtained based on the assumptions that the individual classifiers are uncorrelated and that the optimal weights for weighted soft voting can be solved, yet real situations are more complicated.

4.4 Combining by Learning

4.4.1 Stacking

Stacking [Wolpert, 1992, Breiman, 1996b, Smyth and Wolpert, 1998] is a general procedure where a learner is trained to combine the individual learners. Here, the individual learners are called the *first-level learners*, while the combiner is called the *second-level learner*, or **meta-learner**.

The basic idea is to train the first-level learners using the original training data set, and then generate a new data set for training the second-level learner, where the outputs of the first-level learners are regarded as input features while the original labels are still regarded as labels of the new training data. The first-level learners are often generated by applying different learning algorithms, and so, stacked ensembles are often heterogeneous, though it is also possible to construct homogeneous stacked ensembles. The pseudo-code of a general stacking procedure is summarized in Figure 4.6.

Input: Data set $D = \{(\boldsymbol{x}_1, y_1), (\boldsymbol{x}_2, y_2), \ldots, (\boldsymbol{x}_m, y_m)\}$;
　　　　First-level learning algorithms $\mathfrak{L}_1, \ldots, \mathfrak{L}_T$;
　　　　Second-level learning algorithm $\mathfrak{L}$.

Process:
1.　**for** $t = 1, \ldots, T$:　　% Train a first-level learner by applying the
2.　　$h_t = \mathfrak{L}_t(D)$;　　% first-level learning algorithm $\mathfrak{L}_t$
3.　**end**
4.　$D' = \emptyset$;　　　　% Generate a new data set
5.　**for** $i = 1, \ldots, m$:
6.　　**for** $t = 1, \ldots, T$:
7.　　　$z_{it} = h_t(\boldsymbol{x}_i)$;
8.　　**end**
9.　　$D' = D' \cup ((z_{i1}, \ldots, z_{iT}), y_i)$;
10.　**end**
11.　$h' = \mathfrak{L}(D')$;　　　% Train the second-level learner h' by applying
　　　　　　　　　　% the second-level learning algorithm $\mathfrak{L}$ to the
　　　　　　　　　　% new data set $\mathcal{D}'$.

Output: $H(\boldsymbol{x}) = h'(h_1(\boldsymbol{x}), \ldots, h_T(\boldsymbol{x}))$

FIGURE 4.6: A general Stacking procedure.

On one hand, stacking is a general framework which can be viewed as a generalization of many ensemble methods. On the other hand, it can be viewed as a specific combination method which combines by learning, and this is the reason why we introduce Stacking in this chapter.

In the training phase of stacking, a new data set needs to be generated from the first-level classifiers. If the exact data that are used to train the first-level learner are also used to generate the new data set for training the second-level learner, there will be a high risk of overfitting. Hence, it is suggested that the instances used for generating the new data set are excluded from the training examples for the first-level learners, and a cross-validation or leave-one-out procedure is often recommended.

Take k-fold cross-validation for example. Here, the original training data set D is randomly split into k almost equal parts $D_1, \ldots, D_k$. Define D_j and $D_{(-j)} = D \setminus D_j$ to be the test and training sets for the jth fold. Given T learning algorithms, a first-level learner $h_t^{(-j)}$ is obtained by invoking the tth learning algorithm on $D_{(-j)}$. For each $\boldsymbol{x}_i$ in D_j, the test set of the jth fold, let z_{it} denote the output of the learner $h_t^{(-j)}$ on $\boldsymbol{x}_i$. Then, at the end of the entire cross-validation process, the new data set is generated from the T individual learners as

$$D' = \{(z_{i1}, \ldots, z_{iT}, y_i)\}_{i=1}^m, \qquad (4.52)$$

on which the second-level learning algorithm will be applied, and the resulting learner h' is a function of $(z_1, \ldots, z_T)$ for y. After generating the new data set, generally, the final first-level learners are re-generated by training on the whole training data.

Breiman [1996b] demonstrated the success of stacked regression. He used regression trees of different sizes or linear regression models with different numbers of variables as the first-level learners, and least-square linear regression model as the second-level learner under the constraint that all regression coefficients are non-negative. This non-negativity constraint was found to be crucial to guarantee that the performance of the stacked ensemble would be better than selecting the single best learner.

For stacked classification, Wolpert [1992] indicated that it is crucial to consider the types of features for the new training data, and the types of learning algorithms for the second-level learner.

Ting and Witten [1999] recommended to use *class probabilities* instead of crisp class labels as features for the new data, since this makes it possible to take into account not only the predictions but also the confidences of the individual classifiers. For first-level classifiers that can output class probabilities, the output of the classifier h_k on an instance x is $(h_{k1}(x), \ldots, h_{kl}(x))$, which is a probability distribution over all the possible class labels $\{c_1, \ldots, c_l\}$, and $h_{kj}(x)$ denotes the probability predicted by h_k for the instance x belonging to class c_j. Though h_k predicts only the class c_j with the largest class probability $h_{kj}(x)$ as the class label, the probabilities it obtained for all classes contain helpful information. Thus, the class probabilities from all first-level classifiers on x can be used along with the true class label of x to form a new training example for the second-level learner.

Ting and Witten [1999] also recommended to use **multi-response linear regression** (MLR), which is a variant of the least-square linear regression algorithm [Breiman, 1996b], as the second-level learning algorithm. Any classification problem with real-valued features can be converted into a multi-response regression problem. For a classification problem with l classes $\{c_1, \ldots, c_l\}$, l separate regression problems are formed as follows: for each class c_j, a linear regression model is constructed to predict a binary variable, which equals one if c_j is the correct class label and zero otherwise. The linear regression coefficients are determined based on the least-squares principle. In the prediction stage, given an instance x to classify, all the trained linear regression models will be invoked, and the class label corresponding to the regression model with the largest value will be output. It was found that the non-negativity constraints that are necessary in regression [Breiman, 1996b] are irrelevant to the performance improvement in classification [Ting and Witten, 1999]. Later, Seewald [2002] suggested to use different sets of features for the l linear regression problems in MLR. That is, only the probabilities of class c_j predicted by the different classifiers, i.e., $h_{kj}(x)$ $(k = 1, \ldots, T)$, are used to construct the linear regression model corresponding to c_j. Consequently, each of the linear regression problems has T instead of $l \times T$ features. The Weka implementation of Stacking provides both the standard Stacking algorithm and the StackingC algorithm which implements Seewald [2002]'s suggestion.

Clarke [2003] provided a comparison between Stacking and **Bayesian Model Averaging** (BMA) which assigns weights to different models based on posterior probabilities. In theory, if the correct *data generating model* is among the models under consideration, and if the noise level is low, BMA is never worse and often better than Stacking. However, in practice it is usually not the case since the correct data generating model is often not in the models under consideration and may even be difficult to be approximated well by the considered models. Clarke [2003]'s empirical results showed that stacking is more robust than BMA, and BMA is quite sensitive to model approximation error.

4.4.2 Infinite Ensemble

Most ensemble methods exploit only a small finite subset of hypotheses, while Lin and Li [2008] developed an infinite ensemble framework that constructs ensembles with infinite hypotheses. This framework can be regarded as learning the combination weights for all possible hypotheses. It is based on support vector machines, and by embedding infinitely many hypotheses into a kernel, it can be found that the learning problem reduces to an SVM training problem with specific kernels.

Let $\mathcal{H} = \{h_\alpha : \alpha \in \mathcal{C}\}$ denote the hypothesis space, where $\mathcal{C}$ is a measure space. The kernel that embeds $\mathcal{H}$ is defined as

$$K_{\mathcal{H},r}(\boldsymbol{x}_i, \boldsymbol{x}_j) = \int_{\mathcal{C}} \Phi_{\boldsymbol{x}_i}(\alpha)\Phi_{\boldsymbol{x}_j}(\alpha)d\alpha \,, \tag{4.53}$$

where $\Phi_{\boldsymbol{x}}(\alpha) = r(\alpha)h_\alpha(\boldsymbol{x})$, and $r : \mathcal{C} \mapsto \mathbb{R}^+$ is chosen such that the integral exists for all $\boldsymbol{x}_i, \boldsymbol{x}_j$. Here, α denotes the parameter of the hypothesis h_α, and $Z(\alpha)$ means that Z depends on α. In the following we denote $K_{\mathcal{H},r}$ by $K_{\mathcal{H}}$ when r is clear from the context. It is easy to prove that (4.53) defines a valid kernel [Schölkopf and Smola, 2002].

Following SVM, the framework formulates the following (primal) problem:

$$\min_{w \in \mathcal{L}_2(\mathcal{C}), b \in \mathbb{R}, \xi \in \mathbb{R}^m} \frac{1}{2} \int_{\mathcal{C}} w^2(\alpha)d\alpha + C \sum_{i=1}^{m} \xi_i \tag{4.54}$$

$$\text{s.t.} \quad y_i \left(\int_{\mathcal{C}} w(\alpha)r(\alpha)h_\alpha(\boldsymbol{x})d\alpha + b \right) \geq 1 - \xi_i$$

$$\xi_i \geq 0 \quad (\forall i = 1, \ldots, m).$$

The final classifier obtained from this optimization problem is

$$g(\boldsymbol{x}) = \text{sign} \left(\int_{\mathcal{C}} w(\alpha)r(\alpha)h_\alpha(\boldsymbol{x})d\alpha + b \right). \tag{4.55}$$

Obviously, if $\mathcal{C}$ is uncountable, it is possible that each hypothesis h_α takes an infinitesimal weight $w(\alpha)r(\alpha)d\alpha$ in the ensemble. Thus, the obtained final classifier is very different from those obtained with other ensemble methods. Suppose $\mathcal{H}$ is negation complete, that is, $h \in \mathcal{H} \Leftrightarrow -h \in \mathcal{H}$. Then, every linear combination over $\mathcal{H}$ has an equivalent linear combination with only non-negative weights. By treating b as a constant hypothesis, the classifier in (4.55) can be seen as an ensemble of infinite hypotheses.

By using the *Lagrangian multiplier* method and the kernel trick, the dual problem of (4.54) can be obtained, and the final classifier can be written in terms of the kernel $K_\mathcal{H}$ as

$$g(\boldsymbol{x}) = \text{sign}\left(\sum_{i=1}^{m} y_i \lambda_i K_\mathcal{H}(\boldsymbol{x}_i, \boldsymbol{x}) + b \right) , \qquad (4.56)$$

where $K_\mathcal{H}$ is the kernel embedding the hypothesis set $\mathcal{H}$, and λ_i's are the *Lagrange multipliers*. (4.56) is equivalent to (4.55) and hence it is also an infinite ensemble over $\mathcal{H}$. In practice, if a kernel $K_\mathcal{H}$ can be constructed according to (4.53) with a proper embedding function r, such as the *stump kernel* and the *perceptron kernel* in [Lin and Li, 2008], the learning problem can be reduced to solve an SVM with the kernel $K_\mathcal{H}$, and thus, the final ensemble can be obtained by applying typical SVM solvers.

4.5 Other Combination Methods

There are many other combination methods in addition to averaging, voting and combining by learning. In this section we briefly introduce the *algebraic* methods, *BKS method* and *decision template method*.

4.5.1 Algebraic Methods

Since the class probabilities output from individual classifiers can be regarded as an estimate of the posterior probabilities, it is straightforward to derive combination rules under the probabilistic framework [Kittler et al., 1998].

Denote $h_i^j(\boldsymbol{x})$, the class probability of c_j output from h_i, as h_i^j. According to Bayesian decision theory, given T classifiers, the instance $\boldsymbol{x}$ should be assigned to the class c_j which maximizes the posteriori probability $P(c_j \mid h_1^j, \ldots, h_T^j)$. From the Bayes theorem, it follows that

$$P(c_j \mid h_1^j, \ldots, h_T^j) = \frac{P(c_j)P(h_1^j, \ldots, h_T^j \mid c_j)}{\sum_{i=1}^{l} P(c_i)P(h_1^j, \ldots, h_T^j \mid c_i)} , \qquad (4.57)$$

where $P(h_1^j, \ldots, h_T^j \mid c_j)$ is the joint probability distribution of the outputs from the classifiers.

Assume that the outputs are conditionally independent, i.e.,

$$P(h_1^j, \ldots, h_T^j \mid c_j) = \prod_{i=1}^{T} P(h_i^j \mid c_j). \tag{4.58}$$

Then, from (4.57), it follows that

$$P(c_j \mid h_1^j, \ldots, h_T^j) = \frac{P(c_j) \prod_{i=1}^{T} P(h_i^j \mid c_j)}{\sum_{i=1}^{l} P(c_i) \prod_{k=1}^{T} P(h_k^j \mid c_i)}$$

$$\propto P(c_j)^{-(T-1)} \prod_{i=1}^{T} P(c_j \mid h_i^j). \tag{4.59}$$

Since h_i^j is the probability output, we have $P(c_j \mid h_i^j) = h_i^j$. Thus, if all classes are with equal prior, we get the *product rule* [Kittler et al., 1998] for combination, i.e.,

$$H^j(\boldsymbol{x}) = \prod_{i=1}^{T} h_i^j(\boldsymbol{x}). \tag{4.60}$$

Similarly, Kittler et al. [1998] derived the soft voting method, as well as the *maximum/minimum/median rules*. Briefly speaking, these rules choose the maximum/minimum/median of the individual outputs as the combined output. For example, the *median rule* generates the combined output according to

$$H^j(\boldsymbol{x}) = \underset{i}{\mathrm{med}}(h_i^j(\boldsymbol{x})), \tag{4.61}$$

where $\mathrm{med}(\cdot)$ denotes the median statistic.

4.5.2 Behavior Knowledge Space Method

The Behavior Knowledge Space (BKS) method was proposed by Huang and Suen [1995]. Let $\boldsymbol{\ell} = (\ell_1, \ldots, \ell_T)^\top$ denote the class labels assigned by the individual classifiers $h_1, \ldots, h_T$ to the instance $\boldsymbol{x}$, where $\ell_i = h_i(\boldsymbol{x})$. If we consider $\boldsymbol{\ell}$ as a T-dimensional random variable, the task can be reduced to estimate $P(c_j \mid \boldsymbol{\ell})$. For this, every possible combination of class labels (i.e., every possible value of $\boldsymbol{\ell}$) can be regarded as an index to a cell in the BKS table [Huang and Suen, 1995]. This table is filled using a data set D, and each example $(\boldsymbol{x}_i, y_i)$ is placed in the cell indexed by $(h_1(\boldsymbol{x}_i), \ldots, h_T(\boldsymbol{x}_i))$. The number of examples in each cell are counted; then, the most representative class label is selected for this cell, where ties are broken arbitrarily and the empty cells are labeled at random or by majority. In the testing stage, the BKS method labels $\boldsymbol{x}$ to the class of the cell indexed by $(h_1(\boldsymbol{x}), \ldots, h_T(\boldsymbol{x}))$.

The BKS method performs well if large and representative data sets are available. It suffers from the *small sample size* problem, in which case over-fitting may be serious. To deal with this problem, Raudys and Roli [2003] analyzed the generalization error of the BKS method, and obtained an analytical model which relates error to sample size. Based on the model, they proposed to use linear classifiers in "ambiguous" cells of the BKS table, and this strategy was reported to strongly improve the BKS performance [Raudys and Roli, 2003].

4.5.3 Decision Template Method

The Decision Template method was developed by Kuncheva et al. [2001]. In this method, the outputs of the classifiers on an instance x are organized in a *decision profile* as the matrix

$$DP(x) = \begin{pmatrix} h_1^1(x) & \dots & h_1^j(x) & \dots & h_1^l(x) \\ \vdots & \ddots & \vdots & \ddots & \vdots \\ h_i^1(x) & \dots & h_i^j(x) & \dots & h_i^l(x) \\ \vdots & \ddots & \vdots & \ddots & \vdots \\ h_T^1(x) & \dots & h_T^j(x) & \dots & h_T^l(x) \end{pmatrix}. \quad (4.62)$$

Based on the training data set $D = \{(x_1, y_1), \dots, (x_m, y_m)\}$, the decision templates are estimated as the expected $DP(x)$, i.e.,

$$DT_k = \frac{1}{m_k} \sum_{i:y_i=c_k} DP(x_i), \quad k = 1, \dots, l \quad (4.63)$$

where m_k is the number of training examples in the class c_k.

The testing stage of this method works like a nearest neighbor algorithm. That is, the similarity between $DP(x)$, i.e., the decision profile of the test instance x, and the decision templates DT_k's are calculated based on some similarity measure [Kuncheva et al., 2001], and then the class label of the most similar decision template is assigned to x.

4.6 Relevant Methods

There are some methods which try to make use of multiple learners, yet in a strict sense they can not be recognized as ensemble combination methods. For example, some methods choose one learner to make the final prediction, though the learner is not a fixed one and thus, all individual learners may be chosen upon receiving different test instances; some methods combine multiple learners trained on different sub-problems rather

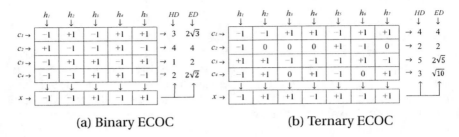

(a) Binary ECOC   (b) Ternary ECOC

FIGURE 4.7: ECOC examples. (a) Binary ECOC for a 4-class problem. An instance x is classified to class c_3 using the Hamming or the Euclidean decoding; (b) Ternary ECOC example, where an instance x is classified to class c_2 according to the Hamming or the Euclidean decoding.

than the exact same problem. This section provides a brief introduction to *ECOC, dynamic classifier selection* and *mixture of experts*.

4.6.1 Error-Correcting Output Codes

Error-Correcting Output Codes (ECOC) is a simple yet powerful approach to deal with a multi-class problem based on the combination of binary classifiers [Dietterich and Bakiri, 1995, Allwein et al., 2000]. In general, the ECOC approach works in two steps:

1. **The coding step**. In this step, a set of B different bipartitions of the class label set $\{c_1, \ldots, c_l\}$ are constructed, and subsequently B binary classifiers $h_1, \ldots, h_B$ are trained over the partitions.

2. **The decoding step**. In this step, given an instance x, a **codeword** is generated by using the outputs of B binary classifiers. Then, the codeword is compared to the *base codeword* of each class, and the instance is assigned to the class with the most similar codeword.

Typically, the partitions of class set are specified by a **coding matrix** M, which can appear in different forms, e.g., binary form [Dietterich and Bakiri, 1995] and ternary form [Allwein et al., 2000].

In the binary form, $\mathbf{M} \in \{-1, +1\}^{l \times B}$ [Dietterich and Bakiri, 1995]. Figure 4.7(a) provides an example of a binary coding matrix, which transforms a four-class problem into five binary classification problems. In the figure, regions coded by $+1$ are considered as a class, while regions coded by -1 are considered as the other class. Consequently, binary classifiers are trained based on these bipartitions. For example, the binary classifier h_2 is trained to discriminate $\{c_1, c_3\}$ against $\{c_2, c_4\}$, that is,

$$h_2(\boldsymbol{x}) = \begin{cases} +1 & \text{if } \boldsymbol{x} \in \{c_1, c_3\} \\ -1 & \text{if } \boldsymbol{x} \in \{c_2, c_4\}. \end{cases} \tag{4.64}$$

In the decoding step, by applying the five binary classifiers, a codeword can be generated for the instance $\boldsymbol{x}$. Then, the codeword is compared with the base codewords defined in the rows of $\mathbf{M}$. For example, in Figure 4.7(a), the instance $\boldsymbol{x}$ is classified to c_3 according to either Hamming distance or Euclidean distance.

In the ternary form, $\mathbf{M} \in \{-1, 0, 1\}^{l \times B}$ [Allwein et al., 2000]. Figure 4.7(b) provides an example of a ternary coding matrix, which transforms a four-class classification problem into seven binary problems. Here, "zero" indicates that the corresponding class is excluded from training the binary classifier. For example, the classifier h_4 is trained to discriminate c_3 against $\{c_1, c_4\}$ without taking into account c_2. Notice that the codeword of a test instance cannot contain zeros since the output of each binary classifier is either -1 or $+1$. In Figure 4.7(b), the instance $\boldsymbol{x}$ is classified to c_2 according to either Hamming distance or Euclidean distance.

Popular binary coding schemes mainly include the **one-versus-rest** scheme and **dense random** scheme [Allwein et al., 2000]. In the one-versus-rest scheme, each binary classifier is trained to discriminate one class against all the other classes. Obviously, the codeword is of length l if there are l classes. In the dense random scheme, each element in the code is usually chosen with a probability of $1/2$ for $+1$ and $1/2$ for -1. Allwein et al. [2000] suggested an optimal codeword length of $10 \log l$. Among a set of dense random matrices, the optimal one is with the largest Hamming decoding distance among each pair of codewords.

Popular ternary coding schemes mainly include the **one-versus-one** scheme and **sparse random** scheme [Allwein et al., 2000]. The one-versus-one scheme considers all pairs of classes, and each classifier is trained to discriminate between two classes. Thus, the codeword length is $l(l-1)/2$. The sparse random scheme is similar to the dense random scheme, except that it includes the zero value in addition to $+1$ and -1. Generally, each element is chosen with probability of $1/2$ for 0, a probability of $1/4$ for $+1$ or -1, and the codeword length is set to $15 \log l$ [Allwein et al., 2000].

The central task of decoding is to find the base codeword $\boldsymbol{w}_i$ (corresponding to class c_i) which is the closest to the codeword $\boldsymbol{v}$ of the given test instance. Popular binary decoding schemes mainly include:

- **Hamming decoder**. This scheme is based on the assumption that the learning task can be modeled as an error-correcting communication problem [Nilsson, 1965]. The measure is given by

$$HD(\boldsymbol{v}, \boldsymbol{w}_i) = \frac{\sum_j (1 - \text{sign}(v^j \cdot w_i^j))}{2}. \tag{4.65}$$

- **Euclidean decoder**. This scheme is directly based on Euclidean distance [Pujol et al., 2006]. The measure is given by

$$ED(v, w_i) = \sqrt{\sum_j (v^j - w_i^j)^2} \,. \tag{4.66}$$

- **Inverse Hamming decoder**. This scheme is based on the matrix Δ which is composed of the Hamming decoding measures between the codewords of M, and $\Delta_{ij} = HD(w_i, w_j)$ [Windeatt and Ghaderi, 2003]. The measure is given by

$$IHD(v, w_i) = \max(\Delta^{-1} D^\top) \,, \tag{4.67}$$

where D denotes the vector of Hamming decoder values of v for each of the base codewords w_i.

Popular ternary decoding schemes mainly include:

- **Attenuated Euclidean decoder**. This is a variant of the Euclidean decoder, which has been redefined to ensure the measure to be unaffected by the positions of the codeword w_i containing zeros [Pujol et al., 2008]. The measure is given by

$$AED(v, w_i) = \sqrt{\sum_j |w_i^j| \cdot (v^j - w_i^j)^2} \,. \tag{4.68}$$

- **Loss-based decoder**. This scheme chooses the class c_i that minimizes a particular loss function [Allwein et al., 2000]. The measure is given by

$$LB(x, w_i) = \sum_j L(h_j(x), w_i^j) \,, \tag{4.69}$$

where $h_j(x)$ is the real-valued prediction on x, and L is the loss function. In practice, the loss function has many choices, while two commonly used ones are $L(h_j(x), w_i^j) = -h_j(x) \cdot w_i^j$ and $L(h_j(x), w_i^j) = \exp(-h_j(x) \cdot w_i^j)$.

- **Probabilistic-based decoder**. This is a probabilistic scheme based on the real-valued output of the binary classifiers [Passerini et al., 2004]. The measure is given by

$$PD(v, w_i) = -\log\left(\prod_{j:w_i^j \neq 0} P(v^j = w_i^j \mid h_j(x)) + C\right) \,, \tag{4.70}$$

where C is a constant, and $P(v^j = w_i^j \mid h_j(x))$ is estimated by

$$P(v^j = w_i^j \mid h_j(x)) = \frac{1}{1 + \exp(w_i^j(a^j \cdot h_j(x) + b^j))} \,, \tag{4.71}$$

where a and b are obtained by solving an optimization problem [Passerini et al., 2004].

4.6.2 Dynamic Classifier Selection

Dynamic Classifier Selection (DCS) is a specific method for exploiting multiple learners. After training multiple individual learners, DCS dynamically selects one learner for each test instance. In contrast to classic learning methods which select the "best" individual learner and discard other individual learners, DCS needs to keep all the individual learners; in contrast to typical ensemble methods which combine individual learners to make predictions, DCS makes predictions by using one individual learner. Considering that DCS keeps all the individual learners for prediction, it can be regarded as a "soft combination" method.

Ho et al. [1994] were the first to introduce DCS. They briefly outlined the DCS procedure and proposed a selection method based on a partition of training examples. The individual classifiers are evaluated on each partition so that the best-performing one for each partition is determined. In the testing stage, the test instance will be categorized into a partition and then classified by the corresponding best classifier.

Woods et al. [1997] proposed a DCS method called DCS-LA. The basic idea is to estimate the accuracy of each individual classifier in local regions surrounding the test instance, and then the most locally accurate classifier is selected to make the classification. In DCS-LA, the local regions are specified in terms of k-*nearest neighbors* in the training data, and the local accuracy can be estimated by *overall local accuracy* or *local class accuracy*. The overall local accuracy is simply the percentage of local examples that are correctly classified; the local class accuracy is the percentage of local examples belonging to the same class that are correctly classified. Giacinto and Roli [1997] developed a similar DCS method based on local accuracy. They estimated the class posterior and calculated a "confidence" for the selection. Didaci et al. [2005] studied the performance bounds of DCS-LA and showed that the upper bounds of DCS-LA are realistic and can be attained by accurate parameter tuning in practice. Their experimental results clearly showed the effectiveness of DCS based on local accuracy estimates.

Giacinto and Roli [2000a,b] placed DCS in the framework of Bayesian decision theory and found that, under the assumptions of *decision regions complementarity* and *decision boundaries complementarity*, the optimal Bayes classifier can be obtained by the selection of non-optimal classifiers. This provides theoretical support for the power of DCS. Following the theoretical analysis, they proposed the *a prior selection* and *a posterior selection* methods which directly exploit probabilistic estimates.

4.6.3 Mixture of Experts

Mixture of experts (ME) [Jacobs et al., 1991, Xu et al., 1995] is an effective approach to exploit multiple learners. In contrast to typical ensemble methods where individual learners are trained for the same problem, ME

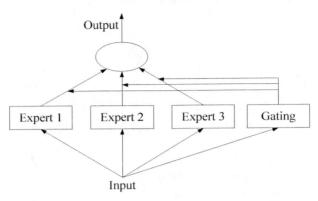

FIGURE 4.8: An illustrative example of mixture of experts. (Plot based on a similar figure in [Jacobs et al., 1991].)

works in a **divide-and-conquer** strategy where a complex task is broken up into several simpler and smaller subtasks, and individual learners (called *experts*) are trained for different subtasks. **Gating** is usually employed to combine the experts. Figure 4.8 illustrates an example for ME which consists of three experts.

Notice that the keys of ME are different from those of typical ensemble methods. In typical ensemble methods, since the individual learners are trained for the same problem, particularly from the same training data set, they are generally highly correlated and a key problem is how to make the individual learners diverse; while in ME, the individual learners are generated for different subtasks and there is no need to devote to diversity. Typical ensemble methods do not divide the task into subtasks; while in ME, a key problem is how to find the natural division of the task and then derive the overall solution from sub-solutions. In literature on ME, much emphasis was given to make the experts local, and this is thought to be crucial to the performance. A basic method for this purpose is to target each expert to a distribution specified by the gating function, rather than the whole original training data distribution.

Without loss of generality, assume that an ME architecture is comprised of T experts, and the output y is a discrete variable with possible values 0 and 1 for binary classification. Given an input x, each local expert h_i tries to approximate the distribution of y and obtains a local output $h_i(y \mid x; \theta_i)$, where θ_i is the parameter of the ith expert h_i. The gating function provides a set of coefficients $\pi_i(x; \alpha)$ that weigh the contributions of experts, and α is the parameter of the gating function. Thus, the final output of the ME is a weighted sum of all the local outputs produced by the experts, i.e.,

$$H(y \mid \boldsymbol{x}; \Psi) = \sum_{i=1}^{T} \pi_i(\boldsymbol{x}; \boldsymbol{\alpha}) \cdot h_i(y \mid \boldsymbol{x}; \boldsymbol{\theta_i}) , \qquad (4.72)$$

where Ψ includes all unknown parameters. The output of the gating function is often modeled by the **softmax function** as

$$\pi_i(\boldsymbol{x}; \boldsymbol{\alpha}) = \frac{\exp(\boldsymbol{v}_i^\top \boldsymbol{x})}{\sum_{j=1}^{T} \exp(\boldsymbol{v}_j^\top \boldsymbol{x})}, \qquad (4.73)$$

where $\boldsymbol{v}_i$ is the weight vector of the ith expert in the gating function, and $\boldsymbol{\alpha}$ contains all the elements in $\boldsymbol{v}_i$'s. In the training stage, $\pi_i(\boldsymbol{x}; \boldsymbol{\alpha})$ states the probability of the instance $\boldsymbol{x}$ appearing in the training set of the ith expert h_i; while in the test stage, it defines the contribution of h_i to the final prediction.

In general, the training procedure tries to achieve two goals: for given experts, to find the optimal gating function; for given gating function, to train the experts on the distribution specified by the gating function. The unknown parameters are usually estimated by the **Expectation Maximization (EM)** algorithm [Jordan and Xu, 1995, Xu et al., 1995, Xu and Jordan, 1996].

4.7 Further Readings

Weighted averaging was shown effective in ensemble learning by [Perrone and Cooper, 1993]. This method is quite basic and was used for combining multiple evidences long time ago, e.g., (4.14) was well known in **portfolio selection** in the 1950s [Markowitz, 1952]. In its early formulation there was no constraint on the weights. Later, it was found that the weights in practice may take large negative and positive values, and hence giving extreme predictions even when the individual learners provide reasonable predictions; moreover, since the training data are used for training the individual learners as well as estimating the weights, the process is very easy to suffer from overfitting. So, Breiman [1996b] suggested to consider the constraints as shown in (4.10), which has become a standard setting.

The expression of majority voting accuracy, (4.16), was first shown by de Concorcet [1785] and later re-developed by many authors. The relation between the majority voting accuracy P_{mv}, the individual accuracy p and the ensemble size T was also given at first by de Concorcet [1785], but for odd sizes only; Lam and Suen [1997] generalized the analysis to even cases, leading to the overall result shown in Section 4.3.1.

Though the effectiveness of plurality voting has been validated by empirical studies, theoretical analysis on plurality voting is somewhat difficult and there are only a few works [Lin et al., 2003, Mu et al., 2009]. In particular, Lin et al. [2003] theoretically compared the recognition/error/rejection rates of plurality voting and majority voting under different conditions, and showed that plurality voting is more efficient to achieve tradeoff between the rejection and error rates.

Kittler et al. [1998], Kittler and Alkoot [2003] showed that voting can be regarded as a special case of averaging, while the averaging rule is more resilient to estimation errors than other combination methods. Kuncheva [2002] theoretically studied six simple classifier combination methods under the assumption that the estimates are independent and identically distributed. Kuncheva et al. [2003] empirically studied majority voting, and showed that dependent classifiers can offer improvement over independent classifiers for majority voting.

The **Dempster-Shafer (DS) theory** [Dempster, 1967, Shafer, 1976] is a theory on evidence aggregation, which is able to represent uncertainties and ignorance (lack of evidence). Several combination methods have been inspired by the DS theory, e.g., [Xu et al., 1992, Rogova, 1994, Al-Ani and Deriche, 2002, Ahmadzadeh and Petrou, 2003, Bi et al., 2008].

Utschick and Weichselberger [2004] proposed to improve the process of binary coding by optimizing a maximum-likelihood objective function; however, they found that the one-versus-rest scheme is still the optimal choice for many multi-class problems. General coding schemes could not guarantee that the coded problems are most suitable for a given task. Crammer and Singer [2002] were the first to design problem-dependent coding schemes, and proved that the problem of finding the optimal discrete coding matrix is NP-complete. Later, several other problem-dependent designs were developed based on exploiting the problem by finding representative binary problems that increase the generalization performance while keeping the code length small. Discriminant ECOC (DECOC) [Pujol et al., 2006] is based on the embedding of discriminant tree structures derived from the problem. Forest-ECOC [Escalera et al., 2007] extends DECOC by including additional classifiers. ECOC-ONE [Pujol et al., 2008] uses a coding process that trains the binary problems guided by a validation set. For binary decoding, Allwein et al. [2000] reported that the practical behavior of the Inverse Hamming decoder is quite similar to the Hamming decoder. For ternary decoding, Escalera et al. [2010b] found that the zero symbol introduces two kinds of biases, and to overcome these problems, they proposed the *Loss-Weighted decoder* (LW) and the *Pessimistic Beta Density Distribution decoder* (β-DEN). An open source ECOC library developed by Escalera et al. [2010a] can be found at http://mloss.org.

The application of Dynamic Classifier Selection is not limited to classification. For example, Zhu et al. [2004] showed that DCS has promising performance in mining data streams with concept drifting or with significant noise. The idea of DCS has even been generalized to *dynamic ensemble selection* by Ko et al. [2008].

Hierarchical mixture of experts (HME) [Jordan and Jacobs, 1992] extends mixture of experts (ME) into a tree structure. In contrast to ME which builds the experts on the input directly, in HME the experts are built from multiple levels of experts and gating functions. The EM algorithm still can be used to train HME. Waterhouse and Robinson [1996] described how to grow the tree structure of HME gradually. Bayesian frameworks for inferring the parameters of ME and HME were developed by Waterhouse et al. [1996] and Bishop and Svensén [2003], respectively.

5

Diversity

5.1 Ensemble Diversity

Ensemble diversity, that is, the difference among the individual learners, is a fundamental issue in ensemble methods.

Intuitively it is easy to understand that to gain from combination, the individual learners must be different, and otherwise there would be no performance improvement if identical individual learners were combined. Tumer and Ghosh [1995] analyzed the performance of *simple soft voting* ensemble using the decision boundary analysis introduced in Section 4.3.5.2, by introducing a term θ to describe the overall correlation among the individual learners. They showed that the expected *added error* of the ensemble is

$$err_{add}^{ssv}(H) = \frac{1 + \theta(T - 1)}{T} \overline{err}_{add}(h) , \qquad (5.1)$$

where $\overline{err}_{add}(h)$ is the expected added error of the individual learners (for simplicity, all individual learners were assumed to have equal error), and T is the ensemble size. (5.1) discloses that if the learners are independent, i.e., $\theta = 0$, the ensemble will achieve a factor of T of error reduction than the individual learners; if the learners are totally correlated, i.e., $\theta = 1$, no gains can be obtained from the combination. This analysis clearly shows that the diversity is crucial to ensemble performance. A similar conclusion can be obtained for other combination methods.

Generating diverse individual learners, however, is not easy. The major obstacle lies in the fact that the individual learners are trained for the same task from the same training data, and thus they are usually highly correlated. Many theoretically plausible approaches, e.g., the optimal solution of weighted averaging (4.14), do not work in practice simply because they are based on the assumption of independent or less correlated learners. The real situation is even more difficult. For example, the derivation of (5.1), though it considers high correlation between individual learners, is based on the assumption that the individual learners produce independent estimates of the posterior probabilities; this is actually not the case in practice.

In fact, the problem of generating diverse individual learners is even more challenging if we consider that the individual learners must not be very poor, and otherwise their combination would not improve and could even worsen the performance. For example, it can be seen from (4.52) that when the performance of individual classifiers is quite poor, the added error of simple soft voted ensemble may become arbitrarily large; similar analytical results can also be obtained for other combination methods.

So, it is desired that the individual learners should be *accurate and diverse*. Combining only accurate learners is often worse than combining some accurate ones together with some relatively weak ones, since complementarity is more important than pure accuracy. Ultimately, the success of ensemble learning lies in achieving a good tradeoff between the individual performance and diversity.

Unfortunately, though diversity is crucial, we still do not have a clear understanding of diversity; for example, currently there is no well-accepted formal definition of diversity. There is no doubt that understanding diversity is the holy grail in the field of ensemble learning.

5.2   Error Decomposition

It is important to see that the generalization error of an ensemble depends on a term related to diversity. For this purpose, this section introduces two famous error decomposition schemes for ensemble methods, that is, the error-ambiguity decomposition and the bias-variance decomposition.

5.2.1   Error-Ambiguity Decomposition

The error-ambiguity decomposition was proposed by Krogh and Vedelsby [1995]. Assume that the task is to use an ensemble of T individual learners $h_1, \ldots, h_T$ to approximate a function $f : R^d \mapsto R$, and the final prediction of the ensemble is obtained through weighted averaging (4.9), i.e.,

$$H(\boldsymbol{x}) = \sum_{i=1}^{T} w_i h_i(\boldsymbol{x})$$

where w_i is the weight for the learner h_i, and the weights are constrained by $w_i \geq 0$ and $\sum_{i=1}^{T} w_i = 1$.

Given an instance $\boldsymbol{x}$, the *ambiguity* of the individual learner h_i is defined as [Krogh and Vedelsby, 1995]

$$ambi(h_i \mid \boldsymbol{x}) = (h_i(\boldsymbol{x}) - H(\boldsymbol{x}))^2 , \qquad (5.2)$$

and the *ambiguity* of the ensemble is

$$\overline{ambi}(h \mid \boldsymbol{x}) = \sum_{i=1}^{T} w_i \cdot ambi(h_i \mid \boldsymbol{x}) = \sum_{i=1}^{T} w_i (h_i(\boldsymbol{x}) - H(\boldsymbol{x}))^2 \,. \qquad (5.3)$$

Obviously, the ambiguity term measures the disagreement among the individual learners on instance $\boldsymbol{x}$. If we use the squared error to measure the performance, then the error of the individual learner h_i and the ensemble H are respectively

$$err(h_i \mid \boldsymbol{x}) = (f(\boldsymbol{x}) - h_i(\boldsymbol{x}))^2 \,, \qquad (5.4)$$

$$err(H \mid \boldsymbol{x}) = (f(\boldsymbol{x}) - H(\boldsymbol{x}))^2 \,. \qquad (5.5)$$

Then, it is easy to get

$$\overline{ambi}(h \mid \boldsymbol{x}) = \sum_{i=1}^{T} w_i err(h_i \mid \boldsymbol{x}) - err(H \mid \boldsymbol{x}) = \overline{err}(h \mid \boldsymbol{x}) - err(H \mid \boldsymbol{x}) \,, \quad (5.6)$$

where $\overline{err}(h \mid \boldsymbol{x}) = \sum_{i=1}^{T} w_i \cdot err(h_i \mid \boldsymbol{x})$ is the weighted average of the individual errors. Since (5.6) holds for every instance $\boldsymbol{x}$, after averaging over the input distribution it still holds that

$$\sum_{i=1}^{T} w_i \int ambi(h_i \mid \boldsymbol{x}) p(\boldsymbol{x}) d\boldsymbol{x} \qquad (5.7)$$

$$= \sum_{i=1}^{T} w_i \int err(h_i \mid \boldsymbol{x}) p(\boldsymbol{x}) d\boldsymbol{x} - \int err(H \mid \boldsymbol{x}) p(\boldsymbol{x}) d\boldsymbol{x} \,,$$

where $p(\boldsymbol{x})$ is the input distribution from which the instances are sampled. The generalization error and the ambiguity of the individual learner h_i can be written respectively as

$$err(h_i) = \int err(h_i \mid \boldsymbol{x}) p(\boldsymbol{x}) d\boldsymbol{x} \,, \qquad (5.8)$$

$$ambi(h_i) = \int ambi(h_i \mid \boldsymbol{x}) p(\boldsymbol{x}) d\boldsymbol{x} \,. \qquad (5.9)$$

Similarly, the generalization error of the ensemble can be written as

$$err(H) = \int err(H \mid \boldsymbol{x}) p(\boldsymbol{x}) d\boldsymbol{x} \,. \qquad (5.10)$$

Based on the above notations and (5.6), we can get the error-ambiguity decomposition [Krogh and Vedelsby, 1995]

$$err(H) = \overline{err}(h) - \overline{ambi}(h), \qquad (5.11)$$

where $\overline{err}(h) = \sum_{i=1}^{T} w_i \cdot err(h_i)$ is the weighted average of individual generalization errors, and $\overline{ambi}(h) = \sum_{i=1}^{T} w_i \cdot ambi(h_i)$ is the weighted average of ambiguities that is also referred to as the ensemble ambiguity.

On the right-hand side of (5.11), the first item $\overline{err}(h)$ is the average error of the individual learners, depending on the generalization ability of individual learners; the second item $\overline{ambi}(h)$ is the ambiguity, which measures the variability among the predictions of individual learners, depending on the ensemble diversity. Since the second term is always positive, and it is subtracted from the first term, it is clear that the error of the ensemble will never be larger than the average error of the individual learners. More importantly, (5.11) shows that the more accurate and the more diverse the individual learners, the better the ensemble.

Notice that (5.11) was derived for the regression setting. It is difficult to get similar results for classification. Furthermore, it is difficult to estimate $\overline{ambi}$ empirically. Usually, the estimate of $\overline{ambi}$ is obtained by subtracting the estimated value of $\overline{err}$ from the estimated value of err, and thus this estimated value just shows the difference between the ensemble error and individual error, not really showing the physical meaning of diversity; moreover, such an estimate often violates the constraint that $\overline{ambi}$ should be positive. Thus, (5.11) does not provide a unified formal formulation of ensemble diversity, though it does offer some important insights.

5.2.2 Bias-Variance-Covariance Decomposition

The **bias-variance-covariance decomposition** [Geman et al., 1992], or popularly called as **bias-variance decomposition**, is an important general tool for analyzing the performance of learning algorithms. Given a learning target and the size of training set, it divides the generalization error of a learner into three components, i.e., **intrinsic noise**, **bias** and **variance**. The intrinsic noise is a lower bound on the expected error of any learning algorithm on the target; the bias measures how closely the average estimate of the learning algorithm is able to approximate the target; the variance measures how much the estimate of the learning approach fluctuates for different training sets of the same size.

Since the intrinsic noise is difficult to estimate, it is often subsumed into the bias term. Thus, the generalization error is broken into the bias term which describes the error of the learner in expectation, and the variance term which reflects the sensitivity of the learner to variations in the training samples.

Let f denote the target and h denote the learner. For squared loss, the decomposition is

$$err(h) = \mathbb{E}\left[(h - f)^2\right]$$
$$= (\mathbb{E}[h] - f)^2 + \mathbb{E}\left[(h - \mathbb{E}[h])^2\right]$$
$$= bias(h)^2 + variance(h), \tag{5.12}$$

where the bias and variance of the learner h is respectively

$$bias(h) = \mathbb{E}[h] - f, \tag{5.13}$$
$$variance(h) = \mathbb{E}\left(h - \mathbb{E}[h]\right)^2. \tag{5.14}$$

The key of estimating the bias and variance terms empirically lies in how to simulate the variation of training samples with the same size. Kohavi and Wolpert [1996]'s method, for example, works in a two-fold cross validation style, where the original data set is split into a training set D_1 and a test set D_2. Then, T training sets are sampled from D_1; the size of these training sets is roughly half of that of D_1 for ensuring that there are not many duplicate training sets in these T training sets even for small D. After that, the learning algorithm is trained on each of those training sets and tested on D_2, from which the bias and variance are estimated. The whole process can be repeated several times to improve the estimates.

For an ensemble of T learners $h_1, \ldots, h_T$, the decomposition of (5.12) can be further expanded, yielding the *bias-variance-covariance decomposition* [Ueda and Nakano, 1996]. Without loss of generality, suppose that the individual learners are combined with equal weights. The averaged bias, averaged variance, and averaged **covariance** of the individual learners are defined respectively as

$$\overline{bias}(H) = \frac{1}{T}\sum_{i=1}^{T}\left(\mathbb{E}[h_i] - f\right), \tag{5.15}$$

$$\overline{variance}(H) = \frac{1}{T}\sum_{i=1}^{T}\mathbb{E}\left(h_i - \mathbb{E}[h_i]\right)^2, \tag{5.16}$$

$$\overline{covariance}(H) = \frac{1}{T(T-1)}\sum_{i=1}^{T}\sum_{\substack{j=1 \\ j\neq i}}^{T}\mathbb{E}\left(h_i - \mathbb{E}[h_i]\right)\mathbb{E}\left(h_j - \mathbb{E}[h_j]\right). \tag{5.17}$$

Then, the bias-variance-covariance decomposition of squared error of ensemble is

$$err(H) = \overline{bias}(H)^2 + \frac{1}{T}\overline{variance}(H) + \left(1 - \frac{1}{T}\right)\overline{covariance}(H). \tag{5.18}$$

(5.18) shows that the squared error of the ensemble depends heavily on the covariance term, which models the correlation between the individual learners. The smaller the covariance, the better the ensemble. It is obvious that if all the learners make similar errors, the covariance will be large, and therefore it is preferred that the individual learners make different errors. Thus, through the covariance term, (5.18) shows that the diversity is important for ensemble performance. Notice that the bias and variance terms are constrained to be positive, while the covariance term can be negative. Also, (5.18) was derived under regression setting, and it is difficult to obtain similar results for classification. So, (5.18) does not provide a formal formulation of ensemble diversity either.

Brown et al. [2005a,b] disclosed the connection between the error-ambiguity decomposition and the bias-variance-covariance decomposition. For simplicity, assume that the individual learners are combined with equal weights. Considering that the left-hand side of (5.11) is the same as the left-hand side of (5.18), by putting the right-hand sides of (5.11) and (5.18) together, it follows that

$$\overline{err}(H) - \overline{ambi}(H) = \mathbb{E}\left[\frac{1}{T}\sum_{i=1}^{T}(h_i - f)^2 - \frac{1}{T}\sum_{i=1}^{T}(h_i - H)^2\right] \tag{5.19}$$

$$= \overline{bias}(H)^2 + \frac{1}{T}\overline{variance}(H) + \left(1 - \frac{1}{T}\right)\overline{covariance}(H) .$$

After some derivations [Brown et al., 2005b,a], we get

$$\overline{err}(H) = \mathbb{E}\left[\frac{1}{T}\sum_{i=1}^{T}(h_i - f)^2\right] = \overline{bias}^2(H) + \overline{variance}(H) , \tag{5.20}$$

$$\overline{ambi}(H) = \mathbb{E}\left[\frac{1}{T}\sum_{i=1}^{T}(h_i - H)^2\right] \tag{5.21}$$

$$= \overline{variance}(H) - variance(H)$$

$$= \overline{variance}(H) - \frac{1}{T}\overline{variance}(H) - \left(1 - \frac{1}{T}\right)\overline{covariance}(H) .$$

Thus, we can see that the term $\overline{variance}$ appears in both the averaged squared error term and the average ambiguity term, and it cancels out if we subtract the ambiguity from the error term. Moreover, the fact that the term $\overline{variance}$ appears in both $\overline{err}$ and $\overline{ambi}$ terms indicates that it is hard to maximize the ambiguity term without affecting the bias term, implying that generating diverse learners is a challenging problem.

5.3 Diversity Measures

5.3.1 Pairwise Measures

To measure ensemble diversity, a classical approach is to measure the pairwise similarity/dissimilarity between two learners, and then average all the pairwise measurements for the overall diversity.

Given a data set $D = \{(x_1, y_1), \ldots, (x_m, y_m)\}$, for binary classification (i.e., $y_i \in \{-1, +1\}$), we have the following **contingency table** for two classifiers h_i and h_j, where $a + b + c + d = m$ are non-negative variables showing the numbers of examples satisfying the conditions specified by the corresponding rows and columns. We will introduce some representative pairwise measures based on these variables.

	$h_i = +1$	$h_i = -1$
$h_j = +1$	a	c
$h_j = -1$	b	d

Disagreement Measure [Skalak, 1996, Ho, 1998] between h_i and h_j is defined as the proportion of examples on which two classifiers make different predictions, i.e.,

$$dis_{ij} = \frac{b+c}{m}. \tag{5.22}$$

The value dis_{ij} is in $[0, 1]$; the larger the value, the larger the diversity.

Q**-Statistic** [Yule, 1900] of h_i and h_j is defined as

$$Q_{ij} = \frac{ad - bc}{ad + bc}. \tag{5.23}$$

It can be seen that Q_{ij} takes value in the range of $[-1, 1]$. Q_{ij} is zero if h_i and h_j are independent; Q_{ij} is positive if h_i and h_j make similar predictions; Q_{ij} is negative if h_i and h_j make different predictions.

Correlation Coefficient [Sneath and Sokal, 1973] of h_i and h_j is defined as

$$\rho_{ij} = \frac{ad - bc}{\sqrt{(a+b)(a+c)(c+d)(b+d)}}. \tag{5.24}$$

This is a classic statistic for measuring the correlation between two binary vectors. It is easy to see that ρ_{ij} and Q_{ij} have the same sign, and $|\rho_{ij}| \geq |Q_{ij}|$.

Kappa-Statistic [Cohen, 1960] is also a classical measure in statistical literature, and it was first used to measure the diversity between two classifiers by [Margineantu and Dietterich, 1997, Dietterich, 2000b]. It is defined as [1]

$$\kappa_p = \frac{\Theta_1 - \Theta_2}{1 - \Theta_2},$$ (5.25)

where Θ_1 and Θ_2 are the probabilities that the two classifiers agree and *agree by chance*, respectively. The probabilities for h_i and h_j can be estimated on the data set D according to

$$\Theta_1 = \frac{a + d}{m},$$ (5.26)

$$\Theta_2 = \frac{(a + b)(a + c) + (c + d)(b + d)}{m^2}.$$ (5.27)

$\kappa_p = 1$ if the two classifiers totally agree on D; $\kappa_p = 0$ if the two classifiers agree by chance; $\kappa_p < 0$ is a rare case where the agreement is even less than what is expected by chance.

The above measures do not require to know the classification correctness. In cases where the correctness of classification is known, the following measure can be used:

Double-Fault Measure [Giacinto and Roli, 2001] is defined as the proportion of examples that have been misclassified by both the classifiers h_i and h_j, i.e.,

$$df_{ij} = \frac{e}{m},$$ (5.28)

where $e = \sum_{k=1}^{m} \mathbb{I}(h_i(\boldsymbol{x}_k) \neq y_k \wedge h_j(\boldsymbol{x}_k) \neq y_k)$.

5.3.2   Non-Pairwise Measures

Non-pairwise measures try to assess the ensemble diversity directly, rather than by averaging pairwise measurements. Given a set of individual classifiers $\{h_1, \ldots, h_T\}$ and a data set $D = \{(\boldsymbol{x}_1, y_1), \ldots, (\boldsymbol{x}_m, y_m)\}$ where $\boldsymbol{x}_i$ is an instance and $y_i \in \{-1, +1\}$ is class label, in the following we will introduce some representative non-pairwise measures.

Kohavi-Wolpert Variance was proposed by Kohavi and Wolpert [1996], and originated from the bias-variance decomposition of the error of a classifier. On an instance $\boldsymbol{x}$, the variability of the predicted class label y is defined as

$$var_{\boldsymbol{x}} = \frac{1}{2}\left(1 - \sum_{y \in \{-1,+1\}} P(y \mid \boldsymbol{x})^2\right).$$ (5.29)

---

[1]The notation κ_p is used for pairwise kappa-statistic, and the interrater agreement measure κ (also called non-pairwise kappa-statistic) will be introduced later.

Kuncheva and Whitaker [2003] modified the variability to measure diversity by considering two classifier outputs: *correct* (denoted by $\tilde{y} = +1$) and *incorrect* (denoted by $\tilde{y} = -1$), and estimated $P(\tilde{y} = +1 \mid \boldsymbol{x})$ and $P(\tilde{y} = -1 \mid \boldsymbol{x})$ over individual classifiers, that is,

$$\hat{P}(\tilde{y} = 1 \mid \boldsymbol{x}) = \frac{\rho(\boldsymbol{x})}{T} \quad \text{and} \quad \hat{P}(\tilde{y} = -1 \mid \boldsymbol{x}) = 1 - \frac{\rho(\boldsymbol{x})}{T}, \tag{5.30}$$

where $\rho(\boldsymbol{x})$ is the number of individual classifiers that classify $\boldsymbol{x}$ correctly. By substituting (5.30) into (5.29) and averaging over the data set D, the following kw measure is obtained:

$$kw = \frac{1}{mT^2} \sum_{k=1}^{m} \rho(\boldsymbol{x}_k)(T - \rho(\boldsymbol{x}_k)) . \tag{5.31}$$

It is easy to see that the larger the kw measurement, the larger the diversity.

Interrater agreement is a measure of interrater (inter-classifier) reliability [Fleiss, 1981]. Kuncheva and Whitaker [2003] used it to measure the level of agreement within a set of classifiers. This measure is defined as

$$\kappa = 1 - \frac{\frac{1}{T} \sum_{k=1}^{m} \rho(\boldsymbol{x}_k)(T - \rho(\boldsymbol{x}_k))}{m(T-1)\bar{p}(1-\bar{p})}, \tag{5.32}$$

where $\rho(\boldsymbol{x}_k)$ is the number of classifiers that classify $\boldsymbol{x}_k$ correctly, and

$$\bar{p} = \frac{1}{mT} \sum_{i=1}^{T} \sum_{k=1}^{m} \mathbb{I}(h_i(\boldsymbol{x}_k) = y_k) \tag{5.33}$$

is the average accuracy of individual classifiers. Similarly with κ_p, $\kappa = 1$ if the classifiers totally agree on D, and $\kappa \leq 0$ if the agreement is even less than what is expected by chance.

Entropy is motivated by the fact that for an instance $\boldsymbol{x}_k$, the disagreement will be maximized if a tie occurs in the votes of individual classifiers. Cunningham and Carney [2000] directly calculated the Shannon's entropy on every instance and averaged them over D for measuring diversity, that is,

$$Ent_{cc} = \frac{1}{m} \sum_{k=1}^{m} \sum_{y \in \{-1,+1\}} -P(y|\boldsymbol{x}_k) \log P(y|\boldsymbol{x}_k) , \tag{5.34}$$

where $P(y|\boldsymbol{x}_k) = \frac{1}{T} \sum_{i=1}^{T} \mathbb{I}(h_i(\boldsymbol{x}_k) = y)$ can be estimated by the proportion of individual classifiers that predict y as the label of $\boldsymbol{x}_k$. It is evident that the calculation of Ent_{cc} does not require to know the correctness of individual classifiers.

Shipp and Kuncheva [2002] assumed to know the correctness of the classifiers, and defined their entropy measure as

$$Ent_{sk} = \frac{1}{m} \sum_{k=1}^{m} \frac{\min(\rho(\boldsymbol{x}_k), T - \rho(\boldsymbol{x}_k))}{T - \lceil T/2 \rceil}, \tag{5.35}$$

where $\rho(\boldsymbol{x})$ is the number of individual classifiers that classify $\boldsymbol{x}$ correctly. The Ent_{sk} value is in the range of $[0, 1]$, where 0 indicates no diversity and 1 indicates the largest diversity. Notice that (5.35) is not a classical entropy, since it does not use the logarithm function. Though it can be transformed into classical form by using a nonlinear transformation, (5.35) is preferred in practice since it is easier to handle and faster to calculate [Shipp and Kuncheva, 2002].

Difficulty was originally proposed by Hansen and Salamon [1990] and explicitly formulated by Kuncheva and Whitaker [2003]. Let a random variable X taking values in $\{0, \frac{1}{T}, \frac{2}{T}, \dots, 1\}$ denote the proportion of classifiers that correctly classify a randomly drawn instance $\boldsymbol{x}$. The probability mass function of X can be estimated by running the T classifiers on the data set D. Considering the distribution shape, if the same instance is *difficult* for all classifiers, and the other instances are *easy* for all classifiers, the distribution shape is with two separated peaks; if the instances that are difficult for some classifiers are easy for other classifiers, the distribution shape is with one off-centered peak; if all instances are equally difficult for all classifiers, the distribution shape is without clear peak. So, by using the variance of X to capture the distribution shape, the difficulty measure is defined as

$$\theta = variance(X). \tag{5.36}$$

It is obvious that the smaller the θ value, the larger the diversity.

Generalized Diversity [Partridge and Krzanowski, 1997] was motivated by the argument that the diversity is maximized when the failure of one classifier is accompanied by the correct prediction of the other. The measure is defined as

$$gd = 1 - \frac{p(2)}{p(1)}, \tag{5.37}$$

where

$$p(1) = \sum_{i=1}^{T} \frac{i}{T} p_i, \tag{5.38}$$

$$p(2) = \sum_{i=1}^{T} \frac{i}{T} \frac{i-1}{T-1} p_i, \tag{5.39}$$

and p_i denotes the probability of i randomly chosen classifiers failing on a randomly drawn instance $\boldsymbol{x}$. The gd value is in the range of $[0, 1]$, and the diversity is minimized when $gd = 0$.

Table 5.1: Summary of ensemble diversity measures, where ↑ (↓) indicates that the larger (smaller) the measurement, the larger the diversity ("Known" indicates whether it requires to know the correctness of individual classifiers).

Diversity Measure	Symbol	↑/↓	Pairwise	Known	Symmetric
Disagreement	dis	↑	Yes	No	Yes
Q-statistic	Q	↓	Yes	No	Yes
Correlation coefficient	ρ	↓	Yes	No	Yes
Kappa-statistic	κ_p	↓	Yes	No	Yes
Double-fault	df	↓	Yes	Yes	No
Interrater agreement	κ	↓	No	Yes	Yes
Kohavi-Wolpert variance	kw	↑	No	Yes	Yes
Entropy (C&C's)	Ent_{cc}	↑	No	No	Yes
Entropy (S&K's)	Ent_{sk}	↑	No	Yes	Yes
Difficulty	θ	↓	No	Yes	No
Generalized diversity	gd	↑	No	Yes	No
Coincident failure	cfd	↑	No	Yes	No

Coincident Failure [Partridge and Krzanowski, 1997] is a modified version of the generalized diversity, defined as

$$cfd = \begin{cases} 0, & p_0 = 1 \\ \frac{1}{1-p_0} \sum_{i=1}^{T} \frac{T-i}{T-1} p_i, & p_0 < 1 . \end{cases} \qquad (5.40)$$

$cfd = 0$ if all classifiers give the same predictions simultaneously, and $cfd = 1$ if each classifier makes mistakes on unique instances.

5.3.3 Summary and Visualization

Table 5.1 provides a summary of the 12 diversity measures introduced above. The table shows whether a measure is pairwise or non-pairwise, whether it requires to know the correctness of classifiers, and whether it is symmetric or non-symmetric. A **symmetric measure** will keep the same when the values of 0 (incorrect) and 1 (correct) in binary classification are swapped [Ruta and Gabrys, 2001].

Kuncheva and Whitaker [2003] showed that the Kohavi-Wolpert variance (kw), the averaged disagreement (dis_{avg}) and the kappa-statistic (κ) are closely related as

$$kw = \frac{T-1}{2T} dis_{avg}, \qquad (5.41)$$

$$\kappa = 1 - \frac{T}{(T-1)\bar{p}(1-\bar{p})} kw, \qquad (5.42)$$

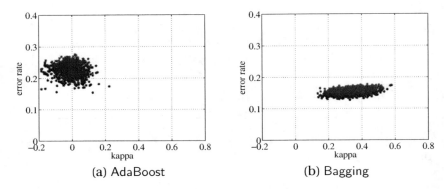

(a) AdaBoost   (b) Bagging

FIGURE 5.1: Examples of kappa-error diagrams on *credit-g* data set, where each ensemble comprises 50 C4.5 decision trees.

where $\bar{p}$ is in (5.33). Moreover, Kuncheva and Whitaker [2003]'s empirical study also disclosed that these diversity measures exhibited reasonably strong relationships.

One advantage of pairwise measures is that they can be visualized in 2d plots. This was first shown by Margineantu and Dietterich [1997]'s **kappa-error diagram**, which is a scatter-plot where each point corresponds to a pair of classifiers, with the x-axis denoting the value of κ_p for the two classifiers, and the y-axis denoting the average error rate of these two classifiers. Figure 5.1 shows examples of the kappa-error diagram. It can be seen that the kappa-error diagram visualizes the accuracy-diversity tradeoff of different ensemble methods. The higher the point clouds, the less accurate the individual classifiers; the more right-hand the point clouds, the less diverse the individual classifiers. It is evident that other pairwise diversity measures can be visualized in a similar way.

5.3.4 Limitation of Diversity Measures

Kuncheva and Whitaker [2003] presented possibly the first doubt on diversity measures. Through a broad range of experiments, they showed that the effectiveness of existing diversity measures are discouraging since there seems to be no clear relation between those diversity measurements and the ensemble performance.

Tang et al. [2006] theoretically analyzed six diversity measures and showed that if the average accuracy of individual learners is fixed and the maximum diversity is achievable, maximizing the diversity among the individual learners is equivalent to maximizing the minimum margin of the ensemble on the training examples. They showed empirically, however, that the maximum diversity is usually not achievable, and the minimum margin of an ensemble is not monotonically increasing with respect to existing diversity measures.

In particular, Tang et al. [2006] showed that, compared to algorithms that seek diversity implicitly, exploiting the above diversity measures explicitly is ineffective in constructing consistently stronger ensembles. On one hand, the change of existing diversity measurements does not provide consistent guidance on whether an ensemble achieves good generalization performance. On the other hand, the measurements are closely related to the average individual accuracies, which is undesirable since it is not expected that the diversity measure becomes another estimate of accuracy.

Notice that it is still well accepted that the motivation of generating diverse individual learners is right. Kuncheva and Whitaker [2003] and Tang et al. [2006] disclosed that though many diversity measures have been developed, the *right* formulation and measures for diversity are unsolved yet, and understanding ensemble diversity remains a holy grail problem.

5.4 Information Theoretic Diversity

Information theoretic diversity [Brown, 2009, Zhou and Li, 2010b] provides a promising recent direction for understanding ensemble diversity. This section will introduce the connection between information theory and ensemble methods first and then introduce two formulations of information theoretic diversity and an estimation method.

5.4.1 Information Theory and Ensemble

The fundamental concept of information theory is the **entropy**, which is a measure of uncertainty. The entropy of a random variable X is defined as

$$Ent(X) = \sum_x -p(x) \log(p(x)), \tag{5.43}$$

where x is the value of X and $p(x)$ is the probability distribution. Based on the concept of entropy, the dependence between two variables X_1 and X_2 can be measured by the **mutual information** [Cover and Thomas, 1991]

$$I(X_1; X_2) = \sum_{x_1, x_2} p(x_1, x_2) \log \frac{p(x_1, x_2)}{p(x_1)p(x_2)}, \tag{5.44}$$

or if given another variable Y, measured by the **conditional mutual information** [Cover and Thomas, 1991]

$$I(X_1; X_2 \mid Y) = \sum_{y, x_1, x_2} p(y)p(x_1, x_2 \mid y) \log \frac{p(x_1, x_2 \mid y)}{p(x_1 \mid y)p(x_2 \mid y)}. \tag{5.45}$$

In the context of information theory, suppose a message Y is sent through a communication channel and the value X is received, the goal is to recover the correct Y by decoding the received value X; that is, a decoding operation $\hat{Y} = g(X)$ is needed. In machine learning, Y is the ground-truth class label, X is the input, and g is the predictor. For ensemble methods, the goal is to recover Y from a set of T classifiers $\{X_1, \ldots, X_T\}$ by a combination function g, and the objective is to minimize the probability of error prediction $p(g(X_{1:T}) \neq Y)$, where $X_{1:T}$ denotes T variables $X_1, \ldots, X_T$. Based on information theory, Brown [2009] bounded the probability of error by two inequalities [Fano, 1961, Hellman and Raviv, 1970] as

$$\frac{Ent(Y) - I(X_{1:T}; Y) - 1}{\log(|Y|)} \leq p(g(X_{1:T}) \neq Y) \leq \frac{Ent(Y) - I(X_{1:T}; Y)}{2}.$$
(5.46)

Thus, to minimize the prediction error, the mutual information $I(X_{1:T}; Y)$ should be maximized. By considering different expansions of the mutual information term, different formulations of information theoretic diversity can be obtained, as will be introduced in the next sections.

5.4.2   Interaction Information Diversity

Interaction information [McGill, 1954] is a multivariate generalization of mutual information for measuring the dependence among multiple variables. The interaction information $I(X_{1:n})$ and the **conditional interaction information** $I(\{X_{1:n}\} \mid Y)$ are respectively defined as

$$I(\{X_{1:n}\}) = \begin{cases} I(X_1; X_2) & \text{for } n = 2 \\ I(\{X_{1:n-1}\} \mid X_n) - I(\{X_{1:n-1}\}) & \text{for } n \geq 3, \end{cases} \quad (5.47)$$

$$I(\{X_{1:n}\} \mid Y) = \mathbb{E}_Y[I(\{X_{1:n}\}) \mid Y]. \quad (5.48)$$

Based on interaction information, Brown [2009] presented an expansion of $I(X_{1:T}; Y)$ as

$$I(X_{1:T}; Y) = \underbrace{\sum_{i=1}^{T} I(X_i; Y)}_{\text{relevancy}} + \underbrace{\sum_{k=2}^{T} \sum_{S_k \subseteq S} I(\{S_k \cup Y\})}_{\text{interaction information diversity}} \quad (5.49)$$

$$= \underbrace{\sum_{i=1}^{T} I(X_i; Y)}_{\text{relevancy}} - \underbrace{\sum_{k=2}^{T} \sum_{S_k \subseteq S} I(\{S_k\})}_{\text{redundancy}} + \underbrace{\sum_{k=2}^{T} \sum_{S_k \subseteq S} I(\{S_k\} | Y)}_{\text{conditional redundancy}} \ ,$$
(5.50)

where S_k is a set of size k. (5.50) shows that the mutual information $I(X_{1:T}; Y)$ can be expanded into three terms.

The first term, $\sum_{i=1}^{T} I(X_i; Y)$, is the sum of the mutual information between each classifier and the target. It is referred to as *relevancy*, which actually gives a bound on the accuracy of the individual classifiers. Since it is additive to the mutual information, a large relevancy is preferred.

The second term, $\sum_{k=2}^{T} \sum_{S_k \subseteq S} I(\{S_k\})$, measures the dependency among all possible subsets of classifiers, and it is independent of the class label Y. This term is referred to as *redundancy*. Notice that it is subtractive to the mutual information. A large $I(\{S_k\})$ indicates strong correlations among classifiers without considering the target Y, which reduces the value of $I(X_{1:T}; Y)$, and hence a small value is preferred.

The third term, $\sum_{k=2}^{T} \sum_{S_k \subseteq S} I(\{S_k\}|Y)$, measures the dependency among the classifiers given the class label. It is referred to as *conditional redundancy*. Notice that it is additive to the mutual information, and a large conditional redundancy is preferred.

It is evident that the relevancy term corresponds to the accuracy, while both the redundancy and the conditional redundancy describe the correlations among classifiers. Thus, the interaction information diversity naturally emerges as (5.49). The interaction information diversity discloses that the correlations among classifiers are not necessarily helpful to ensemble performance, since there are different kinds of correlations and the helpful ones are those which have considered the learning target. It is easy to find that the diversity exists at multiple orders of correlations, not simply pairwise.

One limitation of the interaction information diversity lies in that the expression of the diversity terms, especially the involved interaction information, are quite complicated and there is no effective process for estimating them at multiple orders in practice.

5.4.3 Multi-Information Diversity

Multi-information [Watanabe, 1960, Studeny and Vejnarova, 1998, Slonim et al., 2006] is another multivariate generalization of mutual information. The multi-information $\mathcal{I}(X_{1:n})$ and **conditional multi-information** $\mathcal{I}(X_{1:n} \mid Y)$ are respectively defined as

$$\mathcal{I}(X_{1:n}) = \sum_{x_{1:n}} p(x_1, \cdots, x_n) \log \frac{p(x_1, \cdots, x_n)}{p(x_1)p(x_2) \cdots p(x_n)}, \qquad (5.51)$$

$$\mathcal{I}(X_{1:n} \mid Y) = \sum_{y, x_{1:n}} p(y)p(x_{1:n} \mid y) \log \frac{p(x_{1:n} \mid y)}{p(x_1 \mid y) \cdots p(x_n \mid y)}. \qquad (5.52)$$

It is easy to see that, when $n = 2$ the (conditional) multi-information is reduced to (conditional) mutual information. Moreover,

$$\mathcal{I}(X_{1:n}) = \sum_{i=2}^{n} I(X_i; X_{1:i-1}); \tag{5.53}$$

$$\mathcal{I}(X_{1:n} \mid Y) = \sum_{i=2}^{n} I(X_i; X_{1:i-1} \mid Y). \tag{5.54}$$

Based on multi-information and conditional multi-information, Zhou and Li [2010b] presented an expansion of $I(X_{1:T}; Y)$ as

$$I(X_{1:T}; Y) = \underbrace{\sum_{i=1}^{T} I(X_i; Y)}_{\text{relevance}} + \underbrace{\mathcal{I}(X_{1:T} \mid Y) - \mathcal{I}(X_{1:T})}_{\text{multi-information diversity}} \tag{5.55}$$

$$= \underbrace{\sum_{i=1}^{T} I(X_i; Y)}_{\text{relevance}} - \underbrace{\sum_{i=2}^{T} I(X_i; X_{1:i-1})}_{\text{redundancy}} + \underbrace{\sum_{i=2}^{T} I(X_i; X_{1:i-1} \mid Y)}_{\text{conditional redundancy}}. \tag{5.56}$$

Zhou and Li [2010b] proved that (5.49) and (5.55) are mathematically equivalent, though the formulation of (5.55) is much simpler. One advantage of (5.55) is that its terms are *decomposable* over individual classifiers. Take the redundancy term for example. Given an ensemble of size k, its redundancy is $\mathcal{I}(X_{1:k}) = \sum_{i=2}^{k} I(X_i; X_{1:i-1})$. Then, if a new classifier X_{k+1} is added, the new redundancy becomes $\mathcal{I}(X_{1:k+1}) = \sum_{i=2}^{k+1} I(X_i; X_{1:i-1})$, and the only difference is the mutual information $I(X_{k+1}; X_{1:k})$.

5.4.4 Estimation Method

For the interaction information diversity (5.49), it is obvious that this diversity consists of low-order and high-order components. If we only consider the pairwise components, the following can be obtained:

$$I(X_{1:T}; Y) \approx \sum_{i=1}^{T} I(X_i; Y) - \sum_{i=1}^{T} \sum_{j=i+1}^{T} I(X_i; X_j) + \sum_{i=1}^{T} \sum_{j=i+1}^{T} I(X_i; X_j \mid Y). \tag{5.57}$$

This estimation would not be accurate since it omits higher-order components. If we want to consider higher-order components, however, we need to estimate higher-order interaction information, which is quite difficult and currently there is no effective approach available.

For the multi-information diversity (5.55), Zhou and Li [2010b] presented an approximate estimation approach. Take the redundancy term in (5.55)

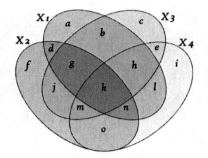

$$I(X_4; X_3, X_2, X_1) = e + h + k + l + m + n + o,$$
$$I(X_4; X_2, X_1) = h + k + l + m + n + o,$$
$$I(X_4; X_3, X_1) = e + h + k + l + m + n,$$
$$I(X_4; X_3, X_2) = e + h + k + m + n + o.$$

FIGURE 5.2: Venn diagram of an illustrative example of Zhou and Li [2010b]'s approximation method.

for example. It is needed to estimate $I(X_i; X_{1:i-1})$ for all i's. Rather than calculating it directly, $I(X_i; X_{1:i-1})$ is approximated by

$$I(X_i; X_{1:i-1}) \approx \max_{\Omega_k \subseteq \Omega} I(X_i; \Omega_k), \tag{5.58}$$

where $\Omega = \{X_{i-1}, \ldots, X_1\}$, and Ω_k is a subset of size k ($1 \leq k \leq i - 1$). As an illustrative example, Figure 5.2 depicts a Venn diagram for four variables, where the ellipses represent the entropies of variables, while the mutual information can be represented by the combination of regions in the diagram. As shown in the right-side of the figure, it can be found that the high-order component $I(X_4; X_3, X_2, X_1)$ shares a large intersection with the low-order component $I(X_4; X_2, X_1)$, where the only difference is region e. Notice that if X_1, X_2 and X_3 are strongly correlated, it is very likely that the uncertainty of X_3 is covered by X_1 and X_2; that is, the regions c and e are very small. Thus, $I(X_4; X_2, X_1)$ provides an approximation to $I(X_4; X_3, X_2, X_1)$. Such a scenario often happens in ensemble construction, since the individual classifiers generally have strong correlations.

Similarly, the conditional redundancy term can be approximated as

$$I(X_i; X_{1:i-1} \mid Y) \approx \max_{\Omega_k \subseteq \Omega} I(X_i; \Omega_k \mid Y). \tag{5.59}$$

Thus, the multi-information diversity can be estimated by

$$I(X_i; X_{1:i-1} \mid Y) - I(X_i; X_{1:i-1}) \approx \max_{\Omega_k \subseteq \Omega} \left[I(X_i; \Omega_k \mid Y) - I(X_i; \Omega_k) \right]. \tag{5.60}$$

It can be proved that this estimation provides a lower-bound of the information theoretic diversity.

To accomplish the estimation, an enumeration over all the Ω_k's is desired. In this way, however, for every i it is needed to estimate $I(X_i; \Omega_k)$ and $I(X_i; \Omega_k \mid Y)$ for C_{i-1}^k number of different Ω_k's. When k is near $(i - 1)/2$, the number will be large, and the estimation of $I(X_i; \Omega_k)$ and $I(X_i; \Omega_k \mid Y)$ will become difficult. Hence, a trade-off is needed, and Zhou and Li [2010b] showed that a good estimation can be achieved even when k is restricted to be small values such as 1 or 2.

5.5 Diversity Generation

Though there is no generally accepted formal formulation and measures for ensemble diversity, there are effective heuristic mechanisms for diversity generation in ensemble construction. The common basic idea is to inject some randomness into the learning process. Popular mechanisms include manipulating the data samples, input features, learning parameters, and output representations.

Data Sample Manipulation. This is the most popular mechanism. Given a data set, multiple different data samples can be generated, and then the individual learners are trained from different data samples. Generally, the data sample manipulation is based on *sampling* approaches, e.g., Bagging adopts *bootstrap sampling* [Efron and Tibshirani, 1993], AdaBoost adopts *sequential sampling*, etc.

Input Feature Manipulation. The training data is usually described by a set of features. Different subsets of features, or called **subspaces**, provide different views on the data. Therefore, individual learners trained from different subspaces are usually diverse. The Random Subspace method [Ho, 1998] shown in Figure 5.3 is a famous ensemble method which employs this mechanism. For data with a lot of redundant features, training a learner in a subspace will be not only effective but also efficient. It is noteworthy that Random Subspace is not suitable for data with only a few features. Moreover, if there are lots of irrelevant features, it is usually better to filter out most irrelevant features before generating the subspaces.

Learning Parameter Manipulation. This mechanism tries to generate diverse individual learners by using different parameter settings for the base learning algorithm. For example, different initial weights can be assigned to individual neural networks [Kolen and Pollack, 1991], different split selections can be applied to individual decision trees [Kwok and Carter, 1988, Liu et al., 2008a], different candidate rule conditions can be applied to individual FOIL rule inducers [Ali and Pazzani, 1996], etc. The Negative Correlation method [Liu and Yao, 1999] explicitly constrains the parameters of individual neural networks to be different by a *regularization* term.

Input: Data set $D = \{(\boldsymbol{x}_1, y_1), (\boldsymbol{x}_2, y_2), \cdots, (\boldsymbol{x}_m, y_m)\}$;
Base learning algorithm $\mathfrak{L}$;
Number of base learners T;
Dimension of subspaces d.

Process:
1. **for** $t = 1, \ldots, T$:
2. $\mathcal{F}_t = \text{RS}(D, d)$ % $\mathcal{F}_t$ is a set of d randomly selected features;
3. $D_t = \text{Map}_{\mathcal{F}_t}(D)$ % D_t keeps only the features in $\mathcal{F}_t$
4. $h_t = \mathfrak{L}(D_t)$ % Train a learner
5. **end**

Output: $H(\boldsymbol{x}) = \arg\max\limits_{y \in \mathcal{Y}} \sum_{t=1}^{T} \mathbb{I}\left(h_t\left(\text{Map}_{\mathcal{F}_t}(\boldsymbol{x})\right) = y\right)$

FIGURE 5.3: The Random Subspace algorithm

Output Representation Manipulation. This mechanism tries to generate diverse individual learners by using different output representations. For example, the ECOC approach [Dietterich and Bakiri, 1995] employs error-correcting output codes, the Flipping Output method [Breiman, 2000] randomly changes the labels of some training instances, the Output Smearing method [Breiman, 2000] converts multi-class outputs to multivariate regression outputs to construct individual learners, etc.

In addition to the above popular mechanisms, there are some other attempts. For example, Melville and Mooney [2005] tried to encourage diversity by using artificial training data. They constructed an ensemble in an iterative way. In each round, a number of artificial instances were generated based on the model of the data distribution. These artificial instances were then assigned the labels that are different maximally from the predictions of the current ensemble. After that, a new learner is trained from the original training data together with the artificial training data. If adding the new learner to the current ensemble increases training error, the new learner will be discarded and another learner will be generated with another set of artificial examples; otherwise, the new learner will be accepted into the current ensemble.

Notice that different mechanisms for diversity generation can be used together. For example, Random Forest [Breiman, 2001] adopts both the mechanisms of data sample manipulation and input feature manipulation.

5.6   Further Readings

In addition to [Kohavi and Wolpert, 1996], there are a number of practically effective bias-variance decomposition approaches, e.g., [Kong and Dietterich, 1995, Breiman, 1996a]. Most approaches focus solely on 0-1 loss and produce quite different definitions. James [2003] proposed a framework which accommodates the essential characteristics of bias and variance, and their decomposition can be generalized to any symmetric loss function.

A comprehensive survey on diversity generation approaches can be found in [Brown et al., 2005a]. Current ensemble methods generally try to generate diverse individual learners from *labeled* training data. Zhou [2009] advocated to try to exploit *unlabeled* training data to enhance diversity, and an effective method was proposed recently by Zhang and Zhou [2010].

Stable learners, e.g., naïve Bayesian and k-nearest neighbor classifiers, which are insensitive to small perturbations on training data, are usually difficult to improve through typical ensemble methods. Zhou and Yu [2005] proposed the FASBIR approach and showed that **multimodal perturbation**, which combines multiple mechanisms of diversity generation, provides a practical way to construct ensembles of stable learners.

6

Ensemble Pruning

6.1 What Is Ensemble Pruning

Given a set of trained individual learners, rather than combining all of them, **ensemble pruning** tries to select a subset of individual learners to comprise the ensemble.

An apparent advantage of ensemble pruning is to obtain ensembles with smaller sizes; this reduces the storage resources required for storing the ensembles and the computational resources required for calculating outputs of individual learners, and thus improves efficiency. There is another benefit, that is, the generalization performance of the pruned ensemble may be even better than the ensemble consisting of all the given individual learners.

The first study on ensemble pruning is possibly [Margineantu and Dietterich, 1997] which tried to prune boosted ensembles. Tamon and Xiang [2000], however, showed that boosting pruning is intractable even to approximate. Instead of pruning ensembles generated by sequential methods, Zhou et al. [2002b] tried to prune ensembles generated by parallel methods such as Bagging, and showed that the pruning can lead to smaller ensembles with better generalization performance. Later, most ensemble pruning studies were devoted to parallel ensemble methods. Caruana et al. [2004] showed that pruning parallel heterogeneous ensembles comprising different types of individual learners is better than taking the original heterogeneous ensembles. In [Zhou et al., 2002b] the pruning of parallel ensembles was called **selective ensemble**; while in [Caruana et al., 2004], the pruning of parallel heterogeneous ensembles was called **ensemble selection**. In this chapter we put all of them under the umbrella of *ensemble pruning*.

Originally, ensemble pruning was defined for the setting where *the individual learners have already been generated*, and no more individual learners will be generated from training data during the pruning process. Notice that traditional **sequential ensemble methods** will discard some individual learners during their training process, but that is not ensemble pruning. These methods typically generate individual learners one by one; once an individual learner is generated, a *sanity check* is applied and the individual learner will be discarded if it cannot pass the check. Such a sanity check is important to ensure the validity of sequential ensembles and prevent them from growing infinitely. For example, in AdaBoost an individual learner will be discarded if its accuracy is below 0.5; however, AdaBoost is not an ensemble pruning method, and boosting pruning [Margineantu and Dietterich, 1997] tries to reduce the number of individual learners after the boosting procedure has stopped and no more individual learners will be generated. It is noteworthy that some recent studies have extended ensemble pruning to all steps of ensemble construction, and individual learners may be pruned even before all individual learners have been generated. Nevertheless, an essential difference between ensemble pruning and sequential ensemble methods remains: for sequential ensemble methods, an individual learner would not be excluded once it is added into the ensemble; while for ensemble pruning methods, any individual learners may be excluded, even for the ones which have been kept in the ensemble for a long time.

Ensemble pruning can be viewed as a special kind of **Stacking**. As introduced in Chapter 4, Stacking tries to apply a meta-learner to combine the individual learners, while the ensemble pruning procedure can be viewed as a special meta-learner. Also, recall that as mentioned in Chapter 4, if we do not worry about how the individual learners are generated, then different ensemble methods can be regarded as different implementations of weighted combination; from this aspect, ensemble pruning can be regarded as a procedure which sets the weights on some learners to zero.

6.2 Many Could Be Better Than All

In order to show that it is possible to get a smaller yet better ensemble through ensemble pruning, this section introduces Zhou et al. [2002b]'s analyses.

We start from the regression setting on which the analysis is easier. Suppose there are N individual learners $h_1, \ldots, h_N$ available, and thus the final ensemble size $T \leq N$. Without loss of generality, assume that the learners are combined via weighted averaging according to (4.9) and the weights are constrained by (4.10). For simplicity, assume that equal weights are used, and thus, from (4.11) we have the generalization error of the ensemble as

$$err = \sum_{i=1}^{N} \sum_{j=1}^{N} C_{ij} / N^2, \qquad (6.1)$$

where C_{ij} is defined in (4.12) and measures the correlation between h_i and h_j. If the kth individual learner is excluded from the ensemble, the generalization error of the pruned ensemble is

$$err' = \sum_{\substack{i=1 \\ i \neq k}}^{N} \sum_{\substack{j=1 \\ j \neq k}}^{N} C_{ij}/(N-1)^2. \tag{6.2}$$

By comparing (6.1) and (6.2), we get the condition under which err is not smaller than err', implying that the pruned ensemble is better than the all-member ensemble, that is,

$$(2N-1) \sum_{i=1}^{N} \sum_{j=1}^{N} C_{ij} \leq 2N^2 \sum_{\substack{i=1 \\ i \neq k}}^{N} C_{ik} + N^2 C_{kk}. \tag{6.3}$$

(6.3) usually holds in practice since the individual learners are often highly correlated. For an extreme example, when all the individual learners are duplicates, (6.3) indicates that the ensemble size can be reduced without sacrificing generalization ability. The simple analysis above shows that in regression, given a number of individual learners, ensembling some instead of all of them may be better.

It is interesting to study the difference between ensemble pruning and *sequential ensemble methods* based on (6.3). As above, let N denote the upper bound of the final ensemble size. Suppose the sequential ensemble method employs the sanity check that the new individual learner h_k ($1 < k \leq N$) will be kept if the ensemble consisting of $h_1, \ldots, h_k$ is better than the ensemble consisting of $h_1, \ldots, h_{k-1}$ on mean squared error. Then, h_k will be discarded if [Perrone and Cooper, 1993]

$$(2k-1) \sum_{i=1}^{k-1} \sum_{j=1}^{k-1} C_{ij} \leq 2(k-1)^2 \sum_{i=1}^{k-1} C_{ik} + (k-1)^2 C_{kk}. \tag{6.4}$$

Comparing (6.3) and (6.4) it is easy to see the following. Firstly, ensemble pruning methods consider the correlation among *all* the individual learners while sequential ensemble methods consider only the correlation between the new individual learner and previously generated ones. For example, assume $N = 100$ and $k = 10$; sequential ensemble methods consider only the correlation between $h_1, \ldots, h_{10}$, while ensemble pruning methods consider the correlations between $h_1, \ldots, h_{100}$. Secondly, when (6.4) holds, sequential ensemble methods will only discard h_k, but $h_1, \ldots, h_{k-1}$ won't be discarded; while any classifier in $h_1, \ldots, h_N$ may be discarded by ensemble pruning methods when (6.3) holds.

Notice that the analysis from (6.1) to (6.4) only applies to regression. Since supervised learning includes regression and classification, analysis of classification setting is needed for a unified result. Again let N denote the number of available individual classifiers, and thus the final ensemble size $T \leq N$. Without loss of generality, consider binary classification with labels $\{-1, +1\}$, and assume that the learners are combined via majority voting introduced in Section 4.3.1 and ties are broken arbitrarily. Given m training instances, the expected output on these instances is $(f_1, \ldots, f_m)^\top$ where f_j is the ground-truth of the jth instance, and the prediction made by the ith classifier h_i on these instances is $(h_{i1}, \ldots, h_{im})^\top$ where h_{ij} is the prediction on the jth instance. Since $f_j, h_{ij} \in \{-1, +1\}$, it is obvious that h_i correctly classifies the jth instance when $h_{ij}f_j = +1$. Thus, the error of the ith classifier on these m instances is

$$err(h_i) = \frac{1}{m} \sum_{j=1}^{m} \eta(h_{ij}f_j), \tag{6.5}$$

where $\eta(\cdot)$ is a function defined as

$$\eta(x) = \begin{cases} 1 & \text{if } x = -1 \\ 0.5 & \text{if } x = 0 \\ 0 & \text{if } x = 1 \end{cases}. \tag{6.6}$$

Let $s = (s_1, \ldots, s_m)^\top$ where $s_j = \sum_{i=1}^{N} h_{ij}$. The output of the all-member ensemble on the jth instance is

$$H_j = \text{sign}(s_j). \tag{6.7}$$

It is obvious that $H_j \in \{-1, 0, +1\}$. The prediction of the all-member ensemble on the jth instance is correct when $H_jf_j = +1$ and wrong when $H_jf_j = -1$, while $H_jf_j = 0$ corresponds to a tie. Thus, the error of the all-member ensemble is

$$err = \frac{1}{m} \sum_{j=1}^{m} \eta(H_jf_j). \tag{6.8}$$

Now, suppose the kth individual classifier is excluded from the ensemble. The prediction made by the pruned ensemble on the jth instance is

$$H'_j = \text{sign}(s_j - h_{kj}), \tag{6.9}$$

and the error of the pruned ensemble is

$$err' = \frac{1}{m} \sum_{j=1}^{m} \eta(H'_jf_j). \tag{6.10}$$

Then, by comparing (6.8) and (6.10), we get the condition under which err is not smaller than err', implying that the pruned ensemble is better than the all-member ensemble; that is,

$$\sum_{j=1}^{m} \left(\eta\left(\text{sign}\left(s_j\right)f_j\right) - \eta\left(\text{sign}\left(s_j - h_{kj}\right)f_j\right) \right) \geq 0. \tag{6.11}$$

Since the exclusion of the kth individual classifier will not change the output of the ensemble if $|s_j| > 1$, and based on the property that

$$\eta(\text{sign}(x)) - \eta(\text{sign}(x - y)) = -\frac{1}{2}\text{sign}(x + y),\qquad(6.12)$$

the condition for the kth individual classifier to be pruned is

$$\sum_{j\in\{\arg_j\,|s_j|\leq 1\}} \text{sign}((s_j + h_{kj})f_j) \leq 0.\qquad(6.13)$$

(6.13) usually holds in practice since the individual classifiers are often highly correlated. For an extreme example, when all the individual classifiers are duplicates, (6.13) indicates that the ensemble size can be reduced without sacrificing generalization ability.

Through combining the analyses on both regression and classification (i.e., (6.3) and (6.13)), we get the theorem of MCBTA (*"many could be better than all"*) [Zhou et al., 2002b], which indicates that for supervised learning, given a set of individual learners, it may be better to ensemble some instead of all of these individual learners.

6.3 Categorization of Pruning Methods

Notice that simply pruning individual learners with poor performance may not lead to a good pruned ensemble. Generally, it is better to keep some accurate individuals together with some not-that-good but complementary individuals. Furthermore, notice that neither (6.3) nor (6.13) provides practical solutions to ensemble pruning since the required computation is usually intractable even when there is only one output in regression and two classes in classification. Indeed, the central problem of ensemble pruning research is how to design practical algorithms leading to smaller ensembles without sacrificing or even improving the generalization performance contrasting to all-member ensembles.

During the past decade, many effective ensemble pruning methods have been proposed. Roughly speaking, those methods can be classified into three categories [Tsoumakas et al., 2009]:

- **Ordering-based pruning**. Those methods try to order the individual learners according to some criterion, and only the learners in the front-part will be put into the final ensemble. Though they work in a sequential style, it is noteworthy that they are quite different from sequential ensemble methods (e.g., AdaBoost) since all the available individual learners are given in advance and no more individual learners will be generated in the pruning process; moreover, any individual learner, not just the latest generated one, may be pruned.

- **Clustering-based pruning**. Those methods try to identify a number of representative *prototype* individual learners to constitute the final ensemble. Usually, a clustering process is employed to partition the individual learners into a number of groups, where individual learners in the same group behave similarly while different groups have large diversity. Then, the prototypes of clusters are put into the final ensemble.

- **Optimization-based pruning**. Those methods formulate the ensemble pruning problem as an optimization problem which aims to find the subset of individual learners that maximizes or minimizes an objective related to the generalization ability of the final ensemble. Many optimization techniques have been used, e.g., heuristic optimization methods, mathematical programming methods, etc.

It is obvious that the boundaries between different categories are not crisp, and there are methods that can be put into more than one category. In particular, though there are many early studies on *pure* ordering-based or clustering-based pruning methods, along with the explosively increasing exploitation of optimization techniques in machine learning, recent ordering-based and clustering-based pruning methods become closer to optimization-based methods.

6.4 Ordering-Based Pruning

Ordering-based pruning originated from Margineantu and Dietterich's [1997] work on *boosting pruning*. Later, most efforts were devoted to pruning ensembles generated by parallel ensemble methods.

Given N individual learners $h_1, \ldots, h_N$, suppose they are combined sequentially in a random order, the generalization error of the ensemble generally decreases monotonically as the ensemble size increases, and approaches an asymptotic constant error. It has been found that [Martínez-Muñoz and Suárez, 2006], however, if an appropriate ordering is devised, the ensemble error generally reaches a minimum with intermediate ensemble size and this minimum is often lower than the asymptotic error, as shown in Figure 6.1. Hence, ensemble pruning can be realized by ordering the N individual learners and then putting the front T individual learners into the final ensemble.

It is generally hard to decide the best T value, but fortunately there are usually many T values that will lead to better performance than the all-member ensemble, and at least the T value can be tuned on training data. A more crucial problem is how to order the individual learners appropri-

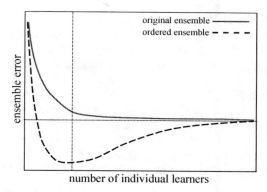

FIGURE 6.1: Illustration of error curves of the original ensemble (aggregated in random order) and ordered ensemble.

ately. During the past decade, many ordering strategies have been proposed. Most of them consider both the accuracy and diversity of individual learners, and a validation data set V with size $|V|$ is usually used (when there are not sufficient data, the training data set D or its sub-samples can be used as validation data). In the following we introduce some representative ordering-based pruning methods.

Reduce-Error Pruning [Margineantu and Dietterich, 1997]. This method starts with the individual learner whose validation error is the smallest. Then, the remaining individual learners are sequentially put into the ensemble, such that the validation error of the resulting ensemble is as small as possible in each round. This procedure is greedy, and therefore, after obtaining the top T individual learners, Margineantu and Dietterich [1997] used Backfitting [Friedman and Stuetzle, 1981] search to improve the ensemble. In each round, it tries to replace one of the already selected individual learners with an unselected individual learner which could reduce the ensemble error. This process repeats until none of the individual learners can be replaced, or the pre-set maximum number of learning rounds is reached. It is easy to see that Backfitting is time-consuming. Moreover, it was reported [Martínez-Muñoz and Suárez, 2006] that Backfitting could not improve the generalization ability significantly for parallel ensemble methods such as Bagging.

Kappa Pruning [Margineantu and Dietterich, 1997]. This method assumes that all the individual learners have similar performance, and uses the κ_p diversity measure introduced in Section 5.3.1 to calculate the diversity of every pair of individual learners on the validation set. It starts with the pair with the smallest κ_p (i.e., the largest diversity among the given individual learners), and then selects pairs of learners in ascending order of κ_p. Finally, the top T individual learners are put into the ensemble. A variant method was proposed by Martínez-Muñoz et al. [2009] later, through replacing the pairwise κ_p diversity measure by the interrater agreement diversity measure κ introduced in Section 5.3.2. The variant method still starts with the pair of individual learners that are with the smallest κ value. Then, at the tth round, it calculates the κ value between each unselected individual learner and the current ensemble H_{t-1}, and takes the individual learner with the smallest κ value to construct the ensemble H_t of size t. The variant method often leads to smaller ensemble error. However, it is computationally much more expensive than the original Kappa pruning. Banfield et al. [2005] proposed another variant method that starts with the all-member ensemble and iteratively removes the individual learner with the largest average κ value.

Kappa-Error Diagram Pruning [Margineantu and Dietterich, 1997]. This method is based on the **kappa-error diagram** introduced in Section 5.3.3. It constructs the *convex hull* of the points in the diagram, which can be regarded as a summary of the entire diagram and includes both the most accurate and the most diverse pairs of individual learners. The pruned ensemble consists of any individual learner that appears in a pair corresponding to a point on the convex hull. From the definition of the kappa-error diagram it is easy to see that this pruning method simultaneously considers the accuracy as well as diversity of individual learners.

Complementariness Pruning [Martínez-Muñoz and Suárez, 2004]. This method favors the inclusion of individual learners that are complementary to the current ensemble. It starts with the individual learner whose validation error is the smallest. Then, at the tth round, given the ensemble H_{t-1} of size $t - 1$, the complementariness pruning method adds the individual learner h_t which satisfies

$$h_t = \arg\max_{h_k} \sum_{(\boldsymbol{x},y)\in V} \mathbb{I}\left(h_k(\boldsymbol{x}) = y \text{ and } H_{t-1}(\boldsymbol{x}) \neq y\right), \tag{6.14}$$

where V is the validation data set, and h_k is picked up from unselected individual learners.

Margin Distance Pruning [Martínez-Muñoz and Suárez, 2004]. This method defines a **signature vector** for each individual learner. For example, the signature vector $c^{(k)}$ of the kth individual learner h_k is a $|V|$-dimensional vector where the ith element is

$$c_i^{(k)} = 2\mathbb{I}\left(h_k\left(\boldsymbol{x}_i\right) = y_i\right) - 1, \tag{6.15}$$

where $(\boldsymbol{x}_i, y_i) \in V$. Obviously, $c_i^{(k)} = 1$ if and only if h_k classifies $\boldsymbol{x}_i$ correctly and -1 otherwise. The performance of the ensemble can be characterized by the average of $c^{(k)}$'s, i.e., $\bar{c} = \frac{1}{N}\sum_{k=1}^{N} c^{(k)}$. The ith instance is correctly classified by the ensemble if the ith element of $\bar{c}$ is positive, and the value of $|\bar{c}_i|$ is the *margin* on the ith instance. If an ensemble correctly classifies all the instances in V, the vector $\bar{c}$ will lie in the first-quadrant of the $|V|$-dimensional hyperspace, that is, every element of $\bar{c}$ is positive. Consequently, the goal is to select the ensemble whose signature vector is near an objective position in the first-quadrant. Suppose the objective position is the point o with equal elements, i.e., $o_i = p$ $(i = 1, \ldots, |V|; 0 < p < 1)$. In practice, the value of p is usually a small value (e.g., $p \in (0.05, 0.25)$). The individual learner to be selected is the one which can reduce the distance between $\bar{c}$ and o to the most.

Orientation Pruning [Martínez-Muñoz and Suárez, 2006]. This method uses the signature vector defined as above. It orders the individual learners increasingly according to the angles between the corresponding signature vectors and the *reference direction*, denoted as c_{ref}, which is the projection of the first-quadrant diagonal onto the hyperplane defined by the signature vector $\bar{c}$ of the all-member ensemble.

Boosting-Based Pruning [Martínez-Muñoz and Suárez, 2007]. This method uses AdaBoost to determine the order of the individual learners. It is similar to the AdaBoost algorithm except that in each round, rather than generating a base learner from the training data, the individual learner with the lowest weighted validation error is selected from the given individual learners. When the weighted error is larger than 0.5, the **Boosting with restart** strategy is used, that is, the weights are reset and another individual learner is selected. Notice that the weights are used in the ordering process, while Martínez-Muñoz and Suárez [2007] reported that there is no significant difference for the pruned ensemble to make prediction with/without the weights.

Reinforcement Learning Pruning [Partalas et al., 2009]. This method models the ensemble pruning problem as an episodic task. Given N individual learners, it assumes that there is an agent which takes N sequential actions each corresponding to either including the individual learner h_k in the final ensemble or not. Then, the Q-learning algorithm [Watkins and Dayan, 1992], a famous **reinforcement learning** technique, is applied to solve an optimal policy of choosing the individual learners.

6.5 Clustering-Based Pruning

An intuitive idea to ensemble pruning is to identify some *prototype* individual learners that are representative yet diverse among the given individual learners, and then use only these prototypes to constitute the ensemble. This category of methods is known as clustering-based pruning because the most straightforward way to identify the prototypes is to use clustering techniques.

Generally, clustering-based pruning methods work in two steps. In the first step, the individual learners are grouped into a number of clusters. Different clustering techniques have been exploited for this purpose. For example, Giacinto et al. [2000] used **hierarchical agglomerative clustering** and regarded the probability that the individual learners do not make coincident validation errors as the distance; Lazarevic and Obradovic [2001] used k-**means clustering** based on Euclidean distance; Bakker and Heskes [2003] used **deterministic annealing** for clustering; etc.

In the second step, prototype individual learners are selected from the clusters. Different strategies have been developed. For example, Giacinto et al. [2000] selected from each cluster the learner which is the most distant to other clusters; Lazarevic and Obradovic [2001] iteratively removed individual learners from the least to the most accurate inside each cluster until the accuracy of the ensemble starts to decrease; Bakker and Heskes [2003] selected the centroid of each cluster; etc.

6.6   Optimization-Based Pruning

Optimization-based pruning originated from [Zhou et al., 2002b] which employs a **genetic algorithm** [Goldberg, 1989] to select individual learners for the pruned ensemble. Later, many other optimization techniques, including heuristic optimization, mathematical programming and probabilistic methods have been exploited. This section introduces several representative methods.

6.6.1   Heuristic Optimization Pruning

Recognizing that the theoretically optimal solution to weighted combination in (4.14) is infeasible in practice, Zhou et al. [2002b] regarded the ensemble pruning problem as an optimization task and proposed a practical method GASEN.

The basic idea is to associate each individual learner with a weight that could characterize the goodness of including the individual learner in the final ensemble. Given N individual learners, the weights can be organized as an N-dimensional weight vector, where small elements in the weight vector suggest that the corresponding individual learners should be excluded. Thus, one weight vector corresponds to one solution to ensemble pruning. In GASEN, a set of weight vectors are randomly initialized at first. Then, a genetic algorithm is applied to the *population* of weight vectors, where the *fitness* of each weight vector is calculated based on the corresponding ensemble performance on validation data. The pruned ensemble is obtained by decoding the optimal weight vector evolved from the genetic algorithm, and excluding individual learners associated with small weights.

There are different GASEN implementations, by using different coding schemes or different genetic operators. For example, Zhou et al. [2002b] used a *floating coding* scheme, while Zhou and Tang [2003] used a *bit coding* scheme which directly takes 0-1 weights and avoids the problem of setting an appropriate threshold to decide which individual learner should be excluded.

In addition to genetic algorithms [Coelho et al., 2003], many other heuristic optimization techniques have been used in ensemble pruning; for example, greedy hill-climbing [Caruana et al., 2004], artificial immune algorithms [Castro et al., 2005, Zhang et al., 2005], case similarity search [Coyle and Smyth, 2006], etc.

6.6.2 Mathematical Programming Pruning

One deficiency of heuristic optimization is the lack of solid theoretical foundations. Along with the great success of using mathematical programming in machine learning, ensemble pruning methods based on mathematical programming optimization have been proposed.

6.6.2.1 SDP Relaxation

Zhang et al. [2006] formulated ensemble pruning as a quadratic integer programming problem. Since finding the optimal solution is computationally infeasible, they provided an approximate solution by **Semi-Definite Programming** (SDP).

First, given N individual classifiers and m training instances, Zhang et al. [2006] recorded the errors in the matrix $\mathbf{P}$ as

$$P_{ij} = \begin{cases} 0 & \text{if } h_j \text{ classifies } x_i \text{ correctly} \\ 1 & \text{otherwise.} \end{cases} \tag{6.16}$$

Let $\mathbf{G} = \mathbf{P}^\top \mathbf{P}$. Then, the diagonal element G_{ii} is the number of mistakes made by h_i, and the off-diagonal element G_{ij} is the number of co-occurred mistakes of h_i and h_j. The matrix elements are normalized according to

$$\tilde{G}_{ij} = \begin{cases} \frac{G_{ij}}{m} & i = j \\ \frac{1}{2}\left(\frac{G_{ij}}{G_{ii}} + \frac{G_{ji}}{G_{jj}}\right) & i \neq j. \end{cases} \tag{6.17}$$

Thus, $\sum_{i=1}^{N} \tilde{G}_{ii}$ measures the overall performance of the individual classifiers, $\sum_{i,j=1;i\neq j}^{N} \tilde{G}_{ij}$ measures the diversity, and a combination of these two terms $\sum_{i,j=1}^{N} \tilde{G}_{ij}$ is a good approximation of the ensemble error.

Consequently, the ensemble pruning problem is formulated as the quadratic integer programming problem

$$\min_{z} z^{\top} \tilde{G} z \quad \text{s.t.} \sum_{i=1}^{N} z_i = T, \ z_i \in \{0, 1\}, \tag{6.18}$$

where the binary variable z_i represents whether the ith classifier h_i is included in the ensemble, and T is the size of the pruned ensemble.

(6.18) is a standard 0-1 optimization problem, which is generally NP-hard. However, let $v_i = 2z_i - 1 \in \{-1, 1\}$,

$$\mathbf{V} = vv^{\top}, \quad \mathbf{H} = \begin{pmatrix} \mathbf{1}^{\top} \tilde{G} \mathbf{1} & \mathbf{1}^{\top} \tilde{G} \\ \tilde{G} \mathbf{1} & \tilde{G} \end{pmatrix}, \text{ and } \mathbf{D} = \begin{pmatrix} N & \mathbf{1}^{\top} \\ \mathbf{1} & \mathbf{I} \end{pmatrix}, \tag{6.19}$$

where $\mathbf{1}$ is all-one column vector and $\mathbf{I}$ is identity matrix, then (6.18) can be rewritten as the equivalent formulation [Zhang et al., 2006]

$$\min_{\mathbf{V}} \quad \mathbf{H} \otimes \mathbf{V} \tag{6.20}$$
$$\text{s.t.} \quad \mathbf{D} \otimes \mathbf{V} = 4T, \ \text{diag}(\mathbf{V}) = \mathbf{1}, \ \mathbf{V} \succeq 0$$
$$\text{rank}(\mathbf{V}) = 1,$$

where $\mathbf{A} \otimes \mathbf{B} = \sum_{ij} A_{ij} B_{ij}$. Then, by dropping the rank constraint, it is relaxed to the following convex SDP problem which can be solved in polynomial time [Zhang et al., 2006]

$$\min_{\mathbf{V}} \quad \mathbf{H} \otimes \mathbf{V} \tag{6.21}$$
$$\text{s.t.} \quad \mathbf{D} \otimes \mathbf{V} = 4T, \ \text{diag}(\mathbf{V}) = \mathbf{1}, \ \mathbf{V} \succeq 0.$$

6.6.2.2 ℓ_1-Norm Regularization

Li and Zhou [2009] proposed a regularized selective ensemble method RSE which reduces the ensemble pruning task to a **Quadratic Programming** (QP) problem.

Given N individual classifiers and considering weighted combination, RSE determines the weight vector $w = [w_1, \ldots, w_N]^{\top}$ by minimizing the regularized risk function

$$R(w) = \lambda V(w) + \Omega(w), \tag{6.22}$$

where $V(w)$ is the empirical loss which measures the misclassification on training data $D = \{(x_1, y_1), \ldots, (x_m, y_m)\}$, $\Omega(w)$ is the *regularization* term which tries to make the final classifier smooth and simple, and λ is a *regularization* parameter which trades off the minimization of $V(w)$ and $\Omega(w)$.

By using the *hinge loss* and *graph Laplacian* regularizer as the empirical loss and *regularization* term, respectively, the problem is formulated as [Li and Zhou, 2009]

$$\min_{\boldsymbol{w}} \quad \boldsymbol{w}^\top \mathbf{PLP}^\top \boldsymbol{w} + \lambda \sum_{i=1}^{m} \max(0, 1 - y_i \boldsymbol{p}_i^\top \boldsymbol{w}) \qquad (6.23)$$

$$\text{s.t.} \quad \mathbf{1}^\top \boldsymbol{w} = 1, \quad \boldsymbol{w} \geq \mathbf{0}$$

where $\boldsymbol{p}_i = (h_1(\boldsymbol{x}_i), \ldots, h_N(\boldsymbol{x}_i))^\top$ encodes the predictions of individual classifiers on $\boldsymbol{x}_i$, $\mathbf{P} \in \{-1, +1\}^{N \times m}$ is the *prediction matrix* which collects predictions of all individual classifiers on all training instances, where $P_{ij} = h_i(\boldsymbol{x}_j)$. $\mathbf{L}$ is the *normalized graph Laplacian* of the neighborhood graph G of the training data. Denote the weighted adjacency matrix of G by $\mathbf{W}$, and $\mathbf{D}$ is a diagonal matrix where $D_{ii} = \sum_{j=1}^{m} W_{ij}$. Then, $\mathbf{L} = \mathbf{D}^{-1/2}(\mathbf{D} - \mathbf{W})\mathbf{D}^{-1/2}$.

By introducing slack variables $\boldsymbol{\xi} = (\xi_1, \ldots, \xi_m)^\top$, (6.23) can be rewritten as

$$\min_{\boldsymbol{w}} \quad \boldsymbol{w}^\top \mathbf{PLP}^\top \boldsymbol{w} + \lambda \mathbf{1}^\top \boldsymbol{\xi} \qquad (6.24)$$

$$\text{s.t.} \quad y_i \boldsymbol{p}_i^\top \boldsymbol{w} + \xi_i \geq 1, \quad (\forall i = 1, \ldots, m)$$

$$\mathbf{1}^\top \boldsymbol{w} = 1, \quad \boldsymbol{w} \geq \mathbf{0}, \quad \boldsymbol{\xi} \geq \mathbf{0}.$$

Obviously, (6.24) is a standard QP problem that can be efficiently solved by existing optimization packages.

Notice that $\mathbf{1}^\top \boldsymbol{w} = 1, \boldsymbol{w} \geq \mathbf{0}$ is a ℓ_1-norm constraint on the weights $\boldsymbol{w}$. The ℓ_1-norm is a sparsity-inducing constraint which will force some w_i's to be zero, and thus, RSE favors an ensemble with small sizes and only a subset of the given individual learners will be included in the final ensemble.

Another advantage of RSE is that it naturally fits the **semi-supervised learning** setting due to the use of the graph Laplacian regularizer, hence it can exploit *unlabeled data* to improve ensemble performance. More information on semi-supervised learning will be introduced in Chapter 8.

6.6.3 Probabilistic Pruning

Chen et al. [2006, 2009] proposed a probabilistic pruning method under the Bayesian framework by introducing a sparsity-inducing prior over the combination weights, where the *maximum a posteriori* (MAP) estimation of the weights is obtained by **Expectation Maximization** (EM) [Chen et al., 2006] and **Expectation Propagation** (EP) [Chen et al., 2009], respectively. Due to the sparsity-inducing prior, many of the posteriors of the weights are sharply distributed at zero, and thus many individual learners are excluded from the final ensemble.

Given N individual learners $h_1, \ldots, h_N$, the output vector of the individual learners on the instance $\boldsymbol{x}$ is $\boldsymbol{h}(\boldsymbol{x}) = (h_1(\boldsymbol{x}), \ldots, h_N(\boldsymbol{x}))^\top$. The output of the all-member ensemble is $H(\boldsymbol{x}) = \boldsymbol{w}^\top \boldsymbol{h}(\boldsymbol{x})$, where $\boldsymbol{w} = [w_1, \ldots, w_N]^\top$ is a non-negative weight vector, $w_i \geq 0$.

To make the weight vector $\boldsymbol{w}$ sparse and non-negative, a left-truncated *Gaussian prior* is introduced to each weight w_i [Chen et al., 2006], that is,

$$p(\boldsymbol{w} \mid \boldsymbol{\alpha}) = \prod_{i=1}^{N} p(w_i \mid \alpha_i) = \prod_{i=1}^{N} \mathcal{N}_t(w_i \mid 0, \alpha_i^{-1}), \tag{6.25}$$

where $\boldsymbol{\alpha} = [\alpha_1, \dots, \alpha_N]^\top$ is the inverse variance of weight vector $\boldsymbol{w}$ and $\mathcal{N}_t(w_i \mid 0, \alpha_i^{-1})$ is a left-truncated Gaussian distribution defined as

$$\mathcal{N}_t(w_i \mid 0, \alpha_i^{-1}) = \begin{cases} 2\mathcal{N}(w_i \mid 0, \alpha_i^{-1}) & \text{if } w_i \geq 0 , \\ 0 & \text{otherwise} . \end{cases} \tag{6.26}$$

For regression, it is assumed that the ensemble output is corrupted by a Gaussian noise $\epsilon_i \sim \mathcal{N}(0, \sigma^2)$ with mean zero and variance σ^2. That is, for each training instance $(\boldsymbol{x}_i, y_i)$, it holds that

$$y_i = \boldsymbol{w}^\top \boldsymbol{h}(\boldsymbol{x}_i) + \epsilon_i . \tag{6.27}$$

Assuming *i.i.d.* training data, the likelihood can be expressed as

$$p(\boldsymbol{y} \mid \boldsymbol{w}, \mathbf{X}, \sigma^2) = (2\pi\sigma^2)^{-m/2} \exp\left\{ -\frac{1}{2\sigma^2} \|\boldsymbol{y}^\top - w^\top \mathbf{H}\| \right\} , \tag{6.28}$$

where $\boldsymbol{y} = [y_1, \dots, y_m]^\top$ is the ground-truth output vector, and $\mathbf{H} = [\boldsymbol{h}(\boldsymbol{x}_1), \dots, \boldsymbol{h}(\boldsymbol{x}_m)]$ is an $N \times m$ matrix which collects all the predictions of individual learners on all the training instances. Consequently, the posterior of $\boldsymbol{w}$ can be written as

$$p(\boldsymbol{w} \mid \mathbf{X}, \boldsymbol{y}, \boldsymbol{\alpha}) \propto \prod_{i=1}^{N} p(w_i \mid \alpha_i) \prod_{i=1}^{m} p(y_i \mid \boldsymbol{x}_i, \boldsymbol{w}) . \tag{6.29}$$

As defined in (6.26), the prior over $\boldsymbol{w}$ is a left-truncated Gaussian, and therefore, exact Bayesian inference is intractable. However, the EM algorithm or EP algorithm can be employed to generate an MAP solution, leading to an approximation of the sparse weight vector [Chen et al., 2006, 2009].

For classification, the ensemble output is formulated as

$$H(\boldsymbol{x}) = \Phi\left(\boldsymbol{w}^\top \boldsymbol{h}(\boldsymbol{x})\right) , \tag{6.30}$$

where $\Phi(x) = \int_{-\infty}^{x} \mathcal{N}(t \mid 0, 1) dt$ is the Gaussian cumulative distribution function. The class label of $\boldsymbol{x}$ is $+1$ if $H(\boldsymbol{x}) \geq 1/2$ and 0 otherwise. As above, the posterior of $\boldsymbol{w}$ can be derived as

$$p(\boldsymbol{w} \mid \mathbf{X}, \boldsymbol{y}, \boldsymbol{\alpha}) \propto \prod_{i=1}^{N} p(w_i \mid \alpha_i) \prod_{i=1}^{m} \Phi(y_i \boldsymbol{w}^\top \boldsymbol{h}(\boldsymbol{x}_i)), \tag{6.31}$$

where both the prior $p(w_i \mid \alpha_i)$ and the likelihood $\Phi(y_i \boldsymbol{w}^\top \boldsymbol{h}(\boldsymbol{x}_i))$ are non-Gaussian, and thus, the EM algorithm or the EP algorithm is used to obtain an MAP estimation of the sparse weight vector [Chen et al., 2006, 2009].

6.7 Further Readings

Tsoumakas et al. [2009] provided a brief review on ensemble pruning methods. Hernández-Lobato et al. [2011] reported a recent empirical study which shows that optimization-based and ordering-based pruning methods, at least for pruning parallel regression ensembles, generally outperform ensembles generated by AdaBoost.R2, Negative Correlation and several other approaches.

In addition to clustering, there are also other approaches for selecting the prototype individual learners, e.g., Tsoumakas et al. [2004, 2005] picked prototype individual learners by using statistical tests to compare their individual performance. Hernández-Lobato et al. [2009] proposed the *instance-based pruning* method, where the individual learners selected for making prediction are determined for each instance separately. Soto et al. [2010] applied the instance-based pruning to pruned ensembles generated by other ensemble pruning methods, yielding the *double pruning* method. A similar idea has been described by Fan et al. [2002].

If each individual learner is viewed as a fancy feature extractor [Kuncheva, 2008, Brown, 2010], it is obvious that ensemble pruning has close relation to **feature selection** [Guyon and Elisseeff, 2003] and new ensemble pruning methods can get inspiration from feature selection techniques. It is worth noting, however, that the different natures of ensemble pruning and feature selection must be considered. For example, in ensemble pruning the individual learners predict the same target and thus have the same physical meaning, while in feature selection the features usually have different physical meanings; the individual learners are usually highly correlated, while this may not be the case for features in feature selection. A breakthrough in computer vision of the last decade, i.e., the *Viola-Jones face detector* [Viola and Jones, 2004], actually can be viewed as a pruning of Harr-feature-based decision stump ensemble, or selection of Harr features by AdaBoost with a cascade architecture.

7

Clustering Ensembles

7.1 Clustering

Clustering aims to find the inherent structure of the unlabeled data by grouping them into clusters of objects [Jain et al., 1999]. A good clustering will produce high quality clusters where the **intra-cluster similarity** is maximized while the **inter-cluster similarity** is minimized. Clustering can be used as a stand-alone exploratory tool to gain insights on the nature of the data, and it can also be used as a preprocessing stage to facilitate subsequent learning tasks. Formally, given the data $D = \{x_1, x_2, \ldots, x_m\}$ where the ith instance $x_i = (x_{i1}, x_{i2}, \ldots, x_{id})^\top \in \mathcal{R}^d$ is a d-dimensional feature vector, the task of clustering is to group D into k disjoint clusters $\{C_j \mid j = 1, \ldots, k\}$ with $\bigcup_{j=1}^{k} C_j = D$ and $C_i \bigcap_{i \neq j} C_j = \emptyset$. The clustering results returned by a clustering algorithm $\mathfrak{L}$ can be represented as a label vector $\lambda \in \mathcal{N}^m$, with the ith element $\lambda_i \in \{1, \ldots, k\}$ indicating the **cluster assignment** of x_i.

7.1.1 Clustering Methods

A lot of clustering methods have been developed and various taxonomies can be defined from different perspectives, such as different data types the algorithms can deal with, different assumptions the methods have adopted, etc. Here, we adopt Han and Kamber [2006]'s taxonomy, which roughly divides clustering methods into the following five categories.

Partitioning Methods. A partitioning method organizes D into k partitions by optimizing an objective partitioning criterion. The most well-known partitioning method is k-**means clustering** [Lloyd, 1982], which optimizes the *square-error* criterion

$$err = \sum_{j=1}^{k} \sum_{x \in C_j} dis(x, \bar{x}_j)^2 \,, \tag{7.1}$$

where $\bar{x}_j = \frac{1}{|C_j|} \sum_{x \in C_j} x$ is the mean of the partition C_j, and $dis(\cdot, \cdot)$ measures the distance between two instances (e.g., Euclidean distance). Notice

135

that finding the optimal partitioning which minimizes err would require exhaustive search of all the possible solutions and is obviously computationally prohibitive due to the combinatorial nature of the search space. To circumvent this difficulty, k-means adopts an *iterative relocation* technique to find the desired solution heuristically. First, it randomly selects k instances from D as the initial cluster centers. Then, every instance in D is assigned to the cluster whose center is the nearest. After that, the cluster centers are updated and the instances are re-assigned to their nearest clusters. The above process will be repeated until convergence.

Hierarchical Methods. A hierarchical method creates a hierarchy of clusterings on D at various granular levels, where a specific clustering can be obtained by thresholding the hierarchy at a specified level of granule. An early attempt toward hierarchical clustering is the SAHN method [Anderberg, 1973, Day and Edelsbrunner, 1984], which forms the hierarchy of clusterings in a *bottom-up* manner. Initially, each data point is placed into a cluster of its own, and an $m \times m$ dissimilarity matrix $\mathbf{D}$ among clusters is set with elements $\mathbf{D}(i,j) = dis(\boldsymbol{x}_i, \boldsymbol{x}_j)$. Then, two closest clusters C_i and C_j are identified based on $\mathbf{D}$ and replaced by the agglomerated cluster C_h. The dissimilarity matrix $\mathbf{D}$ is updated to reflect the deletion of C_i and C_j, as well as the new dissimilarities between C_h and all remaining clusters C_k ($k \neq i, j$):

$$\mathbf{D}(h,k) = \alpha_i \mathbf{D}(i,k) + \alpha_j \mathbf{D}(j,k) + \beta \mathbf{D}(i,j) + \gamma |\mathbf{D}(i,k) - \mathbf{D}(j,k)|, \quad (7.2)$$

where α_i, α_j, β and γ are coefficients characterizing different SAHN implementations. The above merging process is repeated until all the data points fall into a single cluster. Typical implementations of SAHN are named as *single-linkage* ($\alpha_i = 1/2; \alpha_j = 1/2; \beta = 0; \gamma = -1/2$), *complete-linkage* ($\alpha_i = 1/2; \alpha_j = 1/2; \beta = 0; \gamma = 1/2$) and *average-linkage* ($\alpha_i = |C_i|/(|C_i| + |C_j|); \alpha_j = |C_j|/(|C_i| + |C_j|); \beta = 0; \gamma = 0$).

Density-Based Methods. A density-based method constructs clusters on D based on the notion of density, where regions of instances with high density are regarded as clusters which are separated by regions of low density. DBSCAN [Ester et al., 1996] is a representative density-based clustering method, which characterizes the density of the data space with a pair of parameters ($\varepsilon, MinPts$). Given an instance $\boldsymbol{x}$, its neighborhood within a radius ε is called the ε-neighborhood of $\boldsymbol{x}$. $\boldsymbol{x}$ is called a *core object* if its ε-neighborhood contains at least $MinPts$ number of instances. An instance $\boldsymbol{p}$ is *directly density-reachable* to $\boldsymbol{x}$ if $\boldsymbol{p}$ is within the ε-neighborhood of $\boldsymbol{x}$ and $\boldsymbol{x}$ is a core object. First, DBSCAN identifies core objects which satisfy the requirement imposed by the ($\varepsilon, MinPts$) parameters. Then, it forms clusters by iteratively connecting the directly density-reachable instances starting from those core objects. The connecting process terminates when no new data point can be added to any cluster.

Grid-Based Methods. A grid-based method quantizes D into a finite number of cells forming a grid-structure, where the quantization process is usually performed in a multi-resolution style. STING [Wang et al., 1997] is a representative grid-based method, which divides the data space into a number of rectangular cells. Each cell stores statistical information of the instances falling into this cell, such as *count, mean, standard deviation, minimum, maximum, type of distribution*, etc. There are several levels of rectangular cells, each corresponding to a different level of resolution. Here, each cell at a higher level is partitioned into a number of cells at the next lower level, and statistical information of higher-level cells can be easily inferred from its lower-level cells with simple operations such as elementary algebraic calculations.

Model-Based Methods. A model-based method assumes a mathematical model characterizing the properties of D, where the clusters are formed to optimize the fit between the data and the underlying model. The most famous model-based method is **GMM-based clustering** [Redner and Walker, 1984], which works by utilizing the *Gaussian Mixture Model (GMM)*

$$p(\boldsymbol{x}|\boldsymbol{\Theta}) = \sum_{j=1}^{k} \alpha_j \, \mathcal{N}(\boldsymbol{x}|\boldsymbol{\mu}_j, \boldsymbol{\Sigma}_j) \,, \tag{7.3}$$

where each mixture component $\mathcal{N}(\boldsymbol{x}|\boldsymbol{\mu}_j, \boldsymbol{\Sigma}_j)$ $(j = 1, \dots, k)$ employs Gaussian distribution with mean $\boldsymbol{\mu}_j$ and covariance $\boldsymbol{\Sigma}_j$, and participates in constituting the whole distribution $p(\boldsymbol{x}|\boldsymbol{\Theta})$ with non-negative coefficient α_j. In addition, $\sum_{j=1}^{k} \alpha_j = 1$ and $\boldsymbol{\Theta} = \{\alpha_j, \boldsymbol{\mu}_j, \boldsymbol{\Sigma}_j | j = 1, \dots, k\}$. The cluster assignment λ_i for each instance $\boldsymbol{x}_i \in D$ is specified according to the rule

$$\lambda_i = \arg\max_{1 \le l \le k} \frac{\alpha_l \, \mathcal{N}(\boldsymbol{x}_i|\boldsymbol{\mu}_l, \boldsymbol{\Sigma}_l)}{\sum_{j=1}^{k} \alpha_j \, \mathcal{N}(\boldsymbol{x}_i|\boldsymbol{\mu}_j, \boldsymbol{\Sigma}_j)} \,. \tag{7.4}$$

The GMM parameters $\boldsymbol{\Theta}$ are learned from D by employing the popular EM procedure [Dempster et al., 1977] to maximize the following *log-likelihood* function in an iterative manner:

$$p(D|\boldsymbol{\Theta}) = \sum_{i=1}^{m} \ln \left(\sum_{j=1}^{k} \alpha_j \, \mathcal{N}(\boldsymbol{x}_i|\boldsymbol{\mu}_j, \boldsymbol{\Sigma}_j) \right) \,. \tag{7.5}$$

Details on the iterative optimization procedure can be easily found in classical literatures [Jain and Dubes, 1988, Bilmes, 1998, Jain et al., 1999, Duda et al., 2000].

7.1.2 Clustering Evaluation

The task of evaluating the quality of clustering results is commonly referred to as **cluster validity analysis** [Jain and Dubes, 1988, Halkidi et al., 2001]. Existing cluster validity indices for clustering quality assessment can be roughly categorized into two types: **external indices** and **internal indices**.

The external indices evaluate the clustering results by comparing the identified clusters to a pre-specified structure, e.g., the ground-truth clustering. Given the data set $D = \{x_1, \ldots, x_m\}$, let $\mathcal{C} = \{C_1, \ldots, C_k\}$ denote the identified clusters with label vector $\lambda \in \mathcal{N}^m$. Suppose $\mathcal{C}^* = \{C_1^*, \ldots, C_s^*\}$ is the pre-specified clustering structure with label vector λ^*. Then, four complementary terms can be defined to reflect the relationship between $\mathcal{C}$ and $\mathcal{C}^*$:

$$\begin{cases} a = |SS|, & SS = \{(x_i, x_j) \mid \lambda_i = \lambda_j, \lambda_i^* = \lambda_j^*, i < j\}, \\ b = |SD|, & SD = \{(x_i, x_j) \mid \lambda_i = \lambda_j, \lambda_i^* \neq \lambda_j^*, i < j\}, \\ c = |DS|, & DS = \{(x_i, x_j) \mid \lambda_i \neq \lambda_j, \lambda_i^* = \lambda_j^*, i < j\}, \\ d = |DD|, & DD = \{(x_i, x_j) \mid \lambda_i \neq \lambda_j, \lambda_i^* \neq \lambda_j^*, i < j\}, \end{cases} \tag{7.6}$$

where SS contains pairs of instances which belong to the same cluster in both $\mathcal{C}$ and $\mathcal{C}^*$; the meanings of SD, DS and DD can be inferred similarly based on the above definitions. It is evident that $a + b + c + d = m(m-1)/2$.

A number of popular external cluster validity indices are defined as follows [Jain and Dubes, 1988, Halkidi et al., 2001]:

- *Jaccard Coefficient* (JC):

$$\text{JC} = \frac{a}{a + b + c}, \tag{7.7}$$

- *Fowlkes and Mallows Index* (FMI):

$$\text{FMI} = \sqrt{\frac{a}{a + b} \cdot \frac{a}{a + c}}, \tag{7.8}$$

- *Rand Index* (RI):

$$\text{RI} = \frac{2(a + d)}{m(m - 1)}. \tag{7.9}$$

All these cluster validity indices take values between 0 and 1, and the larger the index value, the better the clustering quality.

The internal indices evaluate the clustering results by investigating the inherent properties of the identified clusters without resorting to a reference structure. Given the data set $D = \{x_1, \ldots, x_m\}$, let $\mathcal{C} = \{C_1, \ldots, C_k\}$ denote the identified clusters. The following terms are usually employed:

$$f(C) = \frac{2}{|C|(|C| - 1)} \sum_{i=1}^{|C|-1} \sum_{j=i+1}^{|C|} dis(x_i, x_j), \tag{7.10}$$

$$diam(C) = \max_{x_i, x_j \in C} dis(x_i, x_j), \tag{7.11}$$

$$d_{min}(C_i, C_j) = \min_{x_i \in C_i, x_j \in C_j} dis(x_i, x_j), \tag{7.12}$$

$$d_{cen}(C_i, C_j) = dis(c_i, c_j), \tag{7.13}$$

where $dis(\cdot, \cdot)$ measures the distance between two data points and c_i denotes the centroid of cluster C_i. Therefore, $f(C)$ is the average distance between the instances in cluster C, $diam(C)$ is the diameter of cluster C, $d_{min}(C_i, C_j)$ measures the distance between the two nearest instances in C_i and C_j, and $d_{cen}(C_i, C_j)$ measures the distance between the centroids of C_i and C_j.

A number of popular internal cluster validity indices are defined as follows [Jain and Dubes, 1988, Halkidi et al., 2001]:

- *Davies-Bouldin Index* (DBI):

$$\text{DBI} = \frac{1}{k} \sum_{i=1}^{k} \max_{1 \le j \le k, j \ne i} \left(\frac{f(C_i) + f(C_j)}{d_{cen}(C_i, C_j)} \right) , \qquad (7.14)$$

- *Dunn Index* (DI):

$$\text{DI} = \min_{1 \le i \le k} \left\{ \min_{1 \le j \le k} \left(\frac{d_{min}(C_i, C_j)}{\max_{1 \le l \le k} diam(C_l)} \right) \right\} , \qquad (7.15)$$

- *Silhouette Index* (SI):

$$\text{SI} = \frac{1}{k} \sum_{i=1}^{k} \left(\frac{1}{|C_i|} \sum_{p=1}^{|C_i|} S_p^i \right) , \qquad (7.16)$$

where

$$S_p^i = \frac{a_p^i - b_p^i}{\max\left\{ a_p^i, b_p^i \right\}} , \qquad (7.17)$$

$$a_p^i = \min_{j \ne i} \left\{ \frac{1}{|C_j|} \sum_{q=1}^{|C_j|} dis(\boldsymbol{x}_p, \boldsymbol{x}_q) \right\} , \qquad (7.18)$$

$$b_p^i = \frac{1}{|C_i| - 1} \sum_{q \ne p} dis(\boldsymbol{x}_p, \boldsymbol{x}_q) . \qquad (7.19)$$

For DBI, the smaller the index value, the better the clustering quality; for DI and SI, the larger the index value, the better the clustering quality.

7.1.3 Why Clustering Ensembles

Clustering ensembles, also called **clusterer ensembles** or **consensus clustering**, are a kind of ensemble whose base learners are *clusterings*, also called *clusterers*, generated by clustering methods.

There are several general motivations for investigating clustering ensembles [Fred and Jain, 2002, Strehl and Ghosh, 2002]:

To Improve Clustering Quality. As we have seen in previous chapters, strong generalization ability can be obtained with ensemble methods for supervised learning tasks, as long as the base learners in the ensemble are accurate and diverse. Therefore, it is not surprising that better clustering quality can be anticipated if ensemble methods are also applied under unsupervised learning scenario.

For this purpose, a diverse ensemble of *good* base clusterings should be generated. It is interesting to notice that in clustering, it is less difficult to generate diverse clusterings, since clustering methods have inherent randomness. Diverse clusterings can be obtained by, for example, running clustering methods with different parameter configurations, with different initial data points, or with different data samples, etc. An ensemble is then derived by combining the outputs of the base clusterings, such that useful information encoded in each base clustering is fully leveraged to identify the final clustering with high quality.

To Improve Clustering Robustness. As introduced in Section 7.1.1, a clustering method groups the instances into clusters by assuming a specific structure on the data. Therefore, no single clustering method is guaranteed to be robust across all clustering tasks as the ground-truth structures of different data may vary significantly. Furthermore, due to the inherent randomness of many clustering methods, the clustering results may also be unstable if a single clustering method is applied to the same clustering task several times.

Therefore, it is intuitive to utilize clustering ensemble techniques to generate robust clustering results. Given any data set for clustering analysis, multiple base clusterings can be generated by running diverse clustering methods to accommodate various clustering assumptions, or invoking the same clustering method with different settings to compensate for the inherent randomness. Then, the derived ensemble may play more stably than a single clustering method.

To Enable Knowledge Reuse and Distributed Computing. In many applications, a variety of *legacy* clusterings for the data may already exist and can serve as the knowledge bases to be reused for future data exploration. It is also a common practice that the data are gathered and stored in distributed locations as a result of organizational or operational constraints, while performing clustering analysis by merging them into a centralized location is usually infeasible due to communication, computational and storage costs.

In such situations, it is rather natural to apply clustering ensemble techniques to exploit the multiple base clusterings. The legacy clusterings can directly serve as the base clusterings for further combination. While in the distributed setting, a base clustering can be generated on each distributively stored part of the data, and then the base clustering rather than the original data can be sent to a centralized location for a further exploitation.

7.2 Categorization of Clustering Ensemble Methods

Given the data $D = \{x_1, x_2, \ldots, x_m\}$ where the ith instance $x_i = (x_{i1}, x_{i2}, \ldots, x_{id})^\top \in \mathcal{R}^d$ is a d-dimensional feature vector, like ensemble methods in supervised learning setting, clustering ensemble methods also work in two steps:

1. **Clustering generation**: In this step, each base clusterer $\mathfrak{L}^{(q)}$ ($1 \leq q \leq r$) groups D into $k^{(q)}$ clusters $\{C_j^{(q)} \mid j = 1, 2, \ldots, k^{(q)}\}$. Equivalently, the clustering results returned by $\mathfrak{L}^{(q)}$ can be represented by a label vector $\lambda^{(q)} \in \mathcal{N}^m$, where the ith element $\lambda_i^{(q)} \in \{1, 2, \ldots, k^{(q)}\}$ indicates the cluster assignment of x_i.

2. **Clustering combination**: In this step, given the r base clusterings $\{\lambda^{(1)}, \lambda^{(2)}, \ldots, \lambda^{(r)}\}$, a combination function $\Gamma(\cdot)$ is used to consolidate them into the final clustering $\lambda = \Gamma(\{\lambda^{(1)}, \lambda^{(2)}, \ldots, \lambda^{(r)}\}) \in \mathcal{N}^m$ with k clusters, where $\lambda_i \in \{1, \ldots, k\}$ indicates the cluster assignment of x_i in the final clustering. For example, suppose four base clusterings of seven instances have been generated as follows,

$$\lambda^{(1)} = (1, 1, 2, 2, 2, 3, 3)^\top \qquad \lambda^{(2)} = (2, 3, 3, 2, 2, 1, 1)^\top$$

$$\lambda^{(3)} = (3, 3, 1, 1, 1, 2, 2)^\top \qquad \lambda^{(4)} = (1, 3, 3, 4, 4, 2, 2)^\top$$

where $\lambda^{(1)}$, $\lambda^{(2)}$ and $\lambda^{(3)}$ each groups the seven instances into three clusters, while $\lambda^{(4)}$ results in a clustering with four clusters. Furthermore, though $\lambda^{(1)}$ and $\lambda^{(3)}$ look very different at the first glance, they actually yield the identical clustering results, i.e., $\{\{x_1, x_2\}, \{x_3, x_4, x_5\}, \{x_6, x_7\}\}$. Then, a reasonable consensus (with three clusters) could be $(1, 1, 1, 2, 2, 3, 3)^\top$, or any of its six equivalent labelings such as $(2, 2, 2, 1, 1, 3, 3)^\top$, which shares *as much information as possible* with the four base clusterings in the ensemble [Strehl and Ghosh, 2002].

Generally speaking, clustering generation is relatively easier since any data partition generates a clustering, while the major difficulty of clustering ensembles lies in clustering combination. Specifically, for m instances with k clusters, the number of possible clusterings is $\frac{1}{k!} \sum_{j=1}^{k} C_j^k (-1)^{(k-j)} j^m$, or approximately $k^m/k!$ for $m \gg k$ [Jain and Dubes, 1988]. For example, there will be 171,798,901 ways to form four groups of only 16 instances [Strehl and Ghosh, 2002]. Therefore, a brute-force search over all the possible clusterings to find the optimal combined clustering is apparently infeasible and smart strategies are needed.

Most studies on clustering ensembles focus on the complicated clustering combination part. To successfully derive the ensemble clustering, the key lies in how the information embodied in each base clustering is *expressed* and *aggregated*. During the past decade, many clustering ensemble methods have been proposed. Roughly speaking, these methods can be classified into the following four categories:

- **Similarity-Based Methods**: A similarity-based method expresses the base clustering information as *similarity matrices* and then aggregates multiple clusterings via *matrix averaging*. Examples include [Fred and Jain, 2002, 2005, Strehl and Ghosh, 2002, Fern and Brodley, 2003].

- **Graph-Based Methods**: A graph-based method expresses the base clustering information as an *undirected graph* and then derives the ensemble clustering via *graph partitioning*. Examples include [Ayad and Kamel, 2003, Fern and Brodley, 2004, Strehl and Ghosh, 2002].

- **Relabeling-Based Methods**: A relabeling-based method expresses the base clustering information as *label vectors* and then aggregates via *label alignment*. Examples include [Long et al., 2005, Zhou and Tang, 2006].

- **Transformation-Based Methods**: A transformation-based method expresses the base clustering information as *features for re-representation* and then derives the ensemble clustering via *meta-clustering*. Examples include [Topchy et al., 2003, 2004a].

7.3   Similarity-Based Methods

The basic idea of similarity-based clustering ensemble methods is to exploit the base clusterings to form an $m \times m$ consensus **similarity matrix M**, and then generate the final clustering result based on the consensus similarity matrix. Intuitively, the matrix element $M(i, j)$ characterizes the similarity (or closeness) between the pair of instances x_i and x_j. The general procedure of similarity-based methods is shown in Figure 7.1.

A total of r base similarity matrices $M^{(q)}$ ($q = 1, \ldots, r$) are firstly obtained based on the clustering results of each base clusterer $\mathfrak{L}^{(q)}$ and then *averaged* to form the consensus similarity matrix. Generally, the base similarity matrix $M^{(q)}$ can be instantiated in two different ways according to how $\mathfrak{L}^{(q)}$ returns the clustering results, i.e., *crisp clustering* and *soft clustering*.

Crisp Clustering. In this setting, $\mathfrak{L}^{(q)}$ works by partitioning the data set D into $k^{(q)}$ *crisp* clusters, such as k-means [Strehl and Ghosh, 2002, Fred and

Input: Data set $D = \{x_1, x_2, \ldots, x_m\}$;
       Base clusterer $\mathfrak{L}^{(q)}$ $(q = 1, \ldots, r)$;
       Consensus clusterer $\mathfrak{L}$ on similarity matrix.
Process:
1. **for** $q = 1, \ldots, r$:
2. $\lambda^{(q)} = \mathfrak{L}^{(q)}(D)$; % Form a base clustering from D with $k^{(q)}$ clusters
3.   Derive an $m \times m$ base similarity matrix $\mathbf{M}^{(q)}$ based on $\lambda^{(q)}$;
4. **end**
5. $\mathbf{M} = \frac{1}{r} \sum_{q=1}^{r} \mathbf{M}^{(q)}$; % Form the consensus similarity matrix
6. $\lambda = \mathfrak{L}(\mathbf{M})$; % Form the ensemble clustering based on consensus
              % similarity matrix $\mathbf{M}$
Output: Ensemble clustering λ

FIGURE 7.1: The general procedure of similarity-based clustering ensemble methods.

Jain, 2002, 2005]. Here, each instance belongs to exactly one cluster. The base similarity matrix $\mathbf{M}^{(q)}$ can be set as $\mathbf{M}^{(q)}(i, j) = 1$ if $\lambda_i^{(q)} = \lambda_j^{(q)}$ and 0 otherwise. In other words, $\mathbf{M}^{(q)}$ corresponds to a binary matrix specifying whether each pair of instances co-occurs in the same cluster.

Soft Clustering. In this setting, $\mathfrak{L}^{(q)}$ works by grouping the data set D into $k^{(q)}$ *soft* clusters, such as GMM-based clustering [Fern and Brodley, 2003]. Here, the probability of x_i belonging to the lth cluster can be modeled as $P(l \mid i)$ with $\sum_{l=1}^{k^{(q)}} P(l \mid i) = 1$. The base similarity matrix $\mathbf{M}^{(q)}$ can be set as $\mathbf{M}^{(q)}(i, j) = \sum_{l=1}^{k^{(q)}} P(l \mid i) \cdot P(l \mid j)$. In other words, $\mathbf{M}^{(q)}$ corresponds to a real-valued matrix specifying the probability for each pair of instances to co-occur in any of the clusters.

After obtaining the consensus similarity matrix $\mathbf{M}$, the ensemble clustering λ can be derived from $\mathbf{M}$ by $\mathfrak{L}$ in a number of ways, such as running the single-linkage [Fred and Jain, 2002, 2005], complete-linkage [Fern and Brodley, 2003] or average-linkage [Fred and Jain, 2005] agglomerative clustering over D by taking $1 - \mathbf{M}(i, j)$ as the distance between x_i and x_j, or invoking partitioning clustering method [Strehl and Ghosh, 2002] over a similarity graph with x_i being the vertex and $\mathbf{M}(i, j)$ being the edge weight between vertices.

The most prominent advantage of similarity-based methods lies in their conceptual simplicity, since the similarity matrices are easy to be instantiated and aggregated. The consensus similarity matrix also offers much flexibility for subsequent analysis, where many existing clustering methods which operate on the similarity matrix can be applied to produce the final ensemble clustering.

The major disadvantage of similarity-based methods lies in their efficiency. The computational and storage complexities are both quadratic in m, i.e., the number of instances. Therefore, similarity-based methods can only deal with small or medium-scale problems, and will encounter difficulties in dealing with large-scale data.

7.4 Graph-Based Methods

The basic idea of graph-based clustering ensemble methods is to construct a graph $\mathcal{G} = (V, E)$ to integrate the clustering information conveyed by the base clusterings, and then identify the ensemble clustering by performing graph partitioning of the graph. Intuitively, the intrinsic grouping characteristics among all the instances are implicitly encoded in $\mathcal{G}$.

Given an ensemble of r base clusterings $\{\lambda^{(q)} \mid 1 \leq q \leq r\}$, where each $\lambda^{(q)}$ imposes $k^{(q)}$ clusters over the data set D, let $\mathcal{C} = \{C_l^{(q)} \mid 1 \leq q \leq r, 1 \leq l \leq k^{(q)}\}$ denote the set consisting of all the clusters in the base clusterings. Furthermore, let $k^* = |\mathcal{C}| = \sum_{q=1}^{r} k^{(q)}$ denote the size of $\mathcal{C}$, i.e., the total number of clusters in all base clusterings. Without loss of generality, clusters in $\mathcal{C}$ can be re-indexed as $\{C_j \mid 1 \leq j \leq k^*\}$. There are three alternative ways to construct the graph $\mathcal{G} = (V, E)$ based on how the vertex set V is configured, that is, $V = D$, $V = \mathcal{C}$ and $V = D \cup \mathcal{C}$.

$V = D$. In this setting, each vertex in V corresponds to a single data point $x_i \in D$ [Ayad and Kamel, 2003, Strehl and Ghosh, 2002]. HGPA (HyperGraph-Partitioning Algorithm) [Strehl and Ghosh, 2002] is a representative method within this category, whose pseudo-code is given in Figure 7.2.

Here, $\mathcal{G}$ is a **hypergraph** with equally weighted vertices. Given $\mathcal{C}$, HGPA regards each cluster $C \in \mathcal{C}$ as a **hyperedge** (connecting a set of vertices) and adds it into E. In this way, high-order (≥ 3) rather than only pairwise relationships between instances are incorporated in the hypergraph $\mathcal{G}$. The ensemble clustering λ is obtained by applying the HMETIS hypergraph partitioning package [Karypis et al., 1997] on $\mathcal{G}$, where a cut over a hyperedge C is counted if and only if the vertices in C fall into two or more groups as the partitioning process terminates, and the hyperedge-cut is minimized subject to the constraint that comparable-sized partitioned groups are favored.

$V = \mathcal{C}$. In this setting, each vertex in V corresponds to a set of data points $C \in \mathcal{C}$, i.e., one cluster in the base clusterings. Each edge in E is an ordinary edge connecting two vertices from different base clusterings. MCLA (Meta-

Input: Data set $D = \{x_1, x_2, \ldots, x_m\}$;
   Clusters in all the base clusterings $\mathcal{C} = \{C_j \mid 1 \leq j \leq k^*\}$.
Process:
1. $V = D$; % Set vertices v_i as instances x_i in D
2. $E = \emptyset$;
3. **for** $j = 1, \ldots, k^*$:
4. $E = E \bigcup \{C_j\}$;
5. **end**
6. $\mathcal{G} = (V, E)$;
7. $\lambda = \mathsf{HMETIS}(\mathcal{G})$; % Invoke HMETIS package [Karypis et al., 1997] on $\mathcal{G}$
Output: Ensemble clustering λ

FIGURE 7.2: The HGPA algorithm.

CLustering Algorithm) [Strehl and Ghosh, 2002] is a representative method within this category, whose pseudo-code is given in Figure 7.3.

Here, MCLA constructs $\mathcal{G}$ as a r-partite graph, where r is the number of base clusterings. Each edge is assigned with weight w_{ij} specifying the degree of overlap between two connecting clusters. The METIS package [Karypis and Kumar, 1998] is used to partition $\mathcal{G}$ into k balanced meta-clusters $C_p^{(M)}$ $(p = 1, \ldots, k)$, each characterized by an m-dimensional *indicator vector* $h_p^{(M)} = (h_{p1}^{(M)}, h_{p2}^{(M)}, \ldots, h_{pm}^{(M)})^\top$ expressing the level of association between instances and the meta-cluster. The ensemble clustering λ is then formed by assigning each instance to the meta-cluster mostly associated with it. Notice that it is not guaranteed that every meta-cluster can win for at least one instance, and ties are broken arbitrarily [Strehl and Ghosh, 2002].

$V = D \cup \mathcal{C}$. In this setting, each vertex in V corresponds to either a single data point $x_i \in D$ or a set of data points $C \in \mathcal{C}$. Each edge in E is an ordinary edge connecting two vertices with one from D and another from $\mathcal{C}$. HBGF (Hybrid Bipartite Graph Formulation) [Fern and Brodley, 2003] is a representative method within this category, whose pseudo-code is given in Figure 7.4.

Here, HBGF constructs $\mathcal{G}$ as a bi-partite graph with equally weighted edges. The ensemble clustering λ is obtained by applying the SPEC [Shi and Malik, 2000] or the METIS [Karypis and Kumar, 1998] graph partitioning package [Karypis et al., 1997] on $\mathcal{G}$. Here, the partitioning of the bi-partite graph groups the instance vertices as well as the cluster vertices simultaneously. Therefore, the partitions of the individual instances are returned as the final clustering results.

An appealing advantage of graph-based methods lies in their linear com-

Input: Data set $D = \{x_1, x_2, \ldots, x_m\}$;
　　　　　Clusters in all the base clusterings $\mathcal{C} = \{C_j \mid 1 \leq j \leq k^*\}$.

Process:
1.　$V = \mathcal{C}$; % Set vertices v_i as clusters C_i in $\mathcal{C}$
2.　$E = \emptyset$;
3.　**for** $i = 1, \ldots, k^*$:
4.　　**for** $j = 1, \ldots, k^*$:
5.　　　**if** C_i and C_j belong to different base clusterings
6.　　　**then** $E = E \cup \{e_{ij}\}$; % Add edge $e_{ij} = (v_i, v_j)$
7.　　　　$w_{ij} = |C_i \cap C_j| / (|C_i| + |C_j| - |C_i \cap C_j|)$; % Set weight for e_{ij}
8.　　**end**
9.　**end**
10. $\mathcal{G} = (V, E)$;
11. $\{C_1^{(M)}, C_2^{(M)}, \ldots, C_k^{(M)}\} = \mathsf{METIS}(\mathcal{G})$;
　　　　　% Invoke METIS package [Karypis and Kumar, 1998] on
　　　　　% $\mathcal{G}$ to induce meta-clusters $C_p^{(M)}$ $(p = 1, \ldots, k)$
12. **for** $p = 1, \ldots, k$:
13.　**for** $i = 1, \ldots, m$:
14.　　$h_{pi}^{(M)} = \sum_{C \in C_p^{(M)}} \mathbb{I}(x_i \in C) / |C_p^{(M)}|$;
15.　**end**
16. **end**
17. **for** $i = 1, \ldots, m$:
18.　$\lambda_i = \arg\max_{p \in \{1, \ldots, k\}} h_{pi}^{(M)}$;
19. **end**
Output: Ensemble clustering λ

FIGURE 7.3: The MCLA algorithm.

putational complexity in m, the number of instances. Thus, this category of methods provides a practical choice for clustering analysis on large-scale data. In addition, graph-based methods are able to handle more complicated interactions between instances beyond pairwise relationships, e.g., the high-order relationship encoded by hyperedges in HGPA.

The major deficiency of graph-based methods is that the performance heavily relies on the graph partitioning method that is used to produce the ensemble clustering. Since graph partitioning techniques are not designed for clustering tasks and the partitioned clusters are just by-products of the graph partitioning process, the quality of the ensemble clustering can be impaired. Moreover, most graph partitioning methods such as HMETIS [Karypis et al., 1997] have the constraint that each cluster contains approximately the same number of instances, and thus, the final ensemble clustering would become inappropriate if the intrinsic data clusters are highly

Input: Data set $D = \{x_1, x_2, \ldots, x_m\}$;
Clusters in all the base clusterings $C = \{C_j \mid 1 \leq j \leq k^*\}$;
Graph partitioning package $\mathcal{L}$ (SPEC [Shi and Malik, 2000] or METIS [Karypis and Kumar, 1998]).

Process:
1. $V = D \bigcup C$; % Set vertices v_i as instances x_i in D or clusters C_i in C
2. $E = \emptyset$;
3. **for** $i = 1, \ldots, m$:
4.   **for** $j = 1, \ldots, k^*$:
5.   **if** $v_i \in v_j$ % v_i being an instance in D; v_j being a cluster in C
6.   **then** $E = E \bigcup \{e_{ij}\}$; % Add edge $e_{ij} = (v_i, v_j)$
7. $w_{ij} = 1$; % Set equal weight for e_{ij}
8.   **end**
9. **end**
10. $\mathcal{G} = (V, E)$;
11. $\lambda = \mathcal{L}(\mathcal{G})$; % Invoke the specified graph partitioning package on $\mathcal{G}$
Output: Ensemble clustering λ

FIGURE 7.4: The HBGF algorithm.

imbalanced.

7.5 Relabeling-Based Methods

The basic idea of relabeling-based clustering ensemble methods is to *align* or *relabel* the cluster labels of all base clusterings, such that the same label denotes similar clusters across the base clusterings, and then derive the final ensemble clustering based on the aligned labels.

Notice that unlike supervised learning where the class labels represent specific classes, in unsupervised learning the cluster labels only express grouping characteristics of the data and are not directly comparable across different clusterings. For example, given two clusterings $\lambda^{(1)} = (1, 1, 2, 2, 3, 3, 1)^\top$ and $\lambda^{(2)} = (2, 2, 3, 3, 1, 1, 2)^\top$, though the cluster labels for each instance differ across the two clusterings, $\lambda^{(1)}$ and $\lambda^{(2)}$ are in fact identical. It is obvious that the labels of different clusterings should be aligned, or relabeled, based on label correspondence. Relabeling-based methods have two alternative settings according to the type of label correspondence to be established, i.e., crisp label correspondence and soft label correspondence.

Crisp Label Correspondence. In this setting, each base clustering is as-

---

Input: Data set $D = \{x_1, x_2, \ldots, x_m\}$;
$\qquad$ Base clusterings $\Lambda = \{\lambda^{(1)}, \lambda^{(2)}, \ldots, \lambda^{(r)}\}$ each with k clusters.

Process:

1. Randomly select $\lambda^{(b)} = \{C_l^{(b)} \mid l = 1, \ldots, k\}$ in Λ as *reference* clustering;
2. $\Lambda = \Lambda - \{\lambda^{(b)}\}$;
3. **repeat**
4. $\qquad$ Randomly select $\lambda^{(q)} = \{C_l^{(q)} \mid l = 1, \ldots, k\}$ in Λ to *align* with $\lambda^{(b)}$;
5. $\qquad$ Initialize $k \times k$ matrix $\mathbf{O}$ with $\mathbf{O}(u,v) = \left| C_u^{(b)} \cap C_v^{(q)} \right|$ $(1 \le u, v \le k)$;
$\qquad\qquad$ % Count instances shared by clusters in $\lambda^{(b)}$ and $\lambda^{(q)}$
6. $\qquad \mathcal{I} = \{(u,v) \mid 1 \le u, v \le k\}$;
7. $\qquad$ **repeat**
8. $\qquad\qquad (u', v') = \arg\max_{(u,v)\in\mathcal{I}} \mathbf{O}(u,v)$;
9. $\qquad\qquad$ Relabel $C_{v'}^{(q)}$ as $C_{u'}^{(q)}$;
10. $\qquad\qquad \mathcal{I} = \mathcal{I} - \{(u',w) \mid (u',w) \in \mathcal{I}\} \cup \{(w,v') \mid (w,v') \in \mathcal{I}\}$;
11. $\qquad$ **until** $\mathcal{I} = \emptyset$
12. $\qquad \Lambda = \Lambda - \{\lambda^{(q)}\}$;
13. **until** $\Lambda = \emptyset$;

Output: Relabeled clusterings $\{\lambda^{(q)} \mid 1 \le q \le r\}$ with aligned cluster labels

---

FIGURE 7.5: The relabeling process for crisp label correspondence [Zhou and Tang, 2006].

sumed to group data set $D = \{x_1, x_2, \ldots, x_m\}$ into an equal number of clusters, i.e., $k^{(q)} = k$ $(q = 1, \ldots, r)$. As a representative, the method described in [Zhou and Tang, 2006] aligns cluster labels as shown in Figure 7.5.

In [Zhou and Tang, 2006], clusters in different clusterings are iteratively aligned based on the recognition that similar clusters should contain similar instances. The task of matching two clusterings, e.g., $\lambda^{(q)}$ and $\lambda^{(b)}$, can also be accomplished by formulating it as a standard *assignment problem* [Kuhn, 1955], where the cost of assigning cluster $C_v^{(q)} \in \lambda^{(q)}$ to cluster $C_u^{(b)} \in \lambda^{(b)}$ can be set as $m - |C_u^{(b)} \cap C_v^{(q)}|$. Then, the *minimum cost* one-to-one assignment problem can be solved by the popular *Hungarian algorithm* [Topchy et al., 2004b, Hore et al., 2009].

After the labels of different base clusterings have been relabeled, strategies for combining classifiers can be applied to derive the final ensemble clustering λ. Let $\lambda_i^{(q)} \in \{1, \ldots, k\}$ denote the cluster label of x_i $(i = 1, \ldots, m)$ in the *aligned* base clustering $\lambda^{(q)}$ $(q = 1, \ldots, r)$, four strategies are described in [Zhou and Tang, 2006] to derive λ:

- *Simple Voting*: The ensemble clustering label λ_i of x_i is simply determined by

$$\lambda_i = \underset{l\in\{1,\ldots,k\}}{\arg\max} \sum_{q=1}^{r} \mathbb{I}(\lambda_i^{(q)} = l). \tag{7.20}$$

- *Weighted Voting*: The mutual information between a pair of cluster-ings [Strehl et al., 2000] is employed to derive the weight for each $\lambda^{(q)}$. Given two base clusterings $\lambda^{(p)}$ and $\lambda^{(q)}$, let $m_u = |C_u^{(p)}|$, $m_v = |C_v^{(q)}|$ and $m_{uv} = |C_u^{(p)} \cap C_v^{(q)}|$. The [0,1]-normalized mutual information Φ^{NMI} between $\lambda^{(p)}$ and $\lambda^{(q)}$ can be defined as

$$\Phi^{\mathrm{NMI}}(\lambda^{(p)}, \lambda^{(q)}) = \frac{2}{m} \sum_{u=1}^{k} \sum_{v=1}^{k} m_{uv} \log_{k^2}\left(\frac{m_{uv} \cdot m}{m_u \cdot m_v}\right). \tag{7.21}$$

Other kinds of definitions can be found in [Strehl and Ghosh, 2002, Fred and Jain, 2005]. Then, for each base clustering, the average mutual information can be calculated as

$$\beta^{(q)} = \frac{1}{r-1} \sum_{p=1, p\neq q}^{r} \Phi^{\mathrm{NMI}}(\lambda^{(p)}, \lambda^{(q)}) \ (q = 1, \ldots, r). \tag{7.22}$$

Intuitively, the larger the $\beta^{(q)}$ value, the less statistical information contained in $\lambda^{(q)}$ while not contained in other base clusterings [Zhou and Tang, 2006]. Thus, the weight for $\lambda^{(q)}$ can be defined as

$$w^{(q)} = \frac{1}{Z \cdot \beta^{(q)}} \ (q = 1, \ldots, r), \tag{7.23}$$

where Z is a normalizing factor such that $\sum_{q=1}^{r} w^{(q)} = 1$. Finally, the ensemble clustering label λ_i of x_i is determined by

$$\lambda_i = \underset{l\in\{1,\ldots,k\}}{\arg\max} \sum_{q=1}^{r} w^{(q)} \cdot \mathbb{I}(\lambda_i^{(q)} = l). \tag{7.24}$$

- *Selective Voting*: This is a strategy which incorporates ensemble prun-ing. In [Zhou and Tang, 2006], the mutual information weights $\{w^{(q)} \mid q = 1, \ldots, r\}$ are used to select the base clusterings for combination, where the base clusterings with weights smaller than a threshold w_{thr} are excluded from the ensemble. Zhou and Tang [2006] simply set $w_{thr} = \frac{1}{r}$. Let $\mathcal{Q} = \{q \mid w^{(q)} \geq \frac{1}{r}, 1 \leq q \leq r\}$, then the ensemble clus-tering label λ_i of x_i is determined by

$$\lambda_i = \underset{l\in\{1,\ldots,k\}}{\arg\max} \sum_{q\in\mathcal{Q}} \mathbb{I}(\lambda_i^{(q)} = l). \tag{7.25}$$

- *Selective Weighted Voting*: This is a weighted version of selective voting, where the ensemble clustering label λ_i of x_i is determined by

$$\lambda_i = \underset{l \in \{1,\dots,k\}}{\arg\max} \sum_{q \in Q} w^{(q)} \cdot \mathbb{I}(\lambda_i^{(q)} = l). \tag{7.26}$$

It was reported in [Zhou and Tang, 2006] that the selective weighted voting leads to the best empirical results, where the weighted voting and selective voting both contribute to performance improvement.

Soft Label Correspondence. In this setting, each base clustering is assumed to group the data set D into an *arbitrary* number of clusters, i.e., $k^{(q)} \in \mathcal{N}$ $(q = 1, \dots, r)$. Each base clustering $\lambda^{(q)} = \{C_l^{(q)} \mid l = 1, 2, \dots, k^{(q)}\}$ can be represented as an $m \times k^{(q)}$ matrix $\mathbf{A}^{(q)}$, where $\mathbf{A}^{(q)}(i, l) = 1$ if $x_i \in C_l^{(q)}$ and 0 otherwise. Given two base clusterings $\lambda^{(p)}$ and $\lambda^{(q)}$, a $k^{(p)} \times k^{(q)}$ *soft correspondence* matrix $\mathbf{S}$ is assumed to model the correspondence relationship between clusters of each clustering. Here, $\mathbf{S} \succeq 0$ and $\sum_{v=1}^{k^{(q)}} \mathbf{S}(u, v) = 1$ $(u = 1, 2, \dots, k^{(p)})$. Intuitively, with the help of $\mathbf{S}$, the membership matrix $\mathbf{A}^{(p)}$ for $\lambda^{(p)}$ can be mapped to the membership matrix $\mathbf{A}^{(q)}$ for $\lambda^{(q)}$ by $\mathbf{A}^{(p)}\mathbf{S}$. The quality of this mapping can be measured by the **Frobenius matrix norm** between $\mathbf{A}^{(q)}$ and $\mathbf{A}^{(p)}\mathbf{S}$, i.e., $||\mathbf{A}^{(q)} - \mathbf{A}^{(p)}\mathbf{S}||_F^2$. The smaller the Frobenius norm, the more precisely the soft correspondence matrix $\mathbf{S}$ captures the relation between $\mathbf{A}^{(p)}$ and $\mathbf{A}^{(q)}$.

Given r base clusterings with membership matrices $\mathbf{A}^{(1)} \in \mathcal{R}^{m \times k^{(1)}}, \dots,$ $\mathbf{A}^{(r)} \in \mathcal{R}^{m \times k^{(r)}}$ and the number of k, as a representative, the SCEC (Soft Correspondence Ensemble Clustering) method [Long et al., 2005] aims to find the final ensemble clustering $\mathbf{A} \in \mathcal{R}^{m \times k}$ together with r soft correspondence matrices $\mathbf{S}^{(1)} \in \mathcal{R}^{k^{(1)} \times k}, \dots, \mathbf{S}^{(r)} \in \mathcal{R}^{k^{(r)} \times k}$ by minimizing the objective function

$$\min \sum_{q=1}^{r} ||\mathbf{A} - \mathbf{A}^{(q)}\mathbf{S}^{(q)}||_F^2 \tag{7.27}$$

$$\text{s.t. } \mathbf{S}^{(q)}(u, v) \geq 0 \text{ and } \sum_{v=1}^{k} \mathbf{S}^{(q)}(u, v) = 1 \quad \forall q, u, v.$$

This optimization problem can be solved by the **alternating optimization** strategy, i.e., optimizing $\mathbf{A}$ and each $\mathbf{S}^{(q)}$ one at a time by fixing the others. Rather than directly optimizing (7.27), SCEC chooses to make two modifications to the above objective function. First, as the minimizer of (7.27) may converge to a final ensemble clustering $\mathbf{A}$ with unreasonably small number of clusters (i.e., resulting in many all-zero columns in $\mathbf{A}$), a *column-sparseness* constraint is enforced on each $\mathbf{S}^{(q)}$ to help produce an $\mathbf{A}$ with as many clusters as possible. Specifically, the sum of the variation of each column of $\mathbf{S}^{(q)}$ is a good measure of its column-sparseness [Long et al., 2005],

Input: Data set $D = \{x_1, x_2, \ldots, x_m\}$;
   Base clusterings $\Lambda = \{\lambda^{(1)}, \lambda^{(2)}, \ldots, \lambda^{(r)}\}$ each with $k^{(q)}$ clusters;
   Integer k, coefficients α, β, small positive constant ϵ.

Process:
1. **for** $q = 1, \ldots, r$:
2.   Form an $m \times k^{(q)}$ membership matrix $\mathbf{A}^{(q)}$, where $\mathbf{A}^{(q)}(i, l) = 1$ if $x_i \in C_l^{(q)}$ and 0 otherwise; % $\lambda^{(q)} = \{C_l^{(q)} \mid l = 1, 2, \ldots, k^{(q)}\}$
3.   Randomly initialize a $k^{(q)} \times k$ soft correspondence matrix $\mathbf{S}^{(q)}$ with $\mathbf{S}^{(q)} \succeq 0$;
4. **end**
5. **repeat**
6. $\mathbf{A} = \frac{1}{r} \sum_{q=1}^{r} \mathbf{A}^{(q)} \mathbf{S}^{(q)}$; % By setting $\frac{\partial f}{\partial \mathbf{A}} = 0$ with f being the
          % objective function in (7.28)
7.   **for** $q = 1, \ldots, r$:
8. $\mathbf{S}^{(q)} = \mathbf{S}^{(q)} \odot \frac{(\mathbf{A}^{(q)})^\top \mathbf{A} + \beta k \mathbf{1}_{k^{(q)} k}}{\mathbf{B} + \epsilon \cdot \mathbf{1}_{k^{(q)} k}}$, where
       $\mathbf{B} = (\mathbf{A}^{(q)})^\top \mathbf{A}^{(q)} \mathbf{S}^{(q)} - \alpha \mathbf{S}^{(q)} + \frac{\alpha}{k^{(q)}} \mathbf{1}_{k^{(q)} k^{(q)}} \mathbf{S}^{(q)} + \beta k \mathbf{S}^{(q)} \mathbf{1}_{kk}$
9.   **end**
10. **until** convergence;

Output: Membership matrix $\mathbf{A}$ for ensemble clustering

FIGURE 7.6: The SCEC method.

i.e., the larger the value of $||\mathbf{S}^{(q)} - \frac{1}{k^{(q)}} \mathbf{1}_{k^{(q)} k^{(q)}} \mathbf{S}^{(q)}||_F^2$, the more column-sparse the $\mathbf{S}^{(q)}$. Here, $\mathbf{1}_{k^{(q)} k^{(q)}}$ is a $k^{(q)} \times k^{(q)}$ matrix with all ones. Second, as it is hard to handle the normalization constraint $\sum_{v=1}^{k} \mathbf{S}^{(q)}(u, v) = 1$ efficiently, it is transformed into a soft constraint by adding a penalty term to (7.27) with $\sum_{q=1}^{r} ||\mathbf{S}^{(q)} \mathbf{1}_{kk} - \mathbf{1}_{k^{(q)} k}||_F^2$. Now, the objective function of SCEC becomes

$$\min \sum_{q=1}^{r} ||\mathbf{A} - \mathbf{A}^{(q)} \mathbf{S}^{(q)}||_F^2 \tag{7.28}$$

$$- \alpha ||\mathbf{S}^{(q)} - \frac{1}{k^{(q)}} \mathbf{1}_{k^{(q)} k^{(q)}} \mathbf{S}^{(q)}||_F^2 + \beta ||\mathbf{S}^{(q)} \mathbf{1}_{kk} - \mathbf{1}_{k^{(q)} k}||_F^2$$

$$\text{s.t. } \mathbf{S}^{(q)}(u, v) \geq 0 \ \ \forall q, u, v,$$

where α and β are coefficients balancing different terms. Like (7.27), the modified objective function (7.28) can be solved by the alternative optimization process [Long et al., 2005] as shown in Figure 7.6. Specifically (step 8), the division between two matrices is performed in an element-wise manner, and $\odot$ denotes the *Hadamard product* of two matrices. It has been proven that (7.28) is guaranteed to reach a local minimum based on the given alternative optimization process [Long et al., 2005].

An advantage of relabeling-based methods is that they offer the possibility of investigating the connections between different base clusterings, which may be helpful in studying the implications of the clustering results. In particular, in crisp label correspondence, the reference clustering can be viewed as a profiling structure of the data set; while in soft label correspondence, the learned correspondence matrices provide intuitive interpretations to the relations between the ensemble clustering and each base clustering.

A deficiency of relabeling-based methods is that if there is no reasonable correspondence among the base clusterings, they may not work well. Moreover, the crisp label correspondence methods require each base clustering to have identical number of clusters, and it may result in a final ensemble clustering with fewer clusters than the base clusterings. The soft label correspondence methods need to solve an optimization problem involving numerous variables, and this is prone to get stuck in a local minimum far from the optimal solution.

7.6 Transformation-Based Methods

The basic idea of transformation-based clustering ensemble methods is to re-represent each instance as an r-tuple, where r is the number of base clusterings and the qth element indicates its cluster assignment given by the qth base clustering, and then derive the final ensemble clustering by performing clustering analysis over the transformed r-tuples.

For example, suppose there are four base clusterings over five instances, e.g., $\lambda^{(1)} = \{1,1,2,2,3\}$, $\lambda^{(2)} = \{1,2,2,2,3\}$, $\lambda^{(3)} = \{2,2,3,1,3\}$ and $\lambda^{(4)} = \{3,1,3,2,3\}$. Then, based on the transformation process, $\boldsymbol{x}_i$ will be transformed into the r-tuple $\varphi(\boldsymbol{x}_i)$ ($r = 4$) as: $\varphi(\boldsymbol{x}_1) = (\varphi_1(\boldsymbol{x}_1), \varphi_2(\boldsymbol{x}_1), \varphi_3(\boldsymbol{x}_1), \varphi_4(\boldsymbol{x}_1))^\top = (1,1,2,3)^\top$, and similarly, $\varphi(\boldsymbol{x}_2) = (1,2,2,1)^\top$, $\varphi(\boldsymbol{x}_3) = (2,2,3,3)^\top$, $\varphi(\boldsymbol{x}_4) = (2,2,1,2)^\top$ and $\varphi(\boldsymbol{x}_5) = (3,3,3,3)^\top$.

Each transformed r-tuple $\varphi(\boldsymbol{x}) = (\varphi_1(\boldsymbol{x}), \varphi_2(\boldsymbol{x}), \dots, \varphi_r(\boldsymbol{x}))^\top$ can be regarded as a categorical vector, where $\varphi_q(\boldsymbol{x}) \in \mathcal{K}^{(q)} = \{1, 2, \dots, k^{(q)}\}$ ($q = 1, \dots, r$). Any categorical clustering technique can then be applied to group the transformed r-tuples to identify the final ensemble clustering. For example, one can define a similarity function $sim(\cdot, \cdot)$ between the transformed r-tuples, e.g.,

$$sim(\varphi(\boldsymbol{x}_i), \varphi(\boldsymbol{x}_j)) = \sum_{q=1}^{r} \mathbb{I}(\varphi_q(\boldsymbol{x}_i) = \varphi_q(\boldsymbol{x}_j)), \qquad (7.29)$$

and then use traditional clustering methods such as k-means to identify the final ensemble clustering [Topchy et al., 2003].

The task of clustering categorical data can also be equivalently transformed into the task of creating a clustering ensemble, where the qth categorical feature with $k^{(q)}$ possible values can naturally give rise to a base clustering with $k^{(q)}$ clusters [He et al., 2005].

Besides resorting to categorical clustering techniques, the task of clustering the transformed r-tuples can also be tackled directly in a probabilistic framework [Topchy et al., 2004a], as introduced in the following.

Given r base clusterings $\lambda^{(q)}$ $(q = 1, \ldots, r)$ over the data set D, let $\boldsymbol{y} = (y_1, y_2, \ldots, y_r)^\top \in \mathcal{K}^{(1)} \times \mathcal{K}^{(2)} \cdots \times \mathcal{K}^{(r)}$ denote the r-dimensional *random vector*, and $\boldsymbol{y}_i = \varphi(\boldsymbol{x}_i) = (y_1^i, y_2^i, \ldots, y_r^i)^\top$ denote the transformed r-tuple for $\boldsymbol{x}_i$. The random vector $\boldsymbol{y}$ is modeled by a mixture of *multinomial distributions*, i.e.,

$$P(\boldsymbol{y} \mid \boldsymbol{\Theta}) = \sum_{j=1}^{k} \alpha_j P_j(\boldsymbol{y} \mid \boldsymbol{\theta}_j), \tag{7.30}$$

where k is the number of mixture components which also corresponds to the number of clusters in the final ensemble clustering. Each mixture component is parameterized by $\boldsymbol{\theta}_j$ and $\boldsymbol{\Theta} = \{\alpha_j, \boldsymbol{\theta}_j \mid j = 1, \ldots, k\}$. Assume that the components of $\boldsymbol{y}$ are conditionally independent, i.e.,

$$P_j(\boldsymbol{y} \mid \boldsymbol{\theta}_j) = \prod_{q=1}^{r} P_j^{(q)}(y_q \mid \boldsymbol{\theta}_j^{(q)}) \ (1 \leq j \leq k). \tag{7.31}$$

Moreover, the conditional probability $P_j^{(q)}(y_q \mid \boldsymbol{\theta}_j^{(q)})$ is viewed as the outcome of one multinomial try, i.e.,

$$P_j^{(q)}(y_q \mid \boldsymbol{\theta}_j^{(q)}) = \prod_{l=1}^{k^{(q)}} \vartheta_{qj}(l)^{\delta(y_q, l)}, \tag{7.32}$$

where $k^{(q)}$ is the number of clusters in the qth base clustering and $\delta(\cdot, \cdot)$ represents the Kronecker delta function. The probabilities of the $k^{(q)}$ multinomial outcomes are defined as $\vartheta_{qj}(l)$ with $\sum_{l=1}^{k^{(q)}} \vartheta_{qj}(l) = 1$, and thus, $\boldsymbol{\theta}_j = \{\vartheta_{qj}(l) \mid 1 \leq q \leq r, 1 \leq l \leq k^{(q)}\}$.

Based on the above assumptions, the optimal parameter $\boldsymbol{\Theta}^*$ is found by maximizing the log-likelihood function with regard to the m transformed r-tuples $\boldsymbol{Y} = \{\boldsymbol{y}_i \mid 1 \leq i \leq m\}$, i.e.,

$$\boldsymbol{\Theta}^* = \arg\max_{\boldsymbol{\Theta}} \log L(\boldsymbol{Y} \mid \boldsymbol{\Theta}) = \arg\max_{\boldsymbol{\Theta}} \log \left(\prod_{i=1}^{m} P(\boldsymbol{y}_i \mid \boldsymbol{\Theta}) \right)$$

$$= \arg\max_{\boldsymbol{\Theta}} \sum_{i=1}^{m} \log \left(\sum_{j=1}^{k} \alpha_j P_j(\boldsymbol{y}_i \mid \boldsymbol{\theta}_j) \right). \tag{7.33}$$

Input: Data set $D = \{x_1, x_2, \ldots, x_m\}$;
       Base clusterings $\Lambda = \{\lambda^{(1)}, \lambda^{(2)}, \ldots, \lambda^{(r)}\}$ each with $k^{(q)}$ clusters;
       Integer k.

Process:
1. **for** $i = 1, \ldots, m$:
2.   **for** $q = 1, \ldots, r$:
3. $y_q^i = \lambda_i^{(q)}$;
4.   **end**
5. $\varphi(x_i) = (y_1^i, y_2^i, \ldots, y_r^i)^\top$;   % Set the transformed r-tuple for x_i
6. **end**
7. Initialize α_j $(1 \leq j \leq k)$ with $\alpha_j \geq 0$ and $\sum_{j=1}^{k} \alpha_j = 1$;
8. **for** $j = 1, \ldots, k$:
9.   **for** $q = 1, \ldots, r$:
10.   Initialize $\vartheta_{qj}(l)$ $(1 \leq l \leq k^{(q)})$ with $\vartheta_{qj}(l) \geq 0$ and
         $\sum_{l=1}^{k^{(q)}} \vartheta_{qj}(l) = 1$;
11.   **end**
12. **end**
13. **repeat**

14. $\mathbb{E}[z_{ij}] = \dfrac{\alpha_j \prod_{q=1}^{r} \prod_{l=1}^{k^{(q)}} (\vartheta_{qj}(l))^{\delta(y_q^i, l)}}{\sum_{j=1}^{k} \alpha_j \prod_{q=1}^{r} \prod_{l=1}^{k^{(q)}} (\vartheta_{qj}(l))^{\delta(y_q^i, l)}}$;   % E-step

15. $\alpha_j = \dfrac{\sum_{i=1}^{m} \mathbb{E}[z_{ij}]}{\sum_{i=1}^{m} \sum_{j=1}^{k} \mathbb{E}[z_{ij}]}$; $\vartheta_{qj}(l) = \dfrac{\sum_{i=1}^{m} \delta(y_q^i, l) \mathbb{E}[z_{ij}]}{\sum_{i=1}^{m} \sum_{l=1}^{k^{(q)}} \delta(y_q^i, l) \mathbb{E}[z_{ij}]}$;   % M-step

16. **until** convergence;
17. $\lambda_i = \arg\max_{1 \leq j \leq k} \alpha_j P_j(\varphi(x_i) \mid \theta_j)$;   % c.f.: (7.30)−(7.32)

Output: Ensemble clustering λ

FIGURE 7.7: The EM procedure for the transformation-based method [Topchy et al., 2004a] within probabilistic framework.

The EM algorithm is used to solve (7.33). To facilitate the EM procedure, the hidden variables $\mathbf{Z} = \{z_{ij} \mid 1 \leq i \leq m, \; 1 \leq j \leq k\}$ are introduced, where $z_{ij} = 1$ if y_i belongs to the jth mixture component and 0 otherwise. Figure 7.7 illustrates the detailed EM procedure given in [Topchy et al., 2004a].

An advantage of the transformation-based methods is that they are usually easy to implement, since the re-representation of the instances using the base clustering information is rather direct, and any off-the-shelf categorical clustering techniques can be applied to the transformed tuples to compute the final ensemble clustering.

A deficiency of these methods lies in that when re-representing each instance into a categorical tuple, it is possible that the transformed data could not fully encode the information embodied in the original data representation. Therefore, it is by no means guaranteed that the clustering results obtained from the transformed data resemble exactly the desired ensemble clustering from the original base clusterings.

7.7 Further Readings

A lot of clustering methods have been developed. In addition to k-means, famous partitioning methods include k-medoids [Kaufman and Rousseeuw, 1990] whose cluster centers are exactly training instances, k-modes [Huang, 1998] for categorical data, CLARANS [Ng and Han, 1994] for large-scale data, etc. In addition to SAHN, famous hierarchical clustering methods include AGNES [Kaufman and Rousseeuw, 1990] which can be regarded as a particular version of SAHN, DIANA [Kaufman and Rousseeuw, 1990] which forms the hierarchy in a *top-down* manner, BIRCH [Zhang et al., 1996] which integrates hierarchical clustering with other clustering methods, ROCK [Guha et al., 1999] which was designed for categorical data, etc. In addition to DBSCAN, famous density-based methods include OPTICS [Ankerst et al., 1999] which augments DBSCAN with an ordering of clusters, DENCLUE [Hinneburg and Keim, 1998] which utilizes density distribution functions, etc. In addition to STING, famous grid-based methods include WaveCluster [Sheikholeslami et al., 1998] which exploits wavelet transformation, CLIQUE [Agrawal et al., 1998] which was designed for high-dimensional data, etc. In addition to GMM-based clustering, famous model-based methods include SOM [Kohonen, 1989] which forms clusters by mapping from high-dimensional space into lower-dimensional (2d or 3d) space with the neural network model of *self-organizing maps*, COBWEB [Fisher, 1987] which clusters categorical data incrementally, etc. There are so many clustering methods partially because users may have very different motivations to cluster even the same data, where there is no unique objective, and therefore, once a new criterion is given, a new clustering method can be proposed [Estivill-Castro, 2002].

In addition to the cluster quality indices introduced in Section 7.1.2, Jain and Dubes [1988], Halkidi et al. [2001] also provide introduction to many other indices such as the external indices *adjusted Rand index, Huberts Γ statistic* and the internal indices *C index* and *Hartigan index* .

Clustering ensemble techniques have already been applied to many tasks, such as image segmentation [Zhang et al., 2008], gene expression data analysis [Avogadri and Valentini, 2009, Hu et al., 2009, Yu and Wong, 2009], etc. Though there are many works on developing clustering ensemble methods, only a few studies have been devoted to the theoretical aspects. Topchy et al. [2004c] provided a theoretical justification for the usefulness of clustering ensemble under strong assumptions. Kuncheva and Vetrov [2006] studied the stability issue of clustering ensemble with k-means.

In contrast to supervised learning where the "accuracy" has a clear meaning, in unsupervised learning there is no unique equivalent concept. Therefore, the study of the accuracy-diversity relation of clustering ensemble is rather difficult. Hadjitodorov and Kuncheva [2007], Hadjitodorov et al. [2006], Kuncheva and Hadjitodorov [2004], Kuncheva et al. [2006] presented some attempts towards this direction. There are some recent studies on other advanced topics such as clustering ensemble pruning [Fern and Lin, 2008, Hong et al., 2009], scalable clustering ensemble [Hore et al., 2006, 2009], etc.

8

Advanced Topics

8.1 Semi-Supervised Learning

8.1.1 Usefulness of Unlabeled Data

The great advances in data collection and storage technology enable the accumulation of a large amount of data in many real-world applications. Assigning labels to these data, however, is expensive because the labeling process requires human efforts and expertise. For example, in computer-aided medical diagnosis, a large number of x-ray images can be obtained from routine examination, yet it is difficult to ask physicians to mark all focuses of infection in all images. If we use traditional supervised learning techniques to construct a diagnosis system, then only a small portion of training data, on which the focuses have been marked, are useful. Due to the limited amount of labeled training examples, it may be difficult to attain a strong diagnosis system. Thus, a question naturally arises: Can we leverage the abundant unlabeled data with a few labeled training examples to construct a strong learning system?

Semi-supervised learning deals with methods for exploiting unlabeled data in addition to labeled data automatically to improve learning performance. Suppose the data are drawn from an unknown distribution $\mathcal{D}$ over the instance space $\mathcal{X}$ and the label space $\mathcal{Y}$. In semi-supervised learning, a labeled data set $L = \{(\boldsymbol{x}_1, y_1), (\boldsymbol{x}_2, y_2), \ldots, (\boldsymbol{x}_l, y_l)\}$ and an unlabeled data set $U = \{\boldsymbol{x}_{l+1}, \boldsymbol{x}_{l+2}, \ldots, \boldsymbol{x}_m\}$ are given, where $\boldsymbol{x}_i \in \mathcal{X}$ and $y_i \in \mathcal{Y}$ and generally $l \ll m$, and the task is to learn $H : \mathcal{X} \to \mathcal{Y}$. For simplicity, consider binary classification tasks where $\mathcal{Y} = \{-1, +1\}$.

It is interesting to know why unlabeled data, which do not contain labels, can be helpful to supervised learning. Figure 8.1 provides an illustration. It can be seen that though both the classification boundaries are perfectly consistent with the labeled data points, the boundary obtained by considering unlabeled data is better in generalization. In fact, since both the unlabeled data U and the labeled data L are drawn from the same distribution $\mathcal{D}$, unlabeled data can disclose some information on data distribution which is helpful for constructing a model with good generalization ability.

Indeed, semi-supervised learning approaches work by taking assump-

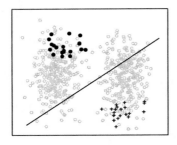   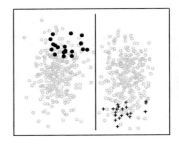

(a) Without unlabeled data   (b) With unlabeled data

FIGURE 8.1: Illustration of the usefulness of unlabeled data. The optimal classification boundary without/with considering unlabeled data are plotted, respectively.

tions on how the distribution information disclosed by unlabeled data is connected with the label information. There are two basic assumptions, i.e., the **cluster assumption** and the **manifold assumption**. The former assumes that data with similar inputs should have similar class labels; the latter assumes that the data live in a low-dimensional manifold while the unlabeled data can help to identify that manifold. The cluster assumption concerns classification, while the manifold assumption can also be applied to tasks other than classification. In some sense, the manifold assumption is a generalization of the cluster assumption, since it is usually assumed that the cluster structure of the data will be more easily found in the lower-dimensional manifold. These assumptions are closely related to **low-density separation**, which specifies that the boundary should not go across high-density regions in the instance space. This assumption has been adopted by many semi-supervised learning approaches. It is evident that unlabeled data can help, at least, to identify the similarity, and thus contribute to the construction of prediction models.

Transductive learning is a concept closely related to semi-supervised learning. The main difference between them lies in the different assumptions on the test data. Transductive learning takes a *closed-world* assumption, i.e., the test data is known in advance and the unlabeled data are exactly the test data. The goal of transductive learning is to optimize the generalization ability on this test data. Semi-supervised learning takes an *open-world* assumption, i.e., the test data is not known and the unlabeled data are not necessarily test data. Transductive learning can be viewed as a special setting of semi-supervised learning, and we do not distinguish them in the following.

8.1.2 Semi-Supervised Learning with Ensembles

This section briefly introduces some semi-supervised ensemble methods. Most semi-supervised ensemble methods work by training learners using the initial labeled data at first, and then using the learners to assign *pseudo-labels* to unlabeled data. After that, new learners are trained by using both the initial labeled data and the pseudo-labeled data. The procedure of training learners and assigning pseudo-labels are repeated until some stopping condition is reached. Based on the categorization of *sequential* and *parallel* ensemble methods (see Section 3.1), the introduction to common semi-supervised ensemble methods is separated into the following two subsections.

8.1.2.1 Semi-Supervised Sequential Ensemble Methods

Semi-supervised sequential ensemble methods mainly include Boosting-style methods, such as SSMBoost, ASSEMBLE and SemiBoost.

SSMBoost [d'Alché-Buc et al., 2002]. This method extends the margin definition to unlabeled data and employs gradient descent to construct an ensemble which minimizes the margin loss function on both labeled and unlabeled data. Here, Boosting is generalized as a linear combination of hypotheses, that is,

$$H(\boldsymbol{x}) = \sum_{i=1}^{T} \beta_i h_i(\boldsymbol{x}), \qquad (8.1)$$

where the output of each base learner h_i is in $[-1, 1]$. The overall loss function ℓ is defined with any decreasing function ℓ of the margin γ as

$$\ell(H) = \sum_{i=1}^{l} \ell\left(\gamma\left(H\left(\boldsymbol{x}_i\right), y_i\right)\right), \qquad (8.2)$$

where $\gamma(H(\boldsymbol{x}_i), y_i) = y_i H(\boldsymbol{x}_i)$ is the margin of the hypothesis H on the labeled example $(\boldsymbol{x}_i, y_i)$. Apparently, the margin measures the confidence of the classification for labeled data. For unlabeled data, however, the margin cannot be calculated, since we do not know the ground-truth labels. One alternative is to use the expected margin

$$\gamma_u\left(H\left(\boldsymbol{x}\right)\right) = \mathbb{E}_y\big(\gamma(H(\boldsymbol{x}), y)\big).$$

Using the output $(H(\boldsymbol{x}) + 1)/2$ as threshold for an estimate of the posterior probability $P(y = +1 \mid \boldsymbol{x})$, the expected margin for unlabeled data in U becomes

$$\gamma_u\left(H\left(\boldsymbol{x}\right)\right) = \frac{H(\boldsymbol{x}) + 1}{2} H(\boldsymbol{x}) + \left(1 - \frac{H\left(\boldsymbol{x}\right) + 1}{2}\right)(-H\left(\boldsymbol{x}\right))$$

$$= \left(H(\boldsymbol{x})\right)^2. \qquad (8.3)$$

Another way is to use the *maximum a posteriori* probability of y directly, and thus,

$$\gamma_u\left(H\left(\boldsymbol{x}\right)\right) = H(\boldsymbol{x})\mathtt{sign}\big(H(\boldsymbol{x})\big) = |H(\boldsymbol{x})|. \tag{8.4}$$

Notice that the margins in both (8.3) and (8.4) require the outputs of the learner on unlabeled data; this is the *pseudo-label* assigned by the ensemble. With the definition of margin for unlabeled data, the overall loss function of SSMBoost at the tth round is defined as

$$\ell(H_t) = \sum_{i=1}^{l} \ell\big(\gamma(H_t(\boldsymbol{x}_i), y_i)\big) + \sum_{i=l+1}^{m} \ell\big(\gamma_u(H_t(\boldsymbol{x}_i))\big). \tag{8.5}$$

Then, in the tth round, SSMBoost tries to create a new base learner h_{t+1} and the corresponding weight β_{t+1} to minimize $\ell(H_t)$. The final ensemble H is obtained when the number of rounds T is reached. Notice that rather than standard AdaBoost, SSMBoost uses the MarginBoost which is a variant of AnyBoost [Mason et al., 2000] to attain base learners in each round.

ASSEMBLE [Bennett et al., 2002]. This method is similar to SSMBoost. It also constructs ensembles in the form of (8.1), and alternates between assigning pseudo-labels to unlabeled data using the existing ensemble and generating the next base classifier to maximize the margin on both labeled and unlabeled data, where the margin on unlabeled data is calculated according to (8.4). The main difference between SSMBoost and ASSEMBLE lies in the fact that SSMBoost requires the base learning algorithm be a semi-supervised learning method, while Bennett et al. [2002] enabled ASSEMBLE to work with any weight-sensitive learner for both binary and multi-class problems. ASSEMBLE using decision trees as base classifiers won the *NIPS 2001 Unlabeled Data Competition*.

SemiBoost [Mallapragada et al., 2009]. Recall that in SSMBoost and ASSEMBLE, in each round the pseudo-labels are assigned to some unlabeled data with high confidence, and the pseudo-labeled data along with the labeled data are used together to train a new base learner in the next round. In this way, the pseudo-labeled data may be only helpful to increase the classification margin, yet provide little novel information about the learning task, since these pseudo-labeled data can be classified by the existing ensemble with high confidence. To overcome this problem, Mallapragada et al. [2009] proposed the SemiBoost method, which uses pairwise similarity measurements to guide the selection of unlabeled data to assign pseudo-labels. They imposed the constraint that similar unlabeled instances must be assigned the same label, and if an unlabeled instance is similar to a labeled instance then it must be assigned the label of the labeled instance. With these constraints, the SemiBoost method is closely related to graph-based semi-supervised learning approaches exploiting the manifold assumption. SemiBoost was generalized for multi-class problems by Valizadegan et al. [2008].

8.1.2.2   Semi-Supervised Parallel Ensemble Methods

Semi-supervised parallel ensemble methods are usually *disagreement-based semi-supervised learning* approaches, such as Tri-Training and Co-Forest.

Tri-Training [Zhou and Li, 2005]. This method can be viewed as an extension of the Co-Training method [Blum and Mitchell, 1998]. Co-Training trains two classifiers from different feature sets, and in each round, each classifier labels some unlabeled data for the other learner to refine. Co-Training works well on data with two *independent* feature sets both containing *sufficient* information for constructing a strong learner. Most data sets contain only a single feature set, and it is difficult to judge which learner should be trusted when they disagree. To address this issue, Zhou and Li [2005] proposed to train three learners, and in each round the unlabeled data are used in a *majority teach minority* way; that is, for an unlabeled instance, if the predictions of two learners agree yet the third learner disagrees, then the unlabeled instance will be labeled by two learners for the third learner. To reduce the risk of "correct minority" being misled by "incorrect majority", a sanity check mechanism was designed in [Zhou and Li, 2005], which is examined in each round. In the testing phase, the prediction is obtained by majority voting. The Tri-Training method can work with any base learners and is easy to implement. Notice that, like ensembles in supervised learning, the three learners need to be diverse. Zhou and Li [2005] generated the initial learners using *bootstrap sampling*, similar to the strategy used in Bagging. Other strategies for augmenting diversity can also be applied, and there is no doubt that Tri-Training can work well with multiple views since different views will provide natural diversity.

Co-Forest [Li and Zhou, 2007]. This method is an extension of Tri-Training to include more base learners. In each round, each learner is refined with unlabeled instances labeled by its *concomitant ensemble*, which comprises all the other learners. The *concomitant ensembles* used in Co-Forest are usually more accurate than the two learners used in Tri-Training. However, by using more learners, it should be noticed that, during the "majority teach minority" procedure the behaviors of the learners will become more and more similar, and thus the diversity of the learners decreases rapidly. This problem can be reduced to some extent by injecting randomness into the learning process. In [Li and Zhou, 2007], a random forest was used to realize the ensemble, and in each round, different subsets of unlabeled instances were sampled from the unlabeled data for different learners; this strategy is not only helpful for augmenting diversity, but also helpful for reducing the risk of being trapped into poor local minima.

8.1.2.3　Augmenting Ensemble Diversity with Unlabeled Data

Conventional ensemble methods work under the supervised setting, trying to achieve a high accuracy and high diversity for individual learners by using the labeled training data. It is noteworthy, however, that pursuing high accuracy and high diversity on the same labeled training data can suffer from a dilemma; that is, the increase of diversity may require a sacrifice of individual accuracy. For an extreme example, if all learners are nearly perfect on training data, to increase the diversity, the training accuracy of most of the learners needs to be reduced.

From the aspect of diversity augmentation, using unlabeled data makes a big difference. For example, given two sets of classifiers, $H = \{h_1, \ldots, h_n\}$ and $G = \{g_1, \ldots, g_n\}$, if we know that all of the classifiers are 100% accurate on labeled training data, there is no basis for choosing between ensemble H and ensemble G. However, if we find that the g_i's make the same predictions on unlabeled data while the h_i's make different predictions on some unlabeled data, we know that the ensemble H would have good chance to be better than G because it is more diverse while still being equally accurate on the training data.

Notice that most semi-supervised ensemble methods, as introduced in Section 8.1.2, exploit unlabeled data to improve the individual accuracy by assigning pseudo-labels to unlabeled data and then using the pseudo-labeled examples together with the original labeled examples to train the individual learners. Recently, Zhou [2009] indicated that it is possible to design new ensemble methods by using unlabeled data to help augment diversity, and Zhang and Zhou [2010] proposed the UDEED method along this direction.

Let $\mathcal{X} = \mathcal{R}^d$ denote the d-dimensional input space, and given labeled training examples $L = \{(\boldsymbol{x}_1, y_1), (\boldsymbol{x}_2, y_2), \ldots, (\boldsymbol{x}_l, y_l)\}$ and unlabeled instances $U = \{\boldsymbol{x}_{l+1}, \boldsymbol{x}_{l+2}, \ldots, \boldsymbol{x}_m\}$, where $\boldsymbol{x}_i \in \mathcal{X}$. For simplicity, consider binary classification problem, that is, $y_i \in \{-1, +1\}$. Let $L_u = \{\boldsymbol{x}_1, \boldsymbol{x}_2, \ldots, \boldsymbol{x}_l\}$ denote the unlabeled data set derived from L by neglecting the label information. Assume that the ensemble comprises T component classifiers $\{h_1, h_2, \ldots, h_T\}$ each taking the form $h_k : \mathcal{X} \to [-1, +1]$. Further, assume that the value of $|h_k(\boldsymbol{x})|$ can be regarded as the confidence of $\boldsymbol{x}$ being positive or negative. As before, use the output $(h_k(\boldsymbol{x}) + 1)/2$ as a threshold for an estimate of the posterior probability $P(y = +1|\boldsymbol{x})$.

The basic idea of the UDEED method is to maximize the *fit* of the classifiers on the labeled data, while maximizing the diversity of the classifiers on the unlabeled data. Therefore, UDEED generates the ensemble $\boldsymbol{h} = (h_1, h_2, \cdots, h_T)$ by minimizing the loss function

$$V(\boldsymbol{h}, L, D) = V_{emp}(\boldsymbol{h}, L) + \alpha \cdot V_{div}(\boldsymbol{h}, D), \qquad (8.6)$$

where $V_{emp}(\boldsymbol{h}, L)$ corresponds to the *empirical loss* of $\boldsymbol{h}$ on L, $V_{div}(\boldsymbol{h}, D)$ corresponds to the *diversity loss* of $\boldsymbol{h}$ on a data set D (e.g., $D = U$) and α is a parameter which trades off these two terms.

Indeed, (8.6) provides a general framework which can be realized with different choices of the loss functions. In [Zhang and Zhou, 2010], $V_{emp}(\boldsymbol{h}, L)$ and $V_{div}(\boldsymbol{h}, D)$ are realized by

$$V_{emp}(\boldsymbol{h}, L) = \frac{1}{T} \cdot \sum_{k=1}^{T} l(h_k, L), \tag{8.7}$$

$$V_{div}(\boldsymbol{h}, D) = \frac{2}{T(T-1)} \cdot \sum_{p=1}^{T-1} \sum_{q=p+1}^{T} d(h_p, h_q, D), \tag{8.8}$$

respectively, where $l(h_k, L)$ measures the empirical loss of h_k on L, and

$$d(h_p, h_q, D) = \frac{1}{|D|} \sum_{\boldsymbol{x} \in D} h_p(\boldsymbol{x}) h_q(\boldsymbol{x}), \tag{8.9}$$

where $d(h_p, h_q, D)$ represents the *prediction difference* between individual classifiers h_p and h_q on D. Notice that the prediction difference is calculated based on the real output $h(\boldsymbol{x})$ instead of the signed output $\text{sign}(h(\boldsymbol{x}))$.

Thus, UDEED aims to find the target model $\boldsymbol{h}^*$ that minimizes the loss function (8.6), that is,

$$\boldsymbol{h}^* = \arg\min_{\boldsymbol{h}} V(\boldsymbol{h}, L, D). \tag{8.10}$$

In [Zhang and Zhou, 2010], logistic regression learners were used as the component learners, and the minimization of the loss function was realized by gradient descent optimization. By studying the ensembles with $D = U$ and $D = L_u$ in (8.10), respectively, it was reported that using unlabeled data in the way of UDEED is quite helpful. Moreover, various ensemble diversity measures were evaluated in [Zhang and Zhou, 2010], and the results verified that the use of unlabeled data in the way of UDEED significantly augmented the ensemble diversity and improved the prediction accuracy.

8.2 Active Learning

8.2.1 Usefulness of Human Intervention

Active learning deals with methods that assume that the learner has some control over the data space, and the goal is to minimize the number of queries on ground-truth labels from an *oracle*, usually human expert, for generating a good learner. In other words, in contrast to **passive learning** where the learner *passively* waits for people to give labels to instances, an active learner will *actively* select some instances to query for their labels, and the central problem in active learning is to achieve a good learner by using the smallest number of queries.

There are two kinds of active learning. In *reservoir-based active learning*, the queries posed by the learner must be drawn from the observed unlabeled instances; while in *synthetic active learning*, the learner is permitted to synthesize new instances and pose them as queries. The observed unlabeled data is helpful to disclose distribution information, like its role in semi-supervised learning, while a synthesized instance might be an instance that does not really exist and the corresponding query might be difficult to answer. Here, we focus on reservoir-based active learning.

It is evident that both active learning and semi-supervised learning try to exploit unlabeled data to improve learning performance, while the major difference is that active learning involves *human intervention*. So, it is interesting to understand how useful human intervention could be. For this purpose, we can study the **sample complexity** of active learning, that is, how many queries are needed for obtaining a good learner.

Generally, the sample complexity of active learning can be studied in two settings, that is, the *realizable case* and *unrealizable case*. The former assumes that there exists a hypothesis perfectly separating the data in the hypothesis class, while the latter assumes that the data could not be perfectly separated by any hypothesis in the hypothesis class because of noise. It is obvious that the latter case is more difficult yet more practical.

During the past decade, many theoretical bounds on the sample complexity of active learning have been proved. In the realizable case, for example, by assuming that the hypothesis class is linear separators through the origin and that the data is distributed uniformly over the unit sphere in $\mathcal{R}^d$, it has been proved that the sample complexity of active learning is $\widetilde{O}(\log \frac{1}{\epsilon})$ taking into account the desired error bound ϵ with confidence $(1 - \delta)$ [Freund et al., 1997, Dasgupta, 2005, 2006, Dasgupta et al., 2005, Balcan et al., 2007]. Here the $\widetilde{O}$ notation is used to hide logarithmic factors $\log \log(\frac{1}{\epsilon})$, $\log(d)$ and $\log(\frac{1}{\delta})$. Notice that the assumed conditions can be satisfied in many situations, and therefore, this theoretical bound implies that in the realizable case, there are many situations where active learning can offer *exponential* improvement in sample complexity compared to passive learning. In the non-realizable case, generally the result is not that optimistic. However, recently Wang and Zhou [2010] proved that there are some situations where active learning can offer *exponential* improvement in the sample complexity compared to passive learning.

Overall, it is well recognized that by using human intervention, active learning can offer significant advantages over passive learning.

8.2.2 Active Learning with Ensembles

One of the major active learning paradigms, **query-by-committee**, also called **committee-based sampling**, is based on ensembles. This paradigm was proposed by Seung et al. [1992] and then implemented by many researchers for different tasks, e.g., [Dagan and Engelson, 1995, Liere and Tadepalli, 1997, McCallum and Nigam, 1998]. In this paradigm, multiple learners are generated, and then the unlabeled instance on which the learners disagree the most is selected to query. For example, suppose there are five learners, among which three learners predict positive and two learners predict negative for an instance x_i, while four learners predict positive and one learner predicts negative for the instance x_j, then these learners disagree more on x_i than on x_j, and therefore x_i will be selected for query rather than x_j.

One of the key issues of query-by-committee is how to generate the multiple learners in the committee. Freund et al. [1997] proved that when the Gibbs algorithm, a randomized learning algorithm which picks a hypothesis from a given hypothesis class according to the *posterior* distribution, is used to generate the learners, query-by-committee can exponentially improve the sample complexity compared to passive learning. The Gibbs algorithm, however, is computationally intractable. Abe and Mamitsuka [1998] showed that popular ensemble methods can be used to generate the committee. As with other ensemble methods, the learners in the committee should be diverse. Abe and Mamitsuka [1998] developed the Query-by-Bagging and Query-by-Boosting methods. Query-by-Bagging employs Bagging to generate the committee. In each round, it re-samples the labeled training data by *bootstrap sampling* and trains a learner on each sample; then, the unlabeled instance on which the learners disagree the most is queried. Query-by-Boosting uses AdaBoost to generate the committee. In each round, it constructs a boosted ensemble; then, the unlabeled instance on which the margin predicted by the boosted ensemble is the minimum is queried.

Notice that the use of the ensemble provides the feasibility of combining active learning with semi-supervised learning. With multiple learners, given a set of unlabeled instances, in each round the unlabeled instance on which the learners disagree the most can be selected to query, while some other unlabeled instances can be exploited by the *majority teach minority* strategy as in semi-supervised parallel ensemble methods such as Tri-Training and Co-Forest (see Section 8.1.2). Zhou et al. [2006] proposed the SSAIRA method based on such an idea, and applied this method to improve the performance of *relevance feedback* in image retrieval. Later, Wang and Zhou [2008] theoretically analyzed the sample complexity of the combination of active learning and semi-supervised learning, and proved that the combination further improves the sample complexity compared to using only semi-supervised learning or only active learning.

8.3 Cost-Sensitive Learning

8.3.1 Learning with Unequal Costs

Conventional learners generally try to minimize the *number of mistakes* they will make in predicting unseen instances. This makes sense when the costs of different types of mistakes are equal. In real-world tasks, however, many problems have unequal costs. For example, in medical diagnosis, the cost of mistakenly diagnosing a patient to be healthy may be far larger than that of mistakenly diagnosing a healthy person as being sick, because the former type of mistake may threaten a life. In such situations, minimizing the number of mistakes may not provide the optimal decision because, for example, three instances that each costs 20 dollars are less important than one instance that costs 120 dollars. So, rather than minimizing the number of mistakes, it is more meaningful to minimize the **total cost**. Accordingly, the total cost, rather than *accuracy* and *error rate*, should be used for evaluating cost-sensitive learning performance.

Cost-sensitive learning deals with methods that work on unequal costs in the learning process, where the goal is to minimize the total cost. A learning process may involve various costs such as the *test cost, teacher cost, intervention cost*, etc. [Turney, 2000], while the most often encountered one is the **misclassification cost**.

Generally, there are two types of misclassification cost, that is, *example-dependent cost* and *class-dependent cost*. The former assumes that the costs are associated with examples, that is, every example has its own misclassification cost; the latter assumes that the costs are associated with classes, that is, every class has its own misclassification cost. Notice that, in most real-world applications, it is feasible to ask a domain expert to specify the cost of misclassifying a class as another class, yet only in some special situations is it convenient to get the cost for every training example. The following will focus on class-dependent costs and hereafter class-dependent will not be mentioned explicitly.

The most popular cost-sensitive learning approach is **Rescaling**, which tries to rebalance the classes such that the influence of each class in the learning process is in proportion to its cost. For binary classification, suppose the cost of misclassifying the ith class to the jth class is $cost_{ij}$, then the *optimal rescaling ratio* of the ith class against the jth class is

$$\tau_{ij} = \frac{cost_{ij}}{cost_{ji}}, \tag{8.11}$$

which implies that after rescaling, the influence of the 1st class should be $cost_{12}/cost_{21}$ times of the influence of the 2nd class. Notice that (8.11) is optimal for cost-sensitive learning, and it can be derived from the Bayes risk theory as shown in [Elkan, 2001].

Rescaling is a general framework which can be implemented in different ways. For example, it can be implemented by **re-weighting**, i.e., assigning different weights to training examples of different classes, and then passing the re-weighted training examples to any *cost-blind* learning algorithms that can handle weighted examples; or by **re-sampling**, i.e., extracting a sample from the training data according to the proportion specified by (8.11), and then passing the re-sampled data to any cost-blind learning algorithms; or by **threshold-moving**, i.e., moving the decision threshold toward the cheaper class according to (8.11). In particular, the threshold-moving strategy has been incorporated into many cost-blind learning methods to generate their cost-sensitive variants. For example, for decision trees, the tree splits can be selected based on a moved decision threshold [Schiffers, 1997], and the tree pruning can be executed based on a moved decision threshold [Drummond and Holte, 2000]; for neural networks, the learning objective can be biased towards the high-cost class based on a moved decision threshold [Kukar and Kononenko, 1998]; for support vector machines, the corresponding optimization problem can be written as [Lin et al., 2002]

$$\min_{\boldsymbol{w},b,\xi} \frac{1}{2}\|\boldsymbol{w}\|_{\mathcal{H}}^2 + C \sum_{i=1}^{m} cost(\boldsymbol{x}_i)\xi_i \qquad (8.12)$$
$$\text{s.t. } y_i(\boldsymbol{w}^T \phi(\boldsymbol{x}_i) + b) \geq 1 - \xi_i$$
$$\xi_i \geq 0 \quad (\forall i = 1, \ldots, m)$$

where ϕ is the feature induced from a kernel function and $cost(\boldsymbol{x}_i)$ is the example-dependent cost for misclassifying $\boldsymbol{x}_i$. It is clear that the classification boundary is moved according to the rescaling ratio specified by the cost terms.

8.3.2   Ensemble Methods for Cost-Sensitive Learning

Many ensemble methods for cost-sensitive learning have been developed. Representative ones mainly include MetaCost and Asymmetric Boosting.

MetaCost [Domingos, 1999]. This method constructs a decision tree ensemble by Bagging to estimate the posterior probability $p(y|\boldsymbol{x})$. Then, it re-labels each training example to the class with the minimum expected risk according to the moved decision threshold. Finally, the relabeled data are used to train a learner to minimize the error rate. The MetaCost algorithm is summarized in Figure 8.2.

Notice that the probability estimates generated by different learning methods are usually different, and therefore, it might be more reliable to use the same learner in both steps of MetaCost. However, the probability estimates produced by classifiers are usually poor, since they are by-products

---

Input: Training data set $D = \{(x_1, y_1), (x_2, y_2), \ldots, (x_m, y_m)\}$;
       Base learning algorithm $\mathfrak{L}$;
       Cost matrix cost, where $cost_{ij}$ is the cost of misclassifying
         examples of the ith class to the jth class;
       Number of subsamples in Bagging T_b;
       Number of examples in each subsample m;
       pb is $True$ *iff* $\mathfrak{L}$ produces class probabilities;
       all is $True$ *iff* all subsamples are to be used for each example.

Process:
1. **for** $i = 1, \ldots, T_b$:
2. D_i is a subsample of D with m examples;
3. $M_i = \mathfrak{L}(D_i)$;
4. **end**
5. **for** each example x in D:
6.   **for** each class j:
7. $p(j|x) = \frac{1}{\sum_i 1} \sum_i p(j|x, M_i)$;
8.   where
9.   **if** pb **then**
10. $p(j|x, M_i)$ is produced by M_i;
11.   **else**
12. $p(j|x, M_i) = \begin{cases} 1 & \text{for the class predicted by } M_i \text{ for } x \text{ ,} \\ 0 & \text{for all other classes.} \end{cases}$
13.   **end**
14.   **if** all **then**
15. i ranges over all M_i's;
16.   **else**
17. i ranges over all M_i's such that $x \notin D_i$;
18.   **end**
19.   **end**
20.   Assign x's class label to be $\arg \min_i \sum_j p(j|x) cost_{ji}$;
21.**end**
22.Build a model M by applying $\mathfrak{L}$ on data set D with new labels.
Output: M

FIGURE 8.2: The MetaCost algorithm.

of classification, and many classifiers do not provide such estimates. Therefore, Bagging is used in MetaCost, while other ensemble methods can also be used to obtain the probability estimates.

Asymmetric Boosting [Masnadi-Shirazi and Vasconcelos, 2007]. This method directly modifies the AdaBoost algorithm such that the cost-sensitive solution is consistent with Bayes optimal risk. Recall the exponential loss function (2.1), the solution (2.4) and its property (2.5), Asymmetric

Input: Training data set $D = \{(\boldsymbol{x}_1, y_1), (\boldsymbol{x}_2, y_2), \dots, (\boldsymbol{x}_m, y_m)\}$;
      Base learning algorithm $\mathfrak{L}$;
      Cost of misclassifying positive/negative examples $cost_+/cost_-$;
      Number of learning trails T;
      Number of iterations in gradient descent N_{gd}.

Process:
1. $\mathcal{I}_+ = \{i | y_i = +1\}$ and $\mathcal{I}_- = \{i | y_i = -1\}$;
2. Initialize weights as $w_i = \frac{1}{2|\mathcal{I}_+|}, \forall i \in \mathcal{I}_+$ and $w_i = \frac{1}{2|\mathcal{I}_-|}, \forall i \in \mathcal{I}_-$;
3. **for** $t = 1$ to T :
4. $k = 1$;
5.   Initialize β_k as a random number in $[0, 1]$;
6.   Using gradient descent to solve f_k from
$$f_k(\boldsymbol{x}) = \arg\min_f [(e^{cost_+\beta_k} - e^{-cost_+\beta_k}) \cdot b + e^{-cost_+\beta_k} T_+$$
$$+ (e^{cost_-\beta_k} - e^{-cost_-\beta_k}) \cdot d + e^{-cost_-\beta_k} T_-]$$
    where
$$T_+ = \sum_{i\in\mathcal{I}_+} w_t(i), \quad T_- = \sum_{i\in\mathcal{I}_-} w_t(i),$$
$$b = \sum_{i\in\mathcal{I}_+} w_t(i)\mathbb{I}(y_i \neq f_{k-1}(\boldsymbol{x}_i)),$$
$$d = \sum_{i\in\mathcal{I}_-} w_t(i)\mathbb{I}(y_i \neq f_{k-1}(\boldsymbol{x}_i));$$
7.   **for** $k = 2$ to N_{gd}:
8.   Solve β_k from
$$2 \cdot cost_+ \cdot b \cdot \cosh(cost_+\beta_k) + 2 \cdot cost_- \cdot d \cdot \cosh(cost_-\beta_k)$$
$$- cost_+ T_+ e^{-cost_+\beta_k} - cost_- T_- e^{-cost_-\beta_k} = 0;$$
9.   Using gradient descent to solve f_k from
$$f_k(\boldsymbol{x}) = \arg\min_f [(e^{cost_+\beta_k} - e^{-cost_+\beta_k}) \cdot b + e^{-cost_+\beta_k} T_+$$
$$+ (e^{cost_-\beta_k} - e^{-cost_-\beta_k}) \cdot d + e^{-cost_-\beta_k} T_-];$$
10.   **end**
11.   Let (h_t, α_t) be (f_k, β_k) with the smallest loss;
12.   Update weights as $w_{t+1}(i) = w_t(i) e^{-cost_{y_i}\alpha_t y_i h_t(\boldsymbol{x}_i)}$
13. **end**

Output: $H(x) = \text{sign}(\sum_{t=1}^T \alpha_t h_t(\boldsymbol{x}))$;

FIGURE 8.3: The Asymmetric Boosting algorithm.

Boosting directly minimizes the loss function

$$\ell_{cost}(h \mid \mathcal{D}) = \mathbb{E}_{\boldsymbol{x}\sim\mathcal{D}}[e^{-yh(\boldsymbol{x})cost(\boldsymbol{x})}] \tag{8.13}$$

$$\approx \frac{1}{m}\sum_{i=1}^m \left[\mathbb{I}(y_i = +1)e^{-y_i h(\boldsymbol{x}_i)cost_+} + \mathbb{I}(y_i = -1)e^{-y_i h(\boldsymbol{x}_i)cost_-}\right],$$

where $y_i \in \{-1, +1\}$ is the ground-truth label of $\boldsymbol{x}_i$, $cost_+$ ($cost_-$) denotes the cost of mistakenly classifying a positive (negative) example to the negative (positive) class, and h is the learner. The optimal solution minimizing

Table 8.1: Summary of major modifications on AdaBoost made by cost-sensitive Boosting methods.

	Weight Update Rule	α
AdaCost	$w_{t+1}(i) = w_t(i)e^{-\alpha_t y_i h_t(\boldsymbol{x}_i)\beta_{\delta_i}}$ $\beta_{+1} = 0.5 - 0.5cost_i$ $\beta_{-1} = 0.5 + 0.5cost_i$	$\alpha = \frac{1}{2}\ln\frac{1+e_t}{1-e_t}$ $e_t = \sum_{i=1}^{m} w_t(i)y_i h_t(\boldsymbol{x}_i)\beta_{\delta_i}$
CSB0	$w_{t+1}(i) = c_{\delta_i}(i)w_t(i)$ $c_{-1}(i) = cost_i,\ \ c_{+1}(i) = 1$	unchanged
CSB1	$w_{t+1}(i) = c_{\delta_i}(i)w_t(i)e^{-y_i h_t(\boldsymbol{x}_i)}$	unchanged
CSB2	$w_{t+1}(i) =$ $C_{\delta_i}(i)w_t(i)e^{-\alpha_t y_i h_t(\boldsymbol{x}_i)}$	unchanged
Asymmetric AdaBoost	$w_{t+1}(i) =$ $w_t(i)e^{-\alpha_t y_i h_t(\boldsymbol{x}_i)}e^{y_i \log\sqrt{K}}$ $K = \frac{cost_+}{cost_-}$ is cost ratio	unchanged
AdaC1	$w_{t+1}(i) =$ $w_t(i)e^{-\alpha_t y_i h_t(\boldsymbol{x}_i)cost_i}$	$\alpha = \frac{1}{2}\ln\frac{1+\sum_{i=1}^{m} cost_i w_t(i)\delta_i}{1-\sum_{i=1}^{m} cost_i w_t(i)\delta_i}$
AdaC2	$w_{t+1}(i) =$ $cost_i w_t(i)e^{-\alpha_t y_i h_t(\boldsymbol{x}_i)}$	$\alpha = \frac{1}{2}\ln\frac{\sum_{y_i = h_t(\boldsymbol{x}_i)} cost_i w_t(i)}{\sum_{y_i \neq h_t(\boldsymbol{x}_i)} cost_i w_t(i)}$
AdaC3	$w_{t+1}(i) =$ $cost_i w_t(i)e^{-\alpha_t y_i h_t(\boldsymbol{x}_i)cost_i}$	$\alpha =$ $\frac{1}{2}\ln\frac{\sum_{i=1}^{m} w_t(i)(cost_i + cost_i^2\delta_i)}{\sum_{i=1}^{m} w_t(i)(cost_i - cost_i^2\delta_i)}$

‡ In the table, $\delta_i = +1$ if $h_t(\boldsymbol{x}_i) = y_i$ and -1 otherwise; $cost_i$ is the misclassification cost of $\boldsymbol{x}_i$; $cost_+$ ($cost_-$) denotes the cost of mistakenly classifying a positive (negative) example to the negative (positive) class. For clarity, in weight update rules, we omit the normalization factor Z_t, which is used to make w_{t+1} a distribution.

the exponential loss ℓ_{cost} is

$$h^* = \frac{1}{cost_+ + cost_-} \ln\frac{p(y = +1|\boldsymbol{x})cost_+}{p(y = -1|\boldsymbol{x})cost_-}, \qquad (8.14)$$

which is consistent with the Bayes optimal solution because

$$\text{sign}(h^*(\boldsymbol{x})) = \underset{y\in\{+1,-1\}}{\arg\max}\ p(y|\boldsymbol{x})cost_{(y)}. \qquad (8.15)$$

Notice that it is difficult to minimize ℓ_{cost} directly by fitting an additive model, and therefore, as the general principle for minimizing convex loss with AdaBoost, Asymmetric Boosting uses gradient descent optimization instead. Figure 8.3 shows the the Asymmetric Boosting algorithm.

There are a number of other cost-sensitive Boosting methods trying to minimize the expected cost. Different from Asymmetric Boosting which is derived directly from the Bayes risk theory, most of those cost-sensitive Boosting methods use heuristics to achieve cost sensitivity, and therefore, their optimal solutions cannot guarantee to be consistent with the Bayes optimal solution. Some of them change the weight update rule of Adaboost by increasing the weights of high-cost examples, such as CSB0, CSB1, CSB2 [Ting, 2000] and Asymmetric AdaBoost [Viola and Jones, 2002]. Some of them change the weight update rule as well as α, the weight of base learners, by associating a cost with the weighted error rate of each class, such as AdaC1, AdaC2, AdaC3 [Sun et al., 2005] and AdaCost [Fan et al., 1999]. Table 8.1 summarizes the major modifications made by these methods on AdaBoost. A thorough comparison of those methods is an important issue to be explored.

8.4 Class-Imbalance Learning

8.4.1 Learning with Class Imbalance

In many real-world tasks, e.g., fraud or failure detection, the data are usually imbalanced; that is, some classes have far more examples than other classes. Consider binary classification for simplicity. The class with more data is called the *majority class* and the other class is called the *minority class*. The *level of imbalance*, i.e., the number of majority class examples divided by that of minority class examples, can be as large as 10^6 [Wu et al., 2008].

It is often meaningless to achieve high accuracy when there is class imbalance, because the minority class would be dominated by the majority class. For example, even when the level of imbalance is just 1,000, which is very common in fraud detection tasks, a trivial solution which simply predicts all unseen instances to belong to the majority class will achieve an accuracy of 99.9%; though the accuracy seems high, the solution is useless since no fraud will be detected.

Notice that an imbalanced data set does not necessarily mean that the learning task must suffer from class-imbalance. If the majority class is more important than the minority class, it is not a problem for the majority class to dominate the learning process. Only when the minority class is more important, or it cannot be sacrificed, the dominance of the majority class is a disaster and **class-imbalance learning** is needed. In other words, there is always an implicit assumption in class-imbalance learning that the minority class has higher cost than the majority class.

Cost-sensitive learning methods are often used in class-imbalance learning. In particular, the Rescaling approach can be adapted to class-imbalance learning by replacing the right-hand side of (8.11) by the ratio of the size of the jth class against that of the ith class; that is, to rebalance the classes according to the level of imbalance, such that the influences of the minority class and the majority class become equal. Notice that, however, the ground-truth level of imbalance is usually unknown, and rescaling according to the level of imbalance in training data does not always work well.

Notice that re-sampling strategies can be further categorized into **under-sampling** which decreases the majority class examples, and **over-sampling** which increases the minority class examples. Either method can be implemented by random sampling with or without replacement. However, randomly duplicating the minority class examples may increase the risk of overfitting, while randomly removing the majority class examples may lose useful information. To relax those problems, many advanced re-sampling methods have been developed.

To improve under-sampling, some methods selectively remove the majority class examples such that more informative examples are kept. For example, the one-sided sampling method [Kubat and Matwin, 1997] tries to find a *consistent* subset D' of the original data D in the sense that the 1-NN rule learned from D' can correctly classify all examples in D. Initially, D' contains all the minority class examples and one randomly selected majority class example. Then, an 1-NN classifier is constructed on D' to classify the examples in D. The misclassified majority examples are added into D'. After that, the **Tomek Link** [Tomek, 1976] is employed to remove borderline or noisy examples in the majority class in D'. Let $d(x_i, x_j)$ denote the distance between x_i and x_j. A pair of examples (x_i, x_j) is called a *Tomek link* if their class labels are different, and no example x_k exists such that $d(x_i, x_k) < d(x_i, x_j)$ or $d(x_j, x_k) < d(x_j, x_i)$. Examples participating in Tomek links are usually either borderline or noisy.

To improve over-sampling, some methods use synthetic examples instead of exact copies to reduce the risk of overfitting. For example, SMOTE [Chawla et al., 2002] generates synthetic examples by randomly interpolating between a minority class example and one of its neighbors from the same class. Data cleaning techniques such as the Tomek link can be applied further to remove the possible noise introduced in the interpolation process.

8.4.2   Performance Evaluation with Class Imbalance

Given data set $D = \{(x_1, y_1), \ldots, (x_m, y_m)\}$, for simplicity, consider binary classification where $y \in \{-1, +1\}$, and suppose the positive class has m_+ examples and negative class has m_- examples, $m_+ + m_- = m$. Assume that the positive class is the minority class, that is, $m_+ < m_-$. The **confusion matrix** of a classifier h is in the form of:

	Ground-truth "+"	Ground-truth "−"
Predicted as "+"	*TP (true positive)*	*FP (false positive)*
Predicted as "−"	*FN (false negative)*	*TN (true negative)*

$$\begin{cases} TP = \sum_{i=1}^{m} \mathbb{I}(y_i = +1)\mathbb{I}(h(\boldsymbol{x}_i) = +1) \\ FP = \sum_{i=1}^{m} \mathbb{I}(y_i = -1)\mathbb{I}(h(\boldsymbol{x}_i) = +1) \\ TN = \sum_{i=1}^{m} \mathbb{I}(y_i = -1)\mathbb{I}(h(\boldsymbol{x}_i) = -1) \\ FN = \sum_{i=1}^{m} \mathbb{I}(y_i = +1)\mathbb{I}(h(\boldsymbol{x}_i) = -1) \end{cases} \tag{8.16}$$

where

$$TP + FN = m_+ , \tag{8.17}$$

$$TN + FP = m_- , \tag{8.18}$$

$$TP + FN + TN + FP = m . \tag{8.19}$$

With these variables, the **accuracy** and **error rate** can be written as

$$acc = P\big(h(\boldsymbol{x}) = y\big) = \frac{TP + TN}{m}, \tag{8.20}$$

$$err = P\big(h(\boldsymbol{x}) \neq y\big) = \frac{FP + FN}{m}, \tag{8.21}$$

respectively, and

$$acc + err = 1. \tag{8.22}$$

It is evident that accuracy and error rate are not adequate for evaluating class-imbalance learning performance, since more attention should be paid to the minority class.

8.4.2.1   ROC Curve and AUC

ROC curve [Green and Swets, 1966, Spackman, 1989] can be used to evaluate learning performance under unknown class distributions or misclassification costs. "ROC" is the abbreviation for *Receiver Operating Characteristic*, which was originally used in radar signal detection in World War II. As illustrated in Figure 8.4, the ROC curve plots how the true positive rate *tpr* on the y-axis changes with the false positive rate *fpr* on the x-axis, where

$$tpr = \frac{TP}{TP + FN} = \frac{TP}{m_+} , \tag{8.23}$$

$$fpr = \frac{FP}{FP + TN} = \frac{FP}{m_-} . \tag{8.24}$$

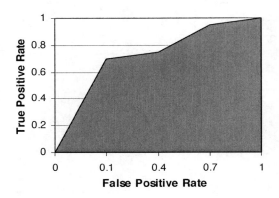

FIGURE 8.4: Illustration of ROC curve. AUC is the area of the dark region.

A classifier corresponds to a point in the ROC space. If it classifies all examples as positive, $tpr = 1$ and $fpr = 1$; if it classifies all examples as negative, $tpr = 0$ and $fpr = 0$; if it classifies all examples correctly, $tpr = 1$ and $fpr = 0$. When the tpr increases, the fpr will be unchanged or increase. If two classifiers are compared, the one located to the upper left is better. A functional hypothesis $h : \mathcal{X} \times \mathcal{Y} \to R$ corresponds to a curve with $(0,0)$ being the start point and $(1,1)$ being the end point, on which a series of (fpr, tpr) points can be generated by applying different thresholds on the outputs of h to separate different classes.

The **AUC** (Area Under ROC Curve) [Metz, 1978, Hanley and McNeil, 1983] is defined as the area under the ROC curve, as shown in Figure 8.4. This criterion integrates the performances of a classifier over all possible values of fpr to represent the overall performance. The statistical interpretation of AUC is the probability of the functional hypothesis $h : \mathcal{X} \times \mathcal{Y} \to R$ assigning a higher score to a positive example than to a negative example, i.e.,

$$AUC(h) = P\big(h(\boldsymbol{x}_+) > h(\boldsymbol{x}_-)\big). \tag{8.25}$$

The *normalized Wilcoxon-Mann-Whitney statistic* gives the maximum likelihood estimate of the true AUC as [Yan et al., 2003]

$$W = \frac{\sum_{\boldsymbol{x}_+} \sum_{\boldsymbol{x}_-} \mathbb{I}\big(h(\boldsymbol{x}_+) > h(\boldsymbol{x}_-)\big)}{m_+ m_-}. \tag{8.26}$$

Therefore, the AUC measures the ranking quality of h. Maximizing the AUC is equivalent to maximizing the number of the pairs satisfying $h(\boldsymbol{x}_+) > h(\boldsymbol{x}_-)$.

8.4.2.2   G-mean, F-measure and Precision-Recall Curve

G-mean, or **Geometric mean**, is the geometric mean of the accuracy of each class, i.e.,

$$G\text{-}mean = \sqrt{\frac{TP}{m_+} \times \frac{TN}{m_-}}, \tag{8.27}$$

where the sizes of different classes have already been considered, and therefore, it is a good candidate for evaluating class-imbalance learning performance.

Precision measures how many examples classified as positive are really positive, while **recall** measures how many positive examples are correctly classified as positive. That is,

$$Precision = \frac{TP}{TP + FP}, \tag{8.28}$$

$$Recall = \frac{TP}{TP + FN} = \frac{TP}{m_+}. \tag{8.29}$$

By these definitions, the precision does not contain any information about FN, and the recall does not contain any information about FP. Therefore, neither provides a complete evaluation of learning performance, while they are complementary to each other.

Though a high precision and a high recall are both desired, there are often conflicts to achieve the two goals together since FP usually becomes larger when TP increases. Being a tradeoff, the **F-measure** is defined as the harmonic mean of precision and recall as [van Rijsbergen, 1979]

$$F_\alpha = \left(\alpha \frac{1}{Recall} + (1 - \alpha) \frac{1}{Precision} \right)^{-1}, \tag{8.30}$$

where α is a parameter to weight the relative importance of precision and recall. By default, α is set to 0.5 to regard the precision and recall as equally important.

To evaluate a learning method in various situations, e.g., with different class distributions, a single pair of (*Precision, Recall*) or a single choice of α for the F-measure is not enough. For this purpose, the **Precision-Recall (PR) curve** can be used. It plots recall on the x-axis and precision on the y-axis, as illustrated in Figure 8.5.

A classifier corresponds to a point in the PR space. If it classifies all examples correctly, $Precision = 1$ and $Recall = 1$; if it classifies all examples as positive, $Recall = 1$ and $Precision = m_+/m$; if it classifies all examples as negative, $Recall = 0$ and $Precision = 1$. If two classifiers are compared, the one located on the upper right is better. A functional hypothesis $h : \mathcal{X} \times \mathcal{Y} \to R$ corresponds to a curve on which a series of (*Precision, Recall*) points can be generated by applying different thresholds on the outputs of h to separate different classes. Discussion on the relationship between the PR and ROC curves can be found in [Davis and Goadrich, 2006].

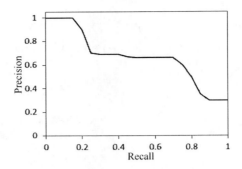

FIGURE 8.5: Illustration of PR curve.

8.4.3   Ensemble Methods for Class-Imbalance Learning

In class-imbalance learning, the ground-truth level of imbalance is usually unknown, and the ground-truth relative importance of the minority class against the majority class is usually unknown also. There are many potential variations, and therefore, it is not strange that ensemble methods have been applied to obtain a more effective and robust performance. This section mainly introduces SMOTEBoost, EasyEnsemble and BalanceCascade.

SMOTEBoost [Chawla et al., 2003]. This method improves the over-sampling method SMOTE [Chawla et al., 2002] by combining it with Ada-Boost.M2. The basic idea is to let the base learners focus more and more on difficult yet rare class examples. In each round, the weights for minority class examples are increased. The SMOTEBoost algorithm is shown in Figure 8.6.

EasyEnsemble [Liu et al., 2009]. The motivation of this method is to keep the high efficiency of under-sampling but reduce the possibility of ignoring potentially useful information contained in the majority class examples. EasyEnsemble adopts a very simple strategy. It randomly generates multiple subsamples $\{N_1, N_2, \ldots, N_T\}$ from the majority class N. The size of each sample is the same as that of the minority class P, i.e., $|N_i| = |P|$. Then, the union of each pair of N_i and P is used to train an AdaBoost ensemble. The final ensemble is formed by combining all the base learners in all the AdaBoost ensembles. The EasyEnsemble algorithm is shown in Figure 8.7.

EasyEnsemble actually generates a Bagged ensemble whose base learners are Boosted ensembles. Such a strategy of combining AdaBoost with Bagging has been adopted in MultiBoosting [Webb and Zheng, 2004], which effectively leverages the power of AdaBoost in reducing bias and the power of Bagging in reducing variance.

BalanceCascade [Liu et al., 2009]. This method tries to use *guided deletion* rather than random deletion of majority class examples. In contrast to

Input: Training data set $D = \{(\boldsymbol{x}_1, y_1), (\boldsymbol{x}_2, y_2), \ldots, (\boldsymbol{x}_m, y_m)\}$;
Minority class examples $P \subseteq D$;
Base learning algorithm $\mathfrak{L}$;
Number of synthetic examples to be generated S;
Number of iterations T.

Process:
1. $B = \{(i, y) : i = 1, \ldots, m, y \neq y_i\}$;
2. Initialize distribution as $w_1(i, y) = 1/|B|$ for $(i, y) \in B$;
3. **for** $i = 1$ to T:
4.   Modify the distribution w_t by creating S synthetic examples from P using SMOTE algorithm;
5.   Train a weak learner by using $\mathfrak{L}$ and w_t;
6.   Compute weak hypothesis $h_t : \mathcal{X} \times \mathcal{Y} \mapsto [0, 1]$;
7.   Compute the pseudo-loss of hypothesis h_t:
$$e_t = \sum_{(i,y) \in B} w_t(i, y) \left(1 - h_t(\boldsymbol{x}_i, y_i) + h_t(\boldsymbol{x}_i, y)\right);$$
8. $\alpha_t = \ln \frac{1 - e_t}{e_t}$;
9. $d_t = \frac{1}{2}(1 - h_t(\boldsymbol{x}_i, y) + h_t(\boldsymbol{x}_i, y_i))$;
10.   Update the distribution $w_{t+1}(i, y) = \frac{1}{Z_t} w_t(i, y) e^{-\alpha_t d_t}$;
11.**end**

Output: $H(x) = \arg\max_{y \in \mathcal{Y}} \sum_{t=1}^{T} \alpha_t h_t(\boldsymbol{x}, y)$.

FIGURE 8.6: The SMOTEBoost algorithm.

EasyEnsemble which generates subsamples of the majority class in an unsupervised parallel manner, BalanceCascade works in a supervised sequential manner. In the ith round, a subsample N_i is generated from the current majority class data set N, with sample size $|N_i| = |P|$. Then, an ensemble H_i is trained from the union of N_i and P by AdaBoost. After that, the majority class examples that are correctly classified by H_i are removed from N. The final ensemble is formed by combining all the base learners in all the AdaBoost ensembles. The BalanceCascade algorithm is shown in Figure 8.8.

BalanceCascade actually works in a cascading-style, which has been used by Viola and Jones [2002] to improve the efficiency of face detection. Notice that both EasyEnsemble and BalanceCascade combine all base learners instead of combining the outputs of the AdaBoost ensembles directly. This strategy is adopted for exploiting the detailed information provided by the base learners. Here, the base learners can actually be viewed as features exposing different aspects of the data.

There are many other ensemble methods for improving over-sampling and under-sampling. For example, the DataBoost-IM method [Guo and Viktor, 2004] identifies hard examples in each boosting round and creates synthetic examples according to the level of imbalance of hard examples; Chan and Stolfo [1998]'s method simply partitions the majority class into

Input: Training data set $D = \{(\boldsymbol{x}_1, y_1), (\boldsymbol{x}_2, y_2), \ldots, (\boldsymbol{x}_m, y_m)\}$;
        Minority class examples $P \subseteq D$;
        Majority class examples $N \subseteq D$;
        Number of subsets T to sample from N;
        Number of iterations s_i to train an AdaBoost ensemble H_i.

Process:
1. **for** $i = 1$ to T:
2.   Randomly sample a subset N_i from N with $|N_i| = |P|$;
3.   Use P and N_i to learn an AdaBoost ensemble H_i, which is with s_i
       weak classifiers $h_{i,j}$ and corresponding weights $\alpha_{i,j}$:
$$H_i(\boldsymbol{x}) = \texttt{sign}\left(\textstyle\sum_{j=1}^{s_i} \alpha_{i,j} h_{i,j}(\boldsymbol{x})\right).$$

4. **end**
Output: $H(\boldsymbol{x}) = \texttt{sign}\left(\sum_{i=1}^{T} \sum_{j=1}^{s_i} \alpha_{i,j} h_{i,j}(\boldsymbol{x})\right).$

FIGURE 8.7: The EasyEnsemble algorithm.

Input: Training data set $D = \{(\boldsymbol{x}_1, y_1), (\boldsymbol{x}_2, y_2), \ldots, (\boldsymbol{x}_m, y_m)\}$;
        Minority class examples $P \subseteq D$;
        Majority class examples $N \subseteq D$;
        Number of subsets T to sample from N;
        Number of iterations s_i to train an AdaBoost ensemble H_i.

Process:
1. $f \Leftarrow {}^{T-1}\sqrt{\frac{|P|}{|N|}}$, f is the false positive rate (the error rate of misclassifying
    a majority class example to the minority class) that H_i should achieve;
2. **for** $i = 1$ to T:
3.   Randomly sample a subset N_i from N with $|N_i| = |P|$;
4.   Use P and N_i to learn an AdaBoost ensemble H_i, which is with s_i
       weak classifiers $h_{i,j}$ and corresponding weights $\alpha_{i,j}$, and adjust θ_i
       such that H_i's false positive rate is f :
$$H_i(\boldsymbol{x}) = \texttt{sign}\left(\textstyle\sum_{j=1}^{s_i} \alpha_{i,j} h_{i,j}(\boldsymbol{x}) - \theta_i\right) ;$$
5.   Remove from N all examples that are correctly classified by H_i.
6. **end**
Output: $H(\boldsymbol{x}) = \texttt{sign}\left(\sum_{i=1}^{T} \sum_{j=1}^{s_i} \alpha_{i,j} h_{i,j}(\boldsymbol{x}) - \sum_{i=1}^{T} \theta_i\right).$

FIGURE 8.8: The BalanceCascade algorithm.

non-overlapping subsets with the size of the minority class and then trains
a base learner based on each pair of the subsets and the minority class.
There are also ensemble methods that combine over-sampling with under-
sampling [Estabrooks et al., 2004] or even combine them with other strate-

gies such as threshold-moving [Zhou and Liu, 2006]. A thorough comparison of those methods is an important issue to be explored. According to incomplete comparisons available currently, the EasyEnsemble method is a good choice in many situations.

8.5 Improving Comprehensibility

In many real-world tasks, in addition to attaining strong generalization ability, the **comprehensibility** of the learned model is also important. It is usually required that the learned model and its predictions are understandable and interpretable. Symbolic rules and decision trees are usually deemed as comprehensible models. For example, every decision made by a decision tree can be explained by the tree branches it goes through.

Comprehensibility is an inherent deficiency of ensemble methods. Even when comprehensible models such as decision trees are used as base learners, the ensemble still lacks comprehensibility, since it aggregates multiple models. This section introduces some techniques for improving ensemble comprehensibility.

8.5.1 Reduction of Ensemble to Single Model

Considering that the comprehensibility of an ensemble is lost mainly because it aggregates multiple models, one possible approach to improving the comprehensibility is to reduce the ensemble to a single model.

CMM [Domingos, 1998]. This method uses the ensemble to label some artificially generated instances, and then applies the base learning algorithm, which was used to train the base learners for the ensemble, on the artificial data together with the original training data to generate a single learner. By adding the artificial data, it is expected that the final single learner can mimic the behavior of ensemble. Notice that the final single learner is trained using the same base learning algorithm. Though this avoids the conflict of different biases of different types of learners, the performance of the final single learner has high risk of overfitting because peculiarity patterns in the training data that affect the base learning algorithm can be strengthened. Also, if the base learners of the ensemble are not comprehensible, CMM will not improve comprehensibility.

Archetype Selection [Ferri et al., 2002]. This method calculates the similarity between each base learner and the ensemble by comparing their predictions on an artificial data set, and then selects the single base learner that is the most similar to the ensemble. Notice that, in many cases there may not exist a base learner that is very close to the ensemble, or the base learners themselves are not comprehensible. In these cases this method will fail.

NeC4.5 [Zhou and Jiang, 2004]. This method is similar to CMM in using the ensemble to generate an artificial data set and then using the artificial data set together with the original training set to generate a single learner. The major difference is that in NeC4.5, the learning algorithm for the final single learner is different from the base learning algorithm of the ensemble. This difference reduces the risk of overfitting, and the final single learner may even be more accurate than the ensemble itself. However, by using different types of learners, the different biases need to be treated well. To obtain an accurate and comprehensible model, NeC4.5 uses a neural network ensemble and a C4.5 decision tree, where the neural networks are targeted to accuracy while the decision tree is used for comprehensibility. It was derived in [Zhou and Jiang, 2004] that when the original training data set does not capture the whole distribution or contains noise, and the first-stage learner (e.g., the ensemble) is more accurate than the second-stage learner (e.g., a C4.5 decision tree trained from the original training data), the procedure of NeC4.5 will be beneficial. Later, such procedure of accomplishing two objectives in two stages with different types of learners is called **twice learning** [Zhou, 2005].

ISM [Assche and Blockeel, 2007]. Considering that it is difficult to generate artificial data in some domains such as those involving *relational* data, this method tries to learn a single decision tree from a tree ensemble without generating an artificial data set. The basic idea is to construct a single tree where each split is decided by considering the utility of this split in similar paths of the trees in the ensemble. Roughly speaking, for each candidate split of a node, a path of feature tests can be obtained from root to the node. Then, similar paths in the trees of the ensemble will be identified, and the utility of the split in each path can be calculated, e.g., according to information gain. The utility values obtained from all the similar paths are aggregated, and finally the candidate split with the largest aggregated utility is selected for the current node.

8.5.2   Rule Extraction from Ensembles

Improving ensemble comprehensibility by rule extraction was inspired by studies on rule extraction from neural networks [Andrews et al., 1995, Tickle et al., 1998, Zhou, 2004], with the goal of using a set of symbolic *if-then* rules to represent the ensemble.

REFNE [Zhou et al., 2003]. This method uses the ensemble to generate an artificial data set. Then, it tries to identify a feature-value pair such as "*color = red*" which is able to make a correct prediction on some artificial examples. If there exists such a feature-value pair, a rule with one antecedent is generated, e.g., *if "color = red" then positive,* and the artificial examples that are classified correctly by the rule are removed. REFNE searches for other one-antecedent rules on the remaining artificial data, and if there is no more, it starts to search for two-antecedent rules such as *if "color = blue" and "shape = round" then positive*; and so on. Numeric features are discretized adaptively, and sanity checks based on statistical tests are executed before each rule is accepted. Notice that REFNE generates *priority rules,* also called *decision list,* which must be applied in the order that the earlier generated, the earlier applied. This method suffers from low efficiency and does not work on large-scale data sets.

C4.5 Rule-PANE [Zhou and Jiang, 2003]. This method improves REFNE by using C4.5 Rule [Quinlan, 1993] to replace the complicated rule generation procedure in REFNE. Though it was named as *C4.5 Rule Preceded by Artificial Neural Ensemble,* similar to REFNE, this method can be applied to extract rules from any type of ensembles comprising any types of base learners.

Notice that, though in most cases the ensemble is more accurate than the extracted rules, there are also cases where the extracted rules are even more accurate than the ensemble. In such cases, there is a conflict between attaining a high *accuracy* and high *fidelity*. If the goal is to explain the ensemble or mimic behaviors of the ensemble, then the higher accuracy of the extracted rules has to be sacrificed. This is the *fidelity-accuracy dilemma* [Zhou, 2004]. However, if the goal is to achieve an accurate and comprehensible model, then it is not needed to care about whether the behaviors of the ensemble can be correctly mimicked; this recognition motivated the *twice learning* paradigm.

8.5.3   Visualization of Ensembles

Visualization is an important approach to help people understand the behaviors of learning methods. Obviously, one of the most straightforward ways is to plot the decision boundary of an ensemble after each learning round. In such a plot, the x-axis and y-axis correspond to any pair of features, while each point corresponds to an instance. For example, Figures 8.9 and 8.10 provide illustrations of the visualization results of Boosted decision stumps and Bagged decision stumps on the *three-Gaussians* data set, respectively.

Notice that visualization with dimensions higher than three is quite difficult. For data with more than three dimensions, dimension reduction may be needed for visualization. In practice, however, the intrinsic dimension of the data is often much larger than two or three, hence visualization can only be performed on some important feature combinations.

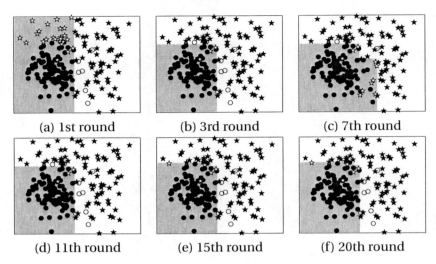

(a) 1st round   (b) 3rd round   (c) 7th round

(d) 11th round   (e) 15th round   (f) 20th round

FIGURE 8.9: Boosted decision stumps on *three-Gaussians*, where circles/stars denote positive/negative examples, and solid/empty mark correct/incorrect classified examples, respectively.

8.6 Future Directions of Ensembles

There are many interesting future research directions for ensembles. Here, we highlight two directions, that is, *understanding ensembles* and *ensembles in the internet world*.

There are two important aspects of understanding ensembles. The first aspect is on *diversity*. It is well accepted that understanding diversity is the holy grail problem in ensemble research. Though some recent advances have been attained [Brown, 2009, Zhou and Li, 2010b], we are still a long way from a complete understanding of diversity. It is not yet known whether diversity is really a driving force, or actually a trap, since it might be just another appearance of accuracy. Moreover, if it is really helpful, can we do better through exploiting it explicitly, for example, by using it as a regularizer for optimization? Recently there is some exploration in this direction [Yu et al., 2011].

The second important aspect is on the *loss view* of ensemble methods. From the view of statistical learning, every learning method is optimizing some kind of loss function. The understanding of the learning method can get help from the understanding of the properties of the loss function. There are some studies on the loss behind AdaBoost [Demiriz et al., 2002, Warmuth et al., 2008]. Though there might exist some deviations, they provided some insight about AdaBoost. Can we conjecture what are the loss

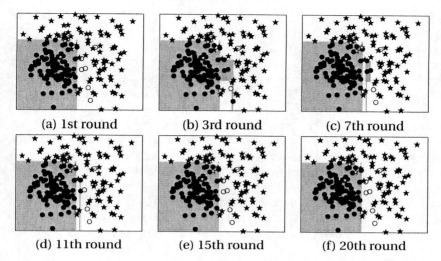

FIGURE 8.10: Bagged decision stumps on *three-Gaussians*, where circles/stars denote positive/negative examples, and solid/empty mark correct/incorrect classified examples, respectively.

functions optimized by other ensemble methods such as Bagging, Random Subspace, etc.? If we know them, can we have practically more effective and efficient ways, rather than ensembles, to optimize them?

There are also two important aspects of ensembles in the internet world. The first one is *on-site ensemble*, which tries to use ensemble methods as tools for exploiting resources scattered over internet. For example, for most tasks there are relevant and helpful data existing at different places of the internet. Merging the data to a single site may suffer from unaffordable communication costs, not to mention other issues such as data ownership and privacy which prevent the data from being exposed to other sites. In such scenarios, each site can maintain its local model. Once the task is being executed, the site can send out a service request, such as the request of making a prediction on an instance, to other sites. The other sites, if they accept the request, will send back only the predictions made by their local models. Finally the initial site can aggregate the remote predictions with its local prediction to get a better result. Li et al. [2010] reported a work in this line of research. There are many issues to be studied, for example, how to make the decision process robust against requests lost on internet, how to identify trustworthy remote predictions, how to make a better combined result based on remote predictions with a little additional information such as simple statistics, how to prevent the initial site from sending so many requests that it can reconstruct the remote models with high confidence and therefore lead to privacy breaches, etc.

The second important aspect is on *reusable ensembles*. This name was inspired by software reuse. Reusable components are functional components of softwares that can be shared as plug-in packages. Ideally, when a user wants to develop a new program, there is no need to start from scratch; instead, the user can search for reusable components and put them together, and only write those functional components that could not be found. Similarly, in the internet world, many sites may like to share their learning models. Thus, when a user wants to construct a learning system, s/he can search for useful reusable models and put them together. For this purpose, there are many issues to be studied, for example, how to establish the specification of the functions and usage of reusable learning models, how to match them with the user requirement, how to put together different learning models trained from different data, etc. Though at present this is just an imagination without support of research results, it is well worth pursuing since it will help learning methods become much easier for common people to use, rather than being like an art that can only be deployed by researchers.

It is also worth highlighting that the utility of variance reduction of ensemble methods would enable them to be helpful to many modern applications, especially those involving dynamic data and environment. For example, for *social network analysis*, a more robust or trustworthy result may be achieved by ensembling the results discovered from different data sources, or even from multiple perturbations of the same data source.

8.7   Further Readings

Many semi-supervised learning approaches have been developed during the past decade. Roughly speaking, they can be categorized into four classes, i.e., generative approaches, S3VMs (Semi-Supervised Support Vector Machines), graph-based approaches and disagreement-based approaches. Generative approaches use a generative model and typically employ EM to model the label estimation and parameter estimation process [Miller and Uyar, 1997, Nigam et al., 2000]. S3VMs use unlabeled data to adjust the SVM decision boundary learned from labeled examples such that it goes through the less dense region while keeping the labeled data correctly classified [Joachims, 1999, Chapelle and Zien, 2005]. Graph-based approaches define a graph on the training data and then enforce the label smoothness over the graph as a *regularization* term [Zhu et al., 2003, Zhou et al., 2004]. Disagreement-based approaches generate more than one learner which collaborate to exploit unlabeled instances, and a large disagreement between the learners is maintained to enable the learning procedure to continue [Blum and Mitchell, 1998, Zhou and Li, 2007]. More introduction on semi-supervised learning can be found in [Chapelle et al., 2006, Zhu, 2006, Zhou and Li, 2010a].

Both ensemble and semi-supervised learning try to achieve strong generalization ability, however, they have almost developed separately and only a few studies have tried to leverage their advantages. This phenomenon was attributed by Zhou [2009] to the fact that the two communities have different philosophies. Zhou [2011] discussed the reasons for combining both.

In addition to query-by-committee, *uncertainty sampling* is another active learning paradigm which tries to query the most *informative* unlabeled instance. In uncertainty sampling, a single learner is trained and then, the unlabeled instance on which the learner is the least confident is selected to query [Lewis and Gale, 1994, Tong and Koller, 2000]. There is another school of active learning that tries to query the most *representative* unlabeled instance, usually by exploiting the cluster structure of data [Nguyen and Smeulders, 2004, Dasgupta and Hsu, 2008]. Recently there are some studies on querying *informative and representative* unlabeled instances [Huang et al., 2010]. Most active learning algorithms focus on querying one instance in each round, while *batch mode* active learning extends the classical setup by selecting multiple unlabeled instances to query in each trial [Guo and Schuurmans, 2008, Hoi et al., 2009]. More introduction on active learning can be found in [Settles, 2009].

Though Rescaling is effective in two-class cost-sensitive learning, its direct extension to multi-class tasks does not work well [Ting, 2002]. Zhou and Liu [2010] disclosed that the Rescaling approach can be applied directly to multi-class tasks only when the cost-coefficients are *consistent*, and otherwise the problem should be decomposed to a series of two-class problems for applying Rescaling directly. In addition to class-dependent cost, there are many studies on example-dependent cost [Zadrozny and Elkan, 2001a, Zadrozny et al., 2003, Brefeld et al., 2003], where some representative methods are also ensemble methods, e.g., the costing method [Zadrozny et al., 2003]. It is worth noting that traditional studies generally assumed that precise cost values are given in advance, while there is a recent work which tried to handle imprecise cost information appearing as cost intervals [Liu and Zhou, 2010].

ROC curve and AUC can be used to study class-imbalance learning as well as cost-sensitive learning, and can be extended to multi-class cases [Hand and Till, 2001, Fawcett, 2006]. **Cost curve** [Drummond and Holte, 2006] is equivalent to ROC curve but makes it easier to visualize cost-sensitive learning performance. It is noteworthy that there are some recent studies that disclose that AUC has significant problems for model selection [Lobo et al., 2008, Hand, 2009].

Some learning methods were developed by directly minimizing a criterion that considers the unequal sizes of different classes. For example, Brefeld and Scheffer [2005] proposed an SVM method to minimize

AUC, while Joachims [2005] proposed an SVM method to minimize F-measure. Those methods can also be used for class-imbalance learning. There are also some class-imbalance learning methods designed based on **one-class learning** or anomaly detection. More introduction on class-imbalance learning can be found in [Chawla, 2006, He and Garcia, 2009]. Notice that, though class imbalance generally occurs simultaneously with unequal costs, most studies do not consider them together, and even for the well-studied Rescaling approach it is not yet known how to do the best in such scenarios [Liu and Zhou, 2006].

Frank and Hall [2003] presented a method to provide a two-dimensional visualization of class probability estimates. Though this method was not specially designed for ensemble methods, there is no doubt that it can be applied to ensembles.

This book does not plan to cover all topics relevant to ensemble methods. For example, **stochastic discrimination** [Kleinberg, 2000] which works by sampling from the space of all subsets of the underlying feature space, and **multiple kernel learning** [Bach et al., 2004] which can be viewed as ensembles of kernels, have not been included in this version. This also applies to **stability selection** [Meinshausen and Bühlmann, 2010], a recent advance in model selection for LASSO [Tibshirani, 1996a], which can be viewed as a Bagging-style ensemble-based feature ranking.

MCS'2010, the 10th MCS Workshop, held a panel[1] on reviewing the past and foreseeing the future of ensemble research. The content of Section 8.6 was presented at that panel by the author of this book.

---

[1]http://www.diee.unica.it/mcs/mcs2010/panel%20discussion.html

References

N. Abe and H. Mamitsuka. Query learning strategies using Boosting and Bagging. In *Proceedings of the 15th International Conference on Machine Learning*, pages 1–9, Madison, WI, 1998.

R. Agrawal, J. Gehrke, D. Gunopulos, and P. Raghavan. Automatic subspace clustering of high dimensional data for data mining applications. In *Proceedings of the ACM SIGMOD International Conference on Management of Data*, pages 94–105, Seattle, WA, 1998.

M. R. Ahmadzadeh and M. Petrou. Use of Dempster-Shafer theory to combine classifiers which use different class boundaries. *Pattern Analysis and Application*, 6(1):41–46, 2003.

A. Al-Ani and M. Deriche. A new technique for combining multiple classifiers using the Dempster-Shafer theory of evidence. *Journal of Artificial Intelligence Research*, 17(1):333–361, 2002.

K. M. Ali and M. J. Pazzani. Error reduction through learning multiple descriptions. *Machine Learning*, 24(3):173–202, 1996.

E. L. Allwein, R. E. Schapire, and Y. Singer. Reducing multiclass to binary: A unifying approach for margin classifiers. *Journal of Machine Learning Research*, 1:113–141, 2000.

E. Alpaydin. *Introduction to Machine Learning*. MIT Press, Cambridge, MA, 2nd edition, 2010.

M. R. Anderberg. *Cluster Analysis for Applications*. Academic, New York, NY, 1973.

R. Andrews, J. Diederich, and A. B. Tickle. Survey and critique of techniques for extracting rules from trained artificial neural networks. *Knowledge-Based Systems*, 8(6):373–389, 1995.

M. Ankerst, M. Breunig, H.-P. Kriegel, and J. Sander. OPTICS: Ordering points to identify the clustering structure. In *Proceedings of the ACM SIGMOD International Conference on Management of Data*, pages 49–60, Philadelphia, PA, 1999.

M. Anthony and N. Biggs. *Computational Learning Theory*. Cambridge University Press, Cambridge, UK, 1992.

M. B. Araújo and M. New. Ensemble forecasting of species distributions. *Trends in Ecology & Evolution*, 22(1):42–47, 2007.

J. A. Aslam and S. E. Decatur. General bounds on statistical query learning and PAC learning with noise via hypothesis boosting. In *Proceedings of the 35th IEEE Annual Symposium on Foundations of Computer Science*, pages 282–291, Palo Alto, CA, 1993.

E. Asmis. *Epicurus' Scientific Method.* Cornell University Press, Ithaca, NY, 1984.

A. V. Assche and H. Blockeel. Seeing the forest through the trees: Learning a comprehensible model from an ensemble. In *Proceedings of the 18th European Conference on Machine Learning*, pages 418–429, Warsaw, Poland, 2007.

S. Avidan. Ensemble tracking. *IEEE Transactions on Pattern Analysis and Machine Intelligence*, 29(2):261–271, 2007.

R. Avogadri and G. Valentini. Fuzzy ensemble clustering based on random projections for DNA microarray data analysis. *Artificial Intelligence in Medicine*, 45(2-3):173–183, 2009.

H. Ayad and M. Kamel. Finding natural clusters using multi-clusterer combiner based on shared nearest neighbors. In *Proceedings of the 4th International Workshop on Multiple Classifier Systems*, pages 166–175, Surrey, UK, 2003.

F. R. Bach, G. R. G. Lanckriet, and M. I. Jordan. Multiple kernel learning, conic duality, and the SMO algorithm. In *Proceedings of the 21st International Conference on Machine Learning*, Banff, Canada, 2004.

B. Bakker and T. Heskes. Clustering ensembles of neural network models. *Neural Networks*, 16(2):261–269, 2003.

M.-F. Balcan, A. Z. Broder, and T. Zhang. Margin based active learning. In *Proceedings of the 20th Annual Conference on Learning Theory*, pages 35–50, San Diego, CA, 2007.

R. E. Banfield, L. O. Hall, K. W. Bowyer, and W. P. Kegelmeyer. Ensemble diversity measures and their application to thinning. *Information Fusion*, 6(1):49–62, 2005.

E. Bauer and R. Kohavi. An empirical comparison of voting classification algorithms: Bagging, boosting, and variants. *Machine Learning*, 36(1-2): 105–139, 1999.

K. Bennett, A. Demiriz, and R. Maclin. Exploiting unlabeled data in ensemble methods. In *Proceedings of the 8th ACM SIGKDD International Conference on Knowledge Discovery and Data Mining*, pages 289–296, Edmonton, Canada, 2002.

J. Bergstra, N. Casagrande, D. Erhan, D. Eck, and B. Kégl. Aggregate features and AdaBoost for music classification. *Machine Learning*, 65(2-3):473–484, 2006.

Y. Bi, J. Guan, and D. Bell. The combination of multiple classifiers using an evidential reasoning approach. *Artificial Intelligence*, 172(15):1731–1751, 2008.

P. J. Bickel, Y. Ritov, and A. Zakai. Some theory for generalized boosting algorithms. *Journal of Machine Learning Research*, 7:705–732, 2006.

J. A. Bilmes. A gentle tutorial of the EM algorithm and its applications to parameter estimation for Gaussian mixture and hidden Markov models. Technical Report TR-97-021, Department of Electrical Engineering and Computer Science, University of California, Berkeley, CA, 1998.

C. M. Bishop. *Neural Networks for Pattern Recognition*. Oxford University Press, New York, NY, 1995.

C. M. Bishop. *Pattern Recognition and Machine Learning*. Springer, New York, NY, 2006.

C. M. Bishop and M. Svensén. Bayesian hierarchical mixtures of experts. In *Proceedings of the 19th Conference in Uncertainty in Artificial Intelligence*, pages 57–64, Acapulco, Mexico, 2003.

A. Blum and T. Mitchell. Combining labeled and unlabeled data with co-training. In *Proceedings of the 11th Annual Conference on Computational Learning Theory*, pages 92–100, Madison, WI, 1998.

J. K. Bradley and R. E. Schapire. FilterBoost: Regression and classification on large datasets. In J. C. Platt, D. Koller, Y. Singer, and S. T. Roweis, editors, *Advances in Neural Information Processing Systems 20*, pages 185–192. MIT Press, Cambridge, MA, 2008.

U. Brefeld and T. Scheffer. AUC maximizing support vector learning. In *Proceedings of the ICML 2005 Workshop on ROC Analysis in Machine Learning*, Bonn, Germany, 2005.

U. Brefeld, P. Geibel, and F. Wysotzki. Support vector machines with example dependent costs. In *Proceedings of the 14th European Conference on Machine Learning*, pages 23–34, Cavtat-Dubrovnik, Croatia, 2003.

L. Breiman. Bias, variance, and arcing classifiers. Technical Report 460, Statistics Department, University of California, Berkeley, CA, 1996a.

L. Breiman. Stacked regressions. *Machine Learning*, 24(1):49–64, 1996b.

L. Breiman. Out-of-bag estimation. Technical report, Department of Statistics, University of California, 1996c.

L. Breiman. Bagging predictors. *Machine Learning*, 24(2):123–140, 1996d.

L. Breiman. Prediction games and arcing algorithms. *Neural Computation*, 11(7):1493–1517, 1999.

L. Breiman. Randomizing outputs to increase prediction accuracy. *Machine Learning*, 40(3):113–120, 2000.

L. Breiman. Random forests. *Machine Learning*, 45(1):5–32, 2001.

L. Breiman. Population theory for boosting ensembles. *Annals of Statistics*, 32(1):1–11, 2004.

L. Breiman, J. Friedman, C. J. Stone, and R. A. Olshen. *Classification and Regression Trees*. Chapman and Hall/CRC, Boca Raton, FL, 1984.

G. Brown. An information theoretic perspective on multiple classifier systems. In *Proceedings of the 8th International Workshop on Multiple Classifier Systems*, pages 344–353, Reykjavik, Iceland, 2009.

G. Brown. Some thoughts at the interface of ensemble methods and feature selection. Keynote at the 9th International Workshop on Multiple Classifier Systems, Cairo, Egypt, 2010.

G. Brown, J. L. Wyatt, R. Harris, and X. Yao. Diversity creation methods: A survey and categorisation. *Information Fusion*, 6(1):5–20, 2005a.

G. Brown, J. L. Wyatt, and P. Tino. Managing diversity in regression ensembles. *Journal of Machine Learning Research*, 6:1621–1650, 2005b.

P. Bühlmann and B. Yu. Analyzing bagging. *Annals of Statistics*, 30(4):927–961, 2002.

P. Bühlmann and B. Yu. Boosting with the l_2 loss: Regression and classification. *Journal of the American Statistical Association*, 98(462):324–339, 2003.

A. Buja and W. Stuetzle. The effect of bagging on variance, bias, and mean squared error. Technical report, AT&T Labs-Research, 2000a.

A. Buja and W. Stuetzle. Smoothing effects of bagging. Technical report, AT&T Labs-Research, 2000b.

A. Buja and W. Stuetzle. Observations on bagging. *Statistica Sinica*, 16(2): 323–351, 2006.

R. Caruana, A. Niculescu-Mizil, G. Crew, and A. Ksikes. Ensemble selection from libraries of models. In *Proceedings of the 21st International Conference on Machine Learning*, pages 18–23, Banff, Canada, 2004.

P. D. Castro, G. P. Coelho, M. F. Caetano, and F. J. V. Zuben. Designing ensembles of fuzzy classification systems: An immune-inspired approach.

In *Proceedings of the 4th International Conference on Artificial Immune Systems*, pages 469–482, Banff, Canada, 2005.

P. Chan and S. Stolfo. Toward scalable learning with non-uniform class and cost distributions: A case study in credit card fraud detection. In *Proceeding of the 4th International Conference on Knowledge Discovery and Data Mining*, pages 164–168, New York, NY, 1998.

P. K. Chan, W. Fan, A. L. Prodromidis, and S. J. Stolfo. Distributed data mining in credit card fraud detection. *IEEE Intelligent Systems*, 14(6):67–74, 1999.

V. Chandola, A. Banerjee, and V. Kumar. Anomaly detection: A survey. *ACM Computing Surveys*, 41(3):1–58, 2009.

O. Chapelle and A. Zien. Semi-supervised learning by low density separation. In *Proceedings of the 10th International Workshop on Artificial Intelligence and Statistics*, pages 57–64. Barbados, 2005.

O. Chapelle, B. Schölkopf, and A. Zien, editors. *Semi-Supervised Learning*. MIT Press, Cambridge, MA, 2006.

N. V. Chawla. Data mining for imbalanced datasets: An overview. In O. Maimon and L. Rokach, editors, *The Data Mining and Knowledge Discovery Handbook*, pages 853–867. Springer, New York, NY, 2006.

N. V. Chawla, K. W. Bowyer, L. O. Hall, and W. P. Kegelmeyer. SMOTE: Synthetic minority oversampling technique. *Journal of Artificial Intelligence Research*, 16:321–357, 2002.

N. V. Chawla, A. Lazarevic, L. O. Hall, and K. W. Bowyer. SMOTEBoost: Improving prediction of the minority class in boosting. In *Proceedings of the 7th European Conference on Principles and Practice of Knowledge Discovery in Databases*, pages 107–119, Cavtat-Dubrovnik, Croatia, 2003.

H. Chen, P. Tiño, and X. Yao. A probabilistic ensemble pruning algorithm. In *Working Notes of ICDM'06 Workshop on Optimization-Based Data Mining Techniques with Applications*, pages 878–882, Hong Kong, China, 2006.

H. Chen, P. Tiño, and X. Yao. Predictive ensemble pruning by expectation propagation. *IEEE Transactions on Knowledge and Data Engineering*, 21 (7):999–1013, 2009.

B. Clarke. Comparing Bayes model averaging and stacking when model approximation error cannot be ignored. *Journal of Machine Learning Research*, 4:683–712, 2003.

A. L. V. Coelho, C. A. M. Lima, and F. J. V. Zuben. GA-based selection of components for heterogeneous ensembles of support vector machines.

In *Proceedings of the Congress on Evolutionary Computation,* pages 2238–2244, Canberra, Australia, 2003.

J. Cohen. A coefficient of agreement for nominal scales. *Educational and Psychological Measurement,* 20(1):37–46, 1960.

I. Corona, G. Giacinto, C. Mazzariello, F. Roli, and C. Sansone. Information fusion for computer security: State of the art and open issues. *Information Fusion,* 10(4):274–284, 2009.

T. M. Cover and P. E. Hart. Nearest neighbor pattern classification. *IEEE Transactions on Information Theory,* 13(1):21–27, 1967.

T. M. Cover and J. A. Thomas. *Elements of Information Theory.* Wiley, New York, NY, 1991.

M. Coyle and B. Smyth. On the use of selective ensembles for relevance classification in case-based web search. In *Proceedings of the 8th European Conference on Case-Based Reasoning,* pages 370–384, Fethiye, Turkey, 2006.

K. Crammer and Y. Singer. On the learnability and design of output codes for multiclass problems. *Machine Learning,* 47(2-3):201–233, 2002.

N. Cristianini and J. Shawe-Taylor. *An Introduction to Support Vector Machines and Other Kernel-Based Learning Methods.* Cambridge University Press, Cambridge, UK, 2000.

P. Cunningham and J. Carney. Diversity versus quality in classification ensembles based on feature selection. Technical Report TCD-CS-2000-02, Department of Computer Science, Trinity College Dublin, 2000.

A. Cutler and G. Zhao. PERT - perfect random tree ensembles. In *Proceedings of the 33rd Symposium on the Interface of Computing Science and Statistics,* pages 490–497, Costa Mesa, CA, 2001.

I. Dagan and S. P. Engelson. Committee-based sampling for training probabilistic classifiers. In *Proceedings of the 12th International Conference on Machine Learning,* pages 150–157, San Francisco, CA, 1995.

F. d'Alché-Buc, Y. Grandvalet, and C. Ambroise. Semi-supervised marginboost. In T. G. Dietterich, S. Becker, and Z. Ghahramani, editors, *Advances in Neural Information Processing Systems 14,* pages 553–560. MIT Press, Cambridge, MA, 2002.

B. V. Dasarathy, editor. *Nearest Neighbor (NN) Norms: NN Pattern Classification Techniques.* IEEE Computer Society Press, Los Alamitos, CA, 1991.

S. Dasgupta. Analysis of a greedy active learning strategy. In L. Saul, Y. Weiss, and L. Bottou, editors, *Advances in Neural Information Processing Systems 17,* pages 337–344. MIT Press, Cambridge, MA, 2005.

S. Dasgupta. Coarse sample complexity bounds for active learning. In Y. Weiss, B. Schölkopf, and J. Platt, editors, *Advances in Neural Information Processing Systems 18*, pages 235–242. MIT Press, Cambridge, MA, 2006.

S. Dasgupta and D. Hsu. Hierarchical sampling for active learning. In *Proceedings of the 25th International Conference on Machine Learning*, pages 208–215, Helsinki, Finland, 2008.

S. Dasgupta, A. T. Kalai, and C. Monteleoni. Analysis of perceptron-based active learning. In *Proceedings of the 18th Annual Conference on Learning Theory*, pages 249–263, Bertinoro, Italy, 2005.

J. Davis and M. Goadrich. The relationship between precision-recall and ROC curves. In *Proceedings of the 23rd International Conference on Machine Learning*, pages 233–240, Pittsburgh, PA, 2006.

W. H. E. Day and H. Edelsbrunner. Efficient algorithms for agglomerative hierarchical clustering methods. *Journal of Classification*, 1:7–24, 1984.

N. C. de Concorcet. *Essai sur l'Application de l'Analyze à la Probabilité des Décisions Rendues à la Pluralité des Voix*. Imprimérie Royale, Paris, France, 1785.

A. Demiriz, K. P. Bennett, and J. Shawe-Taylor. Linear programming boosting via column generation. *Machine Learning*, 46(1-3):225–254, 2002.

A. P. Dempster. Upper and lower probabilities induced by a multivalued mapping. *Annals of Mathematical Statistics*, 38(2):325–339, 1967.

A. P. Dempster, N. M. Laird, and D. B. Rubin. Maximum likelihood from incomplete data via the EM algorithm. *Journal of the Royal Statistical Soceity, Series B*, 39(1):1–38, 1977.

J. Demšar. Statistical comparisons of classifiers over multiple data sets. *Journal of Machine Learning Research*, 7:1–30, 2006.

L. Didaci, G. Giacinto, F. Roli, and G. L. Marcialis. A study on the performances of dynamic classifier selection based on local accuracy estimation. *Pattern Recognition*, 38(11):2188–2191, 2005.

T. G. Dietterich. Approximate statistical tests for comparing supervised classification learning algorithms. *Neural Computation*, 10(7):1895–1923, 1998.

T. G. Dietterich. Ensemble methods in machine learning. In *Proceedings of the 1st International Workshop on Multiple Classifier Systems*, pages 1–15, Sardinia, Italy, 2000a.

T. G. Dietterich. An experimental comparison of three methods for constructing ensembles of decision trees: Bagging, boosting, and randomization. *Machine Learning*, 40(2):139–157, 2000b.

T. G. Dietterich and G. Bakiri. Solving multiclass learning problems via error-correcting output codes. *Journal of Artificial Intelligence Research*, 2:263–286, 1995.

T. G. Dietterich, G. Hao, and A. Ashenfelter. Gradient tree boosting for training conditional random fields. *Journal of Machine Learning Research*, 9: 2113–2139, 2008.

C. Domingo and O. Watanabe. Madaboost: A modification of AdaBoost. In *Proceedings of the 13th Annual Conference on Computational Learning Theory*, pages 180–189, Palo Alto, CA, 2000.

P. Domingos. Knowledge discovery via multiple models. *Intelligent Data Analysis*, 2(1-4):187–202, 1998.

P. Domingos. MetaCost: A general method for making classifiers cost-sensitive. In *Proceedings of the 5th ACM SIGKDD International Conference on Knowledge Discovery and Data Mining*, pages 155–164, San Diego, CA, 1999.

P. Domingos and M. Pazzani. On the optimality of the simple Bayesian classifier under zero-one loss. *Machine Learning*, 29(2-3):103–137, 1997.

C. Drummond and R. C. Holte. Exploiting the cost of (in)sensitivity of decision tree splitting criteria. In *Proceedings of the 17th International Conference on Machine Learning*, pages 239–246, San Francisco, CA, 2000.

C. Drummond and R. C. Holte. Cost curves: An improved method for visualizing classifier performance. *Machine Learning*, 65(1):95–130, 2006.

R. O. Duda, P. E. Hart, and D. G. Stork. *Pattern Classification*. Wiley, New York, NY, 2nd edition, 2000.

B. Efron and R. Tibshirani. *An Introduction to the Bootstrap*. Chapman & Hall, New York, NY, 1993.

C. Elkan. The foundations of cost-sensitive learning. In *Proceedings of the 17th International Joint Conference on Artificial Intelligence*, pages 973–978, Seattle, WA, 2001.

S. Escalera, O. Pujol, and P. Radeva. Boosted landmarks of contextual descriptors and Forest-ECOC: A novel framework to detect and classify objects in clutter scenes. *Pattern Recognition Letters*, 28(13):1759–1768, 2007.

S. Escalera, O. Pujol, and P. Radeva. Error-correcting ouput codes library. *Journal of Machine Learning Research*, 11:661–664, 2010a.

S. Escalera, O. Pujol, and P. Radeva. On the decoding process in ternary error-correcting output codes. *IEEE Transaction on Pattern Analysis and Machine Intelligence*, 32(1):120–134, 2010b.

A. Estabrooks, T. Jo, and N. Japkowicz. A multiple resampling method for learning from imbalanced data sets. *Computational Intelligence*, 20(1): 18–36, 2004.

M. Ester, H.-P. Kriegel, J. Sander, and X. Xu. A density-based algorithm for discovering clusters in large spatial databases. In *Proceedings of the 2nd International Conference on Knowledge Discovery and Data Mining*, pages 226–231, Portland, OR, 1996.

V. Estivill-Castro. Why so many clustering algorithms - A position paper. *SIGKDD Explorations*, 4(1):65–75, 2002.

W. Fan. On the optimality of probability estimation by random decision trees. In *Proceedings of the 19th National Conference on Artificial Intelligence*, pages 336–341, San Jose, CA, 2004.

W. Fan, S. J. Stolfo, J. Zhang, and P. K. Chan. AdaCost: Misclassification cost-sensitive boosting. In *Proceedings of the 16th International Conference on Machine Learning*, pages 97–105, Bled, Slovenia, 1999.

W. Fan, F. Chu, H. Wang, and P. S. Yu. Pruning and dynamic scheduling of cost-sensitive ensembles. In *Proceedings of the 18th National Conference on Artificial Intelligence*, pages 146–151, Edmonton, Canada, 2002.

W. Fan, H. Wang, P. S. Yu, and S. Ma. Is random model better? On its accuracy and efficiency. In *Proceedings of the 3rd IEEE International Conferenceon Data Mining*, pages 51–58, Melbourne, FL, 2003.

R. Fano. *Transmission of Information: Statistical Theory of Communications*. MIT Press, Cambridge, MA, 1961.

T. Fawcett. ROC graphs with instance varying costs. *Pattern Recognition Letters*, 27(8):882–891, 2006.

X. Z. Fern and C. E. Brodley. Random projection for high dimensional data clustering: A cluster ensemble approach. In *Proceedings of the 20th International Conference on Machine Learning*, pages 186–193, Washington, DC, 2003.

X. Z. Fern and C. E. Brodley. Solving cluster ensemble problems by bipartite graph partitioning. In *Proceedings of the 21st International Conference on Machine Learning*, Banff, Canada, 2004.

X. Z. Fern and W. Lin. Cluster ensemble selection. In *Proceedings of the 8th SIAM International Conference on Data Mining*, pages 787–797, Atlanta, GA, 2008.

C. Ferri, J. Hernández-Orallo, and M. J. Ramírez-Quintana. From ensemble methods to comprehensible models. In *Proceedings of the 5th International Conference on Discovery Science*, pages 165–177, Lübeck, Germany, 2002.

D. Fisher. Improving inference through conceptual clustering. In *Proceedings of the 6th National Conference on Artificial Intelligence*, pages 461–465, Seattle, WA, 1987.

J. L. Fleiss. *Statistical Methods for Rates and Proportions*. John Wiley & Sons, New York, NY, 2nd edition, 1981.

E. Frank and M. Hall. Visualizing class probability estimators. In *Proceedings of the 7th European Conference on Principles and Practice of Knowledge Discovery in Databases*, pages 168–179, Cavtat-Dubrovnik, Croatia, 2003.

A. Fred and A. K. Jain. Data clustering using evidence accumulation. In *Proceedings of the 16th International Conference on Pattern Recognition*, pages 276–280, Quebec, Canada, 2002.

A. Fred and A. K. Jain. Combining multiple clusterings using evidence accumulation. *IEEE Transactions on Pattern Analysis and Machine Intelligence*, 27(6):835–850, 2005.

Y. Freund. Boosting a weak learning algorithm by majority. *Information and Computation*, 121(2):256–285, 1995.

Y. Freund. An adaptive version of the boost by majority algorithm. *Machine Learning*, 43(3):293–318, 2001.

Y. Freund. A more robust boosting algorithm. CORR abs/0905.2138, 2009.

Y. Freund and R. E. Schapire. A decision-theoretic generalization of on-line learning and an application to boosting. In *Proceedings of the 2nd European Conference on Computational Learning Theory*, pages 23–37, Barcelona, Spain, 1995.

Y. Freund and R. E. Schapire. A decision-theoretic generalization of on-line learning and an application to boosting. *Journal of Computer and System Sciences*, 55(1):119–139, 1997.

Y. Freund, H. S. Seung, E. Shamir, and N. Tishby. Selective sampling using the query by committee algorithm. *Machine Learning*, 28(2-3):133–168, 1997.

J. Friedman, T. Hastie, and R. Tibshirani. Additive logistic regression: A statistical view of boosting (with discussions). *Annals of Statistics*, 28(2):337–407, 2000.

J. H. Friedman and P. Hall. On bagging and nonlinear estimation. *Journal of Statistical Planning and Inference*, 137(3):669–683, 2007.

J. H. Friedman and W. Stuetzle. Projection pursuit regression. *Journal of American Statistical Association,* 76(376):817–823, 1981.

N. Friedman, D. Geiger, and M. Goldszmidt. Bayesian network classifiers. *Machine Learning,* 29(2):131–163, 1997.

G. Fumera and F. Roli. A theoretical and experimental analysis of linear combiners for multiple classifier systems. *IEEE Transactions on Pattern Analysis and Machine Intelligence,* 27(6):942–956, 2005.

W. Gao and Z.-H. Zhou. Approximation stability and boosting. In *Proceedings of the 21st International Conference on Algorithmic Learning Theory,* pages 59–73, Canberra, Australia, 2010a.

W. Gao and Z.-H. Zhou. On the doubt about margin explanation of boosting. CORR abs/1009.3613, 2012.

C. W. Gardiner. *Handbook of Stochastic Methods.* Springer, New York, NY, 3rd edition, 2004.

S. Geman, E. Bienenstock, and R. Doursat. Neural networks and the bias/variance dilemma. *Neural Computation,* 4(1):1–58, 1992.

P. Geurts, D. Ernst, and L. Wehenkel. Extremely randomized trees. *Machine Learning,* 63(1):3–42, 2006.

G. Giacinto and F. Roli. Adaptive selection of image classifiers. In *Proceedings of the 9th International Conference on Image Analysis and Processing,* pages 38–45, Florence, Italy, 1997.

G. Giacinto and F. Roli. A theoretical framework for dynamic classifier selection. In *Proceedings of the 15th International Conference on Pattern Recognition,* pages 2008–2011, Barcelona, Spain, 2000a.

G. Giacinto and F. Roli. Dynamic classifier selection. In *Proceedings of the 1st International Workshop on Multiple Classifier Systems,* pages 177–189, Cagliari, Italy, 2000b.

G. Giacinto and F. Roli. Design of effective neural network ensembles for image classification purposes. *Image and Vision Computing,* 19(9-10): 699–707, 2001.

G. Giacinto, F. Roli, and G. Fumera. Design of effective multiple classifier systems by clustering of classifiers. In *Proceedings of the 15th International Conference on Pattern Recognition,* pages 160–163, Barcelona, Spain, 2000.

G. Giacinto, F. Roli, and L. Didaci. Fusion of multiple classifiers for intrusion detection in computer networks. *Pattern Recognition Letters,* 24(12): 1795–1803, 2003.

G. Giacinto, R. Perdisci, M. D. Rio, and F. Roli. Intrusion detection in computer networks by a modular ensemble of one-class classifiers. *Information Fusion*, 9(1):69–82, 2008.

T. Gneiting and A. E. Raftery. Atmospheric science: Weather forecasting with ensemble methods. *Science*, 310(5746):248–249, 2005.

K. Goebel, M. Krok, and H. Sutherland. Diagnostic information fusion: Requirements flowdown and interface issues. In *Proceedings of the IEEE Aerospace Conference*, volume 6, pages 155–162, Big Sky, MT, 2000.

D. E. Goldberg. *Genetic Algorithm in Search, Optimization and Machine Learning*. Addison-Wesley, Boston, MA, 1989.

D. M. Green and J. M. Swets. *Signal Detection Theory and Psychophysics*. John Wiley & Sons, New York, NY, 1966.

A. J. Grove and D. Schuurmans. Boosting in the limit: Maximizing the margin of learned ensembles. In *Proceedings of the 15th National Conference on Artificial Intelligence*, pages 692–699, Madison, WI, 1998.

S. Guha, R. Rastogi, and K. Shim. ROCK: A robust clustering algorithm for categorical attributes. In *Proceedings of the 15th International Conference on Data Engineering*, pages 512–521, Sydney, Australia, 1999.

H. Guo and H. L. Viktor. Learning from imbalanced data sets with boosting and data generation: The DataBoost-IM approach. *SIGKDD Explorations*, 6(1):30–39, 2004.

Y. Guo and D. Schuurmans. Discriminative batch mode active learning. In J. C. Platt, D. Koller, Y. Singer, and S. Roweis, editors, *Advances in Neural Information Processing Systems 20*, pages 593–600. MIT Press, Cambridge, MA, 2008.

I. Guyon and A. Elisseeff. An introduction to variable and feature selection. *Journal of Machine Learning Research*, 3:1157–1182, 2003.

S. T. Hadjitodorov and L. I. Kuncheva. Selecting diversifying heuristics for cluster ensembles. In *Proceedings of the 7th International Workshop on Multiple Classifier Systems*, pages 200–209, Prague, Czech, 2007.

S. T. Hadjitodorov, L. I. Kuncheva, and L. P. Todorova. Moderate diversity for better cluster ensembles. *Information Fusion*, 7(3):264–275, 2006.

M. Halkidi, Y. Batistakis, and M. Vazirgiannis. On clustering validation techniques. *Journal of Intelligent Information Systems*, 17(2-3):107–145, 2001.

J. Han and M. Kamber. *Data Mining: Concepts and Techniques*. Morgan Kaufmann, San Francisco, CA, 2nd edition, 2006.

D. Hand, H. Mannila, and P. Smyth. *Principles of Data Mining.* MIT Press, Cambridge, MA, 2001.

D. J. Hand. Measuring classifier performance: A coherent alternative to the area under the ROC curve. *Machine Learning,* 77(1):103–123, 2009.

D. J. Hand and R. J. Till. A simple generalization of the area under the ROC curve to multiple classification problems. *Machine Learning,* 45(2):171–186, 2001.

J. A. Hanley and B. J. McNeil. A method of comparing the areas under receiver operating characteristic curves derived from the same cases. *Radiology,* 148(3):839–843, 1983.

L. K. Hansen and P. Salamon. Neural network ensembles. *IEEE Transactions on Pattern Analysis and Machine Intelligence,* 12(10):993–1001, 1990.

M. Harries. Boosting a strong learner: Evidence against the minimum margin. In *Proceedings of the 16th International Conference on Machine Learning,* pages 171–179, Bled, Slovenia, 1999.

T. Hastie and R. Tibshirani. Classification by pairwise coupling. *Annals of Statistics,* 26(2):451–471, 1998.

T. Hastie, R. Tibshirani, and J. Friedman. *The Elements of Statistical Learning.* Springer, New York, NY, 2001.

S. Haykin. *Neural Networks: A Comprehensive Foundation.* Prentice-Hall, Upper Saddle River, NJ, 2nd edition, 1998.

H. He and E. A. Garcia. Learning from imbalanced data. *IEEE Transactions on Knowledge and Data Engineering,* 21(9):1263–1284, 2009.

Z. He, X. Xu, and S. Deng. A cluster ensemble method for clustering categorical data. *Information Fusion,* 6(2):143–151, 2005.

M. Hellman and J. Raviv. Probability of error, equivocation, and the Chernoff bound. *IEEE Transactions on Information Theory,* 16(4):368–372, 1970.

D. Hernández-Lobato, G. Martínez-Muñoz, and A. Suárez. Statistical instance-based pruning in ensembles of independent classifiers. *IEEE Transaction on Pattern Analysis and Machine Intelligence,* 31(2):364–369, 2009.

D. Hernández-Lobato, G. Martínez-Muñoz, and A. Suárez. Empirical analysis and evaluation of approximate techniques for pruning regression bagging ensembles. *Neurocomputing,* 74(12-13):2250–2264, 2011.

A. Hinneburg and D. A. Keim. An efficient approach to clustering in large multimedia databases with noise. In *Proceedings of the 4th International*

Conference on Knowledge Discovery and Data Mining, pages 58–65, New York, NY, 1998.

T. K. Ho. Random decision forests. In *Proceedings of the 3rd International Conference on Document Analysis and Recognition*, pages 278–282, Montreal, Canada, 1995.

T. K. Ho. The random subspace method for constructing decision forests. *IEEE Transactions on Pattern Analysis and Machine Intelligence*, 20(8): 832–844, 1998.

T. K. Ho, J. J. Hull, and S. N. Srihari. Decision combination in multiple classifier systems. *IEEE Transaction on Pattern Analysis and Machine Intelligence*, 16(1):66–75, 1994.

V. Hodge and J. Austin. A survey of outlier detection methodologies. *Artificial Intelligence Review*, 22(2):85–126, 2004.

S. C. H. Hoi, R. Jin, J. Zhu, and M. R. Lyu. Semisupervised SVM batch mode active learning with applications to image retrieval. *ACM Transactions on Information Systems*, 27(3):1–29, 2009.

Y. Hong, S. Kwong, H. Wang, and Q. Ren. Resampling-based selective clustering ensembles. *Pattern Recognition Letters*, 41(9):2742–2756, 2009.

P. Hore, L. Hall, and D. Goldgof. A cluster ensemble framework for large data sets. In *Proceedings of the IEEE International Conference on Systems, Man and Cybernetics*, pages 3342–3347, Taipei, Taiwan, ROC, 2006.

P. Hore, L. O. Hall, and D. B. Goldgof. A scalable framework for cluster ensembles. *Pattern Recognition*, 42(5):676–688, 2009.

C.-W. Hsu and C.-J. Lin. A comparison of methods for multi-class support vector machines. *IEEE Transactions on Neural Networks*, 13(2):415–425, 2002.

X. Hu, E. K. Park, and X. Zhang. Microarray gene cluster identification and annotation through cluster ensemble and EM-based informative textual summarization. *IEEE Transactions on Information Technology in Biomedicine*, 13(5):832–840, 2009.

F.-J. Huang, Z.-H. Zhou, H.-J. Zhang, and T. Chen. Pose invariant face recognition. In *Proceedings of the 4th IEEE International Conference on Automatic Face and Gesture Recognition*, pages 245–250, Grenoble, France, 2000.

S.-J. Huang, R. Jin, and Z.-H. Zhou. Active learning by querying informative and representative examples. In J. Lafferty, C. K. I. Williams, J. Shawe-Taylor, R. S. Zemel, and A. Culotta, editors, *Advances in Neural Informa-*

tion Processing Systems 23, pages 892–900. MIT Press, Cambridge, MA, 2010.

Y. S. Huang and C. Y. Suen. A method of combining multiple experts for the recognition of unconstrained handwritten numerals. *IEEE Transactions on Pattern Analysis and Machine Intelligence*, 17(1):90–94, 1995.

Z. Huang. Extensions to the k-means algorithm for clustering large data sets with categorical values. *Data Mining and Knowledge Discovery*, 2(3): 283–304, 1998.

R. A. Hutchinson, L.-P. Liu, and T. G. Dietterich. Incorporating boosted regression trees into ecological latent variable models. In *Proceedings of the 25th AAAI Conference on Artificial Intelligence*, pages 1343–1348, San Francisco, CA, 2011.

R. A. Jacobs, M. I. Jordan, S. J. Nowlan, and G. E. Hinton. Adaptive mixtures of local experts. *Neural Computation*, 3(1):79–87, 1991.

A. K. Jain and R. C. Dubes. *Algorithms for Clustering Data*. Prentice Hall, Upper Saddle River, NJ, 1988.

A. K. Jain, M. N. Murty, and P. J. Flynn. Data clustering: A review. *ACM Computing Surveys*, 31(3):264–323, 1999.

G. M. James. Variance and bias for general loss functions. *Machine Learning*, 51(2):115–135, 2003.

T. Joachims. Transductive inference for text classification using support vector machines. In *Proceedings of the 16th International Conference on Machine Learning*, pages 200–209, Bled, Slovenia, 1999.

T. Joachims. A support vector method for multivariate performance measures. In *Proceedings of the 22nd International Conference on Machine Learning*, pages 384–391, Bonn, Germany, 2005.

I. T. Jolliffe. *Principal Component Analysis*. Springer, New York, NY, 2nd edition, 2002.

M. I. Jordan and R. A. Jacobs. Hierarchies of adaptive experts. In J. E. Moody, S. J. Hanson, and R. Lippmann, editors, *Advances in Neural Information Processing Systems 4*, pages 985–992. Morgan Kaufmann, San Francisco, CA, 1992.

M. I. Jordan and L. Xu. Convergence results for the EM approach to mixtures of experts architectures. *Neural Networks*, 8(9):1409–1431, 1995.

G. Karypis and V. Kumar. A fast and high quality multilevel scheme for partitioning irregular graphs. *SIAM Journal on Scientific Computing*, 20(1): 359–392, 1998.

G. Karypis, R. Aggarwal, V. Kumar, and S. Shekhar. Multilevel hypergraph partitioning: Application in VLSI domain. In *Proceedings of the 34th Annual Design Automation Conference*, pages 526–529, Anaheim, CA, 1997.

L. Kaufman and P. J. Rousseeuw. *Finding Groups in Data: An Introduction to Cluster Analysis*. John Wiley & Sons, New York, NY, 1990.

M. Kearns. Efficient noise tolerant learning from statistical queries. *Journal of the ACM*, 45(6):983–1006, 1998.

M. Kearns and L. G. Valiant. Cryptographic limitations on learning Boolean formulae and finite automata. In *Proceedings of the 21st Annual ACM Symposium on Theory of Computing*, pages 433–444, Seattle, WA, 1989.

M. J. Kearns and U. V. Vazirani. *An Introduction to Computational Learning Theory*. MIT Press, Cambridge, MA, 1994.

J. Kittler and F. M. Alkoot. Sum versus vote fusion in multiple classifier systems. *IEEE Transactions on Pattern Analysis and Machine Intelligence*, 25(1):110–115, 2003.

J. Kittler, M. Hatef, R. Duin, and J. Matas. On combining classifiers. *IEEE Transactions on Pattern Analysis and Machine Intelligence*, 20(3):226–239, 1998.

E. M. Kleinberg. On the algorithmic implementation of stochastic discrimination. *IEEE Transactions on Pattern Analysis and Machine Intelligence*, 22(5):473–490, 2000.

D. E. Knuth. *The Art of Computer Programming, Volume 3: Sorting and Searching*. Addison-Wesley, Reading, MA, 2nd edition, 1997.

A. H. Ko, R. Sabourin, and J. A. S. Britto. From dynamic classifier selection to dynamic ensemble selection. *Pattern Recognition*, 41(5):1718–1731, 2008.

R. Kohavi and D. H. Wolpert. Bias plus variance decomposition for zero-one loss functions. In *Proceedings of the 13th International Conference on Machine Learning*, pages 275–283, Bari, Italy, 1996.

T. Kohonen. *Self-Organization and Associative Memory*. Springer-Verlag, Berlin, 3rd edition, 1989.

J. F. Kolen and J. B. Pollack. Back propagation is sensitive to initial conditions. In R. Lippmann, J. E. Moody, and D. S. Touretzky, editors, *Advances in Neural Information Processing Systems 3*, pages 860–867. Morgan Kaufmann, San Francisco, CA, 1991.

J. Z. Kolter and M. A. Maloof. Learning to detect and classify malicious executables in the wild. *Journal of Machine Learning Research*, 7:2721–2744, 2006.

E. B. Kong and T. G. Dietterich. Error-correcting output coding corrects bias and variance. In *Proceedings of the 12th International Conference on Machine Learning*, pages 313–321, Tahoe City, CA, 1995.

A. Krogh and J. Vedelsby. Neural network ensembles, cross validation, and active learning. In G. Tesauro, D. S. Touretzky, and T. K. Leen, editors, *Advances in Neural Information Processing Systems 7*, pages 231–238. MIT Press, Cambridge, MA, 1995.

M. Kubat and S. Matwin. Addressing the curse of imbalanced training sets: One sided selection. In *Proceedings of the 14th Intenational Conference on Machine Learning*, pages 179–186, Nashville, TN, 1997.

H. W. Kuhn. The Hungarian method for the assignment problem. *Naval Research Logistics Quarterly*, 2:83–79, 1955.

M. Kukar and I. Kononenko. Cost-sensitive learning with neural networks. In *Proceedings of the 13th European Conference on Artificial Intelligence*, pages 445–449, Brighton, UK, 1998.

L. I. Kuncheva. A theoretical study on six classifier fusion strategies. *IEEE Transactions on Pattern Analysis and Machine Intelligence*, 24(2):281–286, 2002.

L. I. Kuncheva. *Combining Pattern Classifiers: Methods and Algorithms.* John Wiley & Sons, Hoboken, NJ, 2004.

L. I. Kuncheva. Classifier ensembles: Facts, fiction, faults and future, 2008. Plenary Talk at the 19th International Conference on Pattern Recognition.

L. I. Kuncheva and S. T. Hadjitodorov. Using diversity in cluster ensembles. In *Proceedings of the IEEE International Conference on Systems, Man and Cybernetics*, pages 1214–1219, Hague, The Netherlands, 2004.

L. I. Kuncheva and D. P. Vetrov. Evaluation of stability of k-means cluster ensembles with respect to random initialization. *IEEE Transactions on Pattern Analysis and Machine Intelligence*, 28(11):1798–1808, 2006.

L. I. Kuncheva and C. J. Whitaker. Measures of diversity in classifier ensembles and their relationship with the ensemble accuracy. *Machine Learning*, 51(2):181–207, 2003.

L. I. Kuncheva, J. C. Bezdek, and R. P. Duin. Decision templates for multiple classifier fusion: An experimental comparison. *Pattern Recognition*, 34 (2):299–314, 2001.

L. I. Kuncheva, C. J. Whitaker, C. Shipp, and R. Duin. Limits on the majority vote accuracy in classifier fusion. *Pattern Analysis and Applications*, 6(1): 22–31, 2003.

L. I. Kuncheva, S. T. Hadjitodorov, and L. P. Todorova. Experimental comparison of cluster ensemble methods. In *Proceedings of the 9th International Conference on Information Fusion*, pages 1–7, Florence, Italy, 2006.

S. Kutin and P. Niyogi. Almost-everywhere algorithmic stability and generalization error. In *Proceedings of the 18th Conference on Uncertainty in Artificial Intelligence*, pages 275–282, Edmonton, Canada, 2002.

S. W. Kwok and C. Carter. Multiple decision trees. In *Proceedings of the 4th International Conference on Uncertainty in Artificial Intelligence*, pages 327–338, New York, NY, 1988.

L. Lam and S. Y. Suen. Application of majority voting to pattern recognition: An analysis of its behavior and performance. *IEEE Transactions on Systems, Man and Cybernetics - Part A: Systems and Humans*, 27(5):553–568, 1997.

A. Lazarevic and Z. Obradovic. Effective pruning of neural network classifier ensembles. In *Proceedings of the IEEE/INNS International Joint Conference on Neural Networks*, pages 796–801, Washington, DC, 2001.

D. Lewis and W. Gale. A sequential algorithm for training text classifiers. In *Proceedings of the 17th Annual International ACM SIGIR Conference on Research and Development in Information Retrieval*, pages 3–12, Dublin, Ireland, 1994.

M. Li and Z.-H. Zhou. Improve computer-aided diagnosis with machine learning techniques using undiagnosed samples. *IEEE Transactions on Systems, Man and Cybernetics - Part A: Systems and Humans*, 37(6):1088–1098, 2007.

M. Li, W. Wang, and Z.-H. Zhou. Exploiting remote learners in internet environment with agents. *Science China: Information Sciences*, 53(1):64–76, 2010.

N. Li and Z.-H. Zhou. Selective ensemble under regularization framework. In *Proceedings of the 8th International Workshop Multiple Classifier Systems*, pages 293–303, Reykjavik, Iceland, 2009.

S. Z. Li, Q. Fu, L. Gu, B. Schölkopf, and H. J. Zhang. Kernel machine based learning for multi-view face detection and pose estimation. In *Proceedings of the 8th International Conference on Computer Vision*, pages 674–679, Vancouver, Canada, 2001.

R. Liere and P. Tadepalli. Active learning with committees for text categorization. In *Proceedings of the 14th National Conference on Artificial Intelligence*, pages 591–596, Providence, RI, 1997.

H.-T. Lin and L. Li. Support vector machinery for infinite ensemble learning. *Journal of Machine Learning Research*, 9:285–312, 2008.

X. Lin, S. Yacoub, J. Burns, and S. Simske. Performance analysis of pattern classifier combination by plurality voting. *Pattern Recognition Letters*, 24 (12):1959–1969, 2003.

Y. M. Lin, Y. Lee, and G. Wahba. Support vector machines for classification in nonstandard situations. *Machine Learning*, 46(1):191–202, 2002.

F. T. Liu, K. M. Ting, and W. Fan. Maximizing tree diversity by building complete-random decision trees. In *Proceedings of the 9th Pacific-Asia Conference on Knowledge Discovery and Data Mining*, pages 605–610, Hanoi, Vietnam, 2005.

F. T. Liu, K. M. Ting, Y. Yu, and Z.-H. Zhou. Spectrum of variable-random trees. *Journal of Artificial Intelligence Research*, 32(1):355–384, 2008a.

F. T. Liu, K. M. Ting, and Z.-H. Zhou. Isolation forest. In *Proceedings of the 8th IEEE International Conference on Data Mining*, pages 413–422, Pisa, Italy, 2008b.

F. T. Liu, K. M. Ting, and Z.-H. Zhou. On detecting clustered anomalies using SCiForest. In *Proceedings of the European Conference on Machine Learning and Principles and Practice of Knowledge Discovery in Databases*, pages 274–290, Barcelona, Spain, 2010.

X.-Y. Liu and Z.-H. Zhou. The influence of class imbalance on cost-sensitive learning: An empirical study. In *Proceedings of the 6th IEEE International Conference on Data Mining*, pages 970–974, Hong Kong, China, 2006.

X.-Y. Liu and Z.-H. Zhou. Learning with cost intervals. In *Proceedings of the 16th ACM SIGKDD International Conference on Knowledge Discovery and Data Mining*, pages 403–412, Washington, DC, 2010.

X.-Y. Liu, J. Wu, and Z.-H. Zhou. Exploratory undersampling for class-imbalance learning. *IEEE Transactions on Systems, Man, and Cybernetics - Part B: Cybernetics*, 39(2):539–550, 2009.

Y. Liu and X. Yao. Ensemble learning via negative correlation. *Neural Networks*, 12(10):1399–1404, 1999.

S. P. Lloyd. Least squares quantization in PCM. *IEEE Transactions on Information Theory*, 28(2):128–137, 1982.

J. M. Lobo, A. Jiménez-Valverde, and R. Real. AUC: A misleading measure of the performance of predictive distribution models. *Global Ecology and Biogeography*, 17(2):145–151, 2008.

B. Long, Z. Zhang, and P. S. Yu. Combining multiple clusterings by soft correspondence. In *Proceedings of the 4th IEEE International Conference on Data Mining*, pages 282–289, Brighton, UK, 2005.

P. K. Mallapragada, R. Jin, A. K. Jain, and Y. Liu. Semiboost: Boosting for semi-supervised learning. *IEEE Transactions on Pattern Analysis and Machine Intelligence*, 30(11):2000–2014, 2009.

I. Maqsood, M. R. Khan, and A. Abraham. An ensemble of neural networks for weather forecasting. *Neural Computing & Applications*, 13(2):112–122, 2004.

D. D. Margineantu and T. G. Dietterich. Pruning adaptive boosting. In *Proceedings of the 14th International Conference on Machine Learning*, pages 211–218, Nashville, TN, 1997.

H. Markowitz. Portfolio selection. *Journal of Finance*, 7(1):77–91, 1952.

G. Martínez-Muñoz and A. Suárez. Aggregation ordering in bagging. In *Proceedings of the IASTED International Conference on Artifical Intelligence and Applications*, pages 258–263, Innsbruck, Austria, 2004.

G. Martínez-Muñoz and A. Suárez. Pruning in ordered bagging ensembles. In *Proceedings of the 23rd International Conference on Machine Learning*, pages 609–616, Pittsburgh, PA, 2006.

G. Martínez-Muñoz and A. Suárez. Using boosting to prune bagging ensembles. *Pattern Recognition Letters*, 28(1):156–165, 2007.

G. Martínez-Muñoz, D. Hernández-Lobato, and A. Suárez. An analysis of ensemble pruning techniques based on ordered aggregation. *IEEE Transaction on Pattern Analysis and Machine Intelligence*, 31(2):245–259, 2009.

H. Masnadi-Shirazi and N. Vasconcelos. Asymmetric Boosting. In *Proceedings of the 24th International Conference on Machine Learning*, pages 609–616, Corvallis, OR, 2007.

L. Mason, J. Baxter, P. L. Bartlett, and M. Frean. Functional gradient techniques for combining hypotheses. In P. J. Bartlett, B. Schölkopf, D. Schuurmans, and A. J. Smola, editors, *Advances in Large-Margin Classifiers*, pages 221–246. MIT Press, Cambridge, MA, 2000.

A. Maurer and M. Pontil. Empirical Bernstein bounds and sample-variance penalization. In *Proceedings of the 22nd Conference on Learning Theory*, Montreal, Canada, 2009.

A. McCallum and K. Nigam. Employing EM and pool-based active learning for text classification. In *Proceedings of the 15th International Conference on Machine Learning*, pages 350–358, Madison, WI, 1998.

R. A. McDonald, D. J. Hand, and I. A. Eckley. An empirical comparison of three boosting algorithms on real data sets with artificial class noise. In *Proceedings of the 4th International Workshop on Multiple Classifier Systems*, pages 35–44, Guilford, UK, 2003.

W. McGill. Multivariate information transmission. *IEEE Transactions on Information Theory*, 4(4):93–111, 1954.

D. Mease and A. Wyner. Evidence contrary to the statistical view of boosting (with discussions). *Journal of Machine Learning Research*, 9:131–201, 2008.

N. Meinshausen and P. Bühlmann. Stability selection. *Journal of the Royal Statistical Society: Series B*, 72(4):417–473, 2010.

P. Melville and R. J. Mooney. Creating diversity in ensembles using artificial data. *Information Fusion*, 6(1):99–111, 2005.

C. E. Metz. Basic principles of ROC analysis. *Seminars in Nuclear Medicine*, 8(4):283–298, 1978.

D. J. Miller and H. S. Uyar. A mixture of experts classifier with learning based on both labelled and unlabelled data. In M. Mozer, M. I. Jordan, and T. Petsche, editors, *Advances in Neural Information Processing Systems 9*, pages 571–577. MIT Press, Cambridge, MA, 1997.

T. M. Mitchell. *Machine Learning*. McGraw-Hill, New York, NY, 1997.

X. Mu, P. Watta, and M. H. Hassoun. Analysis of a plurality voting-based combination of classifiers. *Neural Processing Letters*, 29(2):89–107, 2009.

I. Mukherjee and R. Schapire. A theory of multiclass boosting. In J. Lafferty, C. K. I. Williams, J. Shawe-Taylor, R. S. Zemel, and A. Culotta, editors, *Advances in Neural Information Processing Systems 23*, pages 1714–1722. MIT Press, Cambridge, MA, 2010.

S. K. Murthy, S. Kasif, and S. Salzberg. A system for the induction of oblique decision trees. *Journal of Artificial Intelligence Research*, 2:1–33, 1994.

A.M. Narasimhamurthy. A framework for the analysis of majority voting. In *Proceedings of the 13th Scandinavian Conference on Image Analysis*, pages 268–274, Halmstad, Sweden, 2003.

A. Narasimhamurthy. Theoretical bounds of majority voting performance for a binary classification problem. *IEEE Transactions on Pattern Analysis and Machine Intelligence*, 27(12):1988–1995, 2005.

S. Nash and A. Sofer. *Linear and Nonlinear Programming*. McGraw-Hill, New York, NY, 1996.

R. Ng and J. Han. Efficient and effective clustering method for spatial data mining. In *Proceedings of the 20th International Conference on Very Large Data Bases*, pages 144–155, Santiago, Chile, 1994.

H. T. Nguyen and A. W. M. Smeulders. Active learning using pre-clustering. In *Proceedings of the 21st International Conference on Machine Learning*, pages 623–630, Banff, Canada, 2004.

K. Nigam, A. McCallum, S. Thrun, and T. Mitchell. Text classification from labeled and unlabeled documents using EM. *Machine Learning*, 39(2-3): 103–134, 2000.

N. J. Nilsson. *Learning Machines: Foundations of Trainable Pattern-Classifying Systems*. McGraw-Hill, New York, NY, 1965.

D. Opitz and R. Maclin. Popular ensemble methods: An empirical study. *Journal of Artificial Intelligence Research*, 11:169–198, 1999.

S. Panigrahi, A. Kundu, S. Sural, and A. K. Majumdar. Credit card fraud detection: A fusion approach using Dempster-Shafer theory and Bayesian learning. *Information Fusion*, 10(4):354–363, 2009.

I. Partalas, G. Tsoumakas, and I. Vlahavas. Pruning an ensemble of classifiers via reinforcement learning. *Neurocomputing*, 72(7-9):1900–1909, 2009.

D. Partridge and W. J. Krzanowski. Software diversity: Practical statistics for its measurement and exploitation. *Information & Software Technology*, 39(10):707–717, 1997.

A. Passerini, M. Pontil, and P. Frasconi. New results on error correcting output codes of kernel machines. *IEEE Transactions on Neural Networks*, 15 (1):45–54, 2004.

M. P. Perrone and L. N. Cooper. When networks disagree: Ensemble method for neural networks. In R. J. Mammone, editor, *Artificial Neural Networks for Spech and Vision*, pages 126–142. Chapman & Hall, New York, NY, 1993.

J. C. Platt. Probabilities for SV machines. In *Advances in Large Margin Classifiers*, pages 61–74. MIT Press, Cambridge, MA, 2000.

R. Polikar, A. Topalis, D. Parikh, D. Green, J. Frymiare, J. Kounios, and C. M. Clark. An ensemble based data fusion approach for early diagnosis of Alzheimer's disease. *Information Fusion*, 9(1):83–95, 2008.

B. R. Preiss. *Data Structures and Algorithms with Object-Oriented Design Patterns in Java*. Wiley, Hoboken, NJ, 1999.

O. Pujol, P. Radeva, and J. Vitrià. Discriminant ECOC: A heuristic method for application dependent design of error correcting output codes. *IEEE Transactions on Pattern Analysis and Machine Intelligence*, 28(6):1007–1012, 2006.

O. Pujol, S. Escalera, and P. Radeva. An incremental node embedding technique for error correcting output codes. *Pattern Recognition*, 41(2):713–725, 2008.

J. R. Quinlan. *C4.5: Programs for Machine Learning.* Morgan Kaufmann, San Francisco, CA, 1993.

J. R. Quinlan. Induction of decision trees. *Machine Learning*, 1(1):81–106, 1998.

Š. Raudys and F. Roli. The behavior knowledge space fusion method: Analysis of generalization error and strategies for performance improvement. In *Proceedings of the 4th International Workshop on Multiple Classifier Systems*, pages 55–64, Guildford, UK, 2003.

R. A. Redner and H. F. Walker. Mixture densities, maximum likelihood and the EM algorithm. *SIAM Review*, 26(2):195–239, 1984.

L. Reyzin and R. E. Schapire. How boosting the margin can also boost classifier complexity. In *Proceedings of the 23rd International Conference on Machine Learning*, pages 753–760, Pittsburgh, PA, 2006.

B. Ripley. *Pattern Recognition and Neural Networks.* Cambridge University Press, Cambridge, UK, 1996.

M. Robnik-Šikonja. Improving random forests. In *Proceedings of the 15th European Conference on Machine Learning*, pages 359–370, Pisa, Italy, 2004.

J. J. Rodriguez, L. I. Kuncheva, and C. J. Alonso. Rotation forest: A new classifier ensemble method. *IEEE Transactions on Pattern Analysis and Machine Intelligence*, 28(10):1619–1630, 2006.

G. Rogova. Combining the results of several neural network classifiers. *Neural Networks*, 7(5):777–781, 1994.

L. Rokach. *Pattern Classification Using Ensemble Methods.* World Scientific, Singapore, 2010.

D. E. Rumelhart, G. E. Hinton, and R. J. Williams. Learning internal representations by error propagation. In D. E. Rumelhart and J. L. McClelland, editors, *Parallel Distributed Processing: Explorations in the Microstructure of Cognition*, volume 1, pages 318–362. MIT Press, Cambridge, MA, 1986.

D. Ruta and B. Gabrys. Application of the evolutionary algorithms for classifier selection in multiple classifier systems with majority voting. In *Proceedings of the 2nd International Workshop on Multiple Classifier Systems*, pages 399–408, Cambridge, UK, 2001.

R. E. Schapire. The strength of weak learnability. *Machine Learning*, 5(2):197–227, 1990.

R. E. Schapire and Y. Singer. Improved boosting algorithms using confidence-rated predictions. *Machine Learning*, 37(3):297–336, 1999.

R. E. Schapire, Y. Freund, P. Bartlett, and W. S. Lee. Boosting the margin: A new explanation for the effectiveness of voting methods. *Annals of Statistics*, 26(5):1651–1686, 1998.

J. Schiffers. A classification approach incorporating misclassification costs. *Intelligent Data Analysis*, 1(1):59–68, 1997.

B. Schölkopf and A. J. Smola. *Learning with Kernels*. MIT Press, Cambridge, MA, 2002.

B. Schölkopf, C. J. C. Burges, and A. J. Smola, editors. *Advances in Kernel Methods: Support Vector Learning*. MIT Press, Cambridge, MA, 1999.

M. G. Schultz, E. Eskin, E. Zadok, and S. J. Stolfo. Data mining methods for detection of new malicious executables. In *Proceedings of the IEEE Symposium on Security and Privacy*, pages 38–49, Oakland, CA, 2001.

A. K. Seewald. How to make stacking better and faster while also taking care of an unknown weakness. In *Proceedings of the 19th International Conference on Machine Learning*, pages 554–561, Sydney, Australia, 2002.

B. Settles. Active learning literature survey. Technical Report 1648, Department of Computer Sciences, University of Wisconsin at Madison, Madison, WI, 2009.

H. S. Seung, M. Opper, and H. Sompolinsky. Query by committee. In *Proceedings of the 5th Annual ACM Conference on Computational Learning Theory*, pages 287–294, Pittsburgh, PA, 1992.

G. Shafer. *A Mathematical Theory of Evidence*. Princeton University Press, Princeton, NJ, 1976.

G. Sheikholeslami, S. Chatterjee, and A. Zhang. WaveCluster: A multiresolution clustering approach for very large spatial databases. In *Proceedings of the 24th International Conference on Very Large Data Bases*, pages 428–439, New York, NY, 1998.

H. B. Shen and K. C. Chou. Ensemble classifier for protein fold pattern recognition. *Bioinformatics*, 22(14):1717–1722, 2006.

J. Shi and J. Malik. Normalized cuts and image segmentation. *IEEE Transactions on Pattern Analysis and Machine Intelligence*, 22(8):888–905, 2000.

C. A. Shipp and L. I. Kuncheva. Relationships between combination methods and measures of diversity in combining classifiers. *Information Fusion*, 3(2):135–148, 2002.

D. B. Skalak. The sources of increased accuracy for two proposed boosting algorithms. In *Working Notes of the AAAI'96 Workshop on Integrating Multiple Learned Models*, Portland, OR, 1996.

N. Slonim, N. Friedman, and N. Tishby. Multivariate information bottleneck. *Neural Computation*, 18(8):1739–1789, 2006.

P. Smyth and D. Wolpert. Stacked density estimation. In M. I. Jordan, M. J. Kearns, and S. A. Solla, editors, *Advances in Neural Information Processing Systems 10*, pages 668–674. MIT Press, Cambridge, MA, 1998.

P. H. A. Sneath and R. R. Sokal. *Numerical Taxonomy: The Principles and Practice of Numerical Classification*. W. H. Freeman, San Francisco, CA, 1973.

V. Soto, G. Martínez-Muñoz, D. Hernández-Lobato, and A. Suárez. A double pruning algorithm for classification ensembles. In *Proceedings of 9th International Workshop Multiple Classifier Systems*, pages 104–113, Cairo, Egypt, 2010.

K. A. Spackman. Signal detection theory: Valuable tools for evaluating inductive learning. In *Proceedings of the 6th International Workshop on Machine Learning*, pages 160–163, Ithaca, NY, 1989.

A. Strehl and J. Ghosh. Cluster ensembles - A knowledge reuse framework for combining multiple partitions. *Journal of Machine Learning Research*, 3:583–617, 2002.

A. Strehl, J. Ghosh, and R. J. Mooney. Impact of similarity measures on webpage clustering. In *Proceedings of the AAAI'2000 Workshop on AI for Web Search*, pages 58–64, Austin, TX, 2000.

M. Studeny and J. Vejnarova. The multi-information function as a tool for measuring stochastic dependence. In M. I. Jordan, editor, *Learning in Graphical Models*, pages 261–298. Kluwer, Norwell, MA, 1998.

Y. Sun, A. K. C. Wong, and Y. Wang. Parameter inference of cost-sensitive boosting algorithms. In *Proceedings of the 4th International Conference on Machine Learning and Data Mining in Pattern Recognition*, pages 21–30, Leipzig, Germany, 2005.

C. Tamon and J. Xiang. On the boosting pruning problem. In *Proceedings of the 11th European Conference on Machine Learning*, pages 404–412, Barcelona, Spain, 2000.

A. C. Tan, D. Gilbert, and Y. Deville. Multi-class protein fold classification using a new ensemble machine learning approach. *Genome Informatics*, 14:206–217, 2003.

P.-N. Tan, M. Steinbach, and V. Kumar. *Introduction to Data Mining*. Addison-Wesley, Upper Saddle River, NJ, 2006.

E. K. Tang, P. N. Suganthan, and X. Yao. An analysis of diversity measures. *Machine Learning*, 65(1):247–271, 2006.

J. W. Taylor and R. Buizza. Neural network load forecasting with weather ensemble predictions. *IEEE Transactions on Power Systems*, 17(3):626–632, 2002.

S. Theodoridis and K. Koutroumbas. *Pattern Recognition*. Academic Press, New York, NY, 4th edition, 2009.

R. Tibshirani. Regression shrinkage and selection via the lasso. *Journal of the Royal Statistical Society: Series B*, 58(1):267–288, 1996a.

R. Tibshirani. Bias, variance and prediction error for classification rules. Technical report, Department of Statistics, University of Toronto, 1996b.

A. B. Tickle, R. Andrews, M. Golea, and J. Diederich. The truth will come to light: Directions and challenges in extracting the knowledge embedded within trained artificial neural networks. *IEEE Transactions on Neural Networks*, 9(6):1057–1067, 1998.

K. M. Ting. A comparative study of cost-sensitive boosting algorithms. In *Proceedings of the 17th International Conference on Machine Learning*, pages 983–990, San Francisco, CA, 2000.

K. M. Ting. An instance-weighting method to induce cost-sensitive trees. *IEEE Transactions on Knowledge and Data Engineering*, 14(3):659–665, 2002.

K. M. Ting and I. H. Witten. Issues in stacked generalization. *Journal of Artificial Intelligence Research*, 10:271–289, 1999.

I. Tomek. Two modifications of CNN. *IEEE Transactions on Systems, Man and Cybernetics*, 6(11):769–772, 1976.

S. Tong and D. Koller. Support vector machine active learning with applications to text classification. In *Proceedings of the 17th International Conference on Machine Learning*, pages 999–1006, San Francisco, CA, 2000.

A. Topchy, A. K. Jain, and W. Punch. Combining multiple weak clusterings. In *Proceedings of the 3rd IEEE International Conference on Data Mining*, pages 331–338, Melbourne, FL, 2003.

A. Topchy, A. K. Jain, and W. Punch. A mixture model for clustering ensembles. In *Proceedings of the 4th SIAM International Conference on Data Mining*, pages 379–390, Lake Buena Vista, FL, 2004a.

A. Topchy, B. Minaei-Bidgoli, A. K. Jain, and W. F. Punch. Adaptive clustering ensembles. In *Proceedings of the 17th International Conference on Pattern Recognition*, pages 272–275, Cambridge, UK, 2004b.

A. P. Topchy, M. H. C. Law, A. K. Jain, and A. L. Fred. Analysis of consensus partition in cluster ensemble. In *Proceedings of the 4th IEEE International Conference on Data Mining*, pages 225–232, Brighton, UK, 2004c.

G. Tsoumakas, I. Katakis, and I. Vlahavas. Effective voting of heterogeneous classifiers. In *Proceedings of the 15th European Conference on Machine Learning*, pages 465–476, Pisa, Italy, 2004.

G. Tsoumakas, L. Angelis, and I. P. Vlahavas. Selective fusion of heterogeneous classifiers. *Intelligent Data Analysis*, 9(6):511–525, 2005.

G. Tsoumakas, I. Partalas, and I. Vlahavas. An ensemble pruning primer. In O. Okun and G. Valentini, editors, *Applications of Supervised and Unsupervised Ensemble Methods*, pages 155–165. Springer, Berlin, 2009.

K. Tumer. *Linear and Order Statistics Combiners for Reliable Pattern Classification*. PhD thesis, The University of Texas at Austin, 1996.

K. Tumer and J. Ghosh. Theoretical foundations of linear and order statistics combiners for neural pattern classifiers. Technical Report TR-95-02-98, Computer and Vision Research Center, University of Texas, Austin, 1995.

K. Tumer and J. Ghosh. Analysis of decision boundaries in linearly combined neural classifiers. *Pattern Recognition*, 29(2):341–348, 1996.

P. D. Turney. Types of cost in inductive concept learning. In *Proceedings of the ICML'2000 Workshop on Cost-Sensitive Learning*, pages 15–21, San Francisco, CA, 2000.

N. Ueda and R. Nakano. Generalization error of ensemble estimators. In *Proceedings of the IEEE International Conference on Neural Networks*, pages 90–95, Washington, DC, 1996.

W. Utschick and W. Weichselberger. Stochastic organization of output codes in multiclass learning problems. *Neural Computation*, 13(5):1065–1102, 2004.

L. G. Valiant. A theory of the learnable. *Communications of the ACM*, 27 (11):1134–1142, 1984.

H. Valizadegan, R. Jin, and A. K. Jain. Semi-supervised boosting for multiclass classification. In *Proceedings of the 19th European Conference on Machine Learning*, pages 522–537, Antwerp, Belgium, 2008.

C. van Rijsbergen. *Information Retrieval*. Butterworths, London, 1979.

V. N. Vapnik. *Statistical Learning Theory*. Wiley, New York, NY, 1998.

P. Viola and M. Jones. Rapid object detection using a boosted cascade of simple features. In *Proceedings of the IEEE Computer Society Conference on Computer Vision and Pattern Recognition*, pages 511–518, Kauai, HI, 2001.

P. Viola and M. Jones. Fast and robust classification using asymmetric Adaboost and a detector cascade. In T. G. Dietterich, S. Becker, and

Z. Ghahramani, editors, *Advances in Neural Information Processing Systems 14*, pages 1311–1318. MIT Press, Cambridge, MA, 2002.

P. Viola and M. Jones. Robust real-time object detection. *International Journal of Computer Vision*, 57(2):137–154, 2004.

L. Wang, M. Sugiyama, C. Yang, Z.-H. Zhou, and J. Feng. On the margin explanation of boosting algorithm. In *Proceedings of the 21st Annual Conference on Learning Theory*, pages 479–490, Helsinki, Finland, 2008.

W. Wang and Z.-H. Zhou. On multi-view active learning and the combination with semi-supervised learning. In *Proceedings of the 25th International Conference on Machine Learning*, pages 1152–1159, Helsinki, Finland, 2008.

W. Wang and Z.-H. Zhou. Multi-view active learning in the non-realizable case. In J. Lafferty, C. K. I. Williams, J. Shawe-Taylor, R. S. Zemel, and A. Culotta, editors, *Advances in Neural Information Processing Systems 23*, pages 2388–2396. MIT Press, Cambridge, MA, 2010.

W. Wang, J. Yang, and R. Muntz. STING: A statistical information grid approach to spatial data mining. In *Proceedings of the 23rd International Conference on Very Large Data Bases*, pages 186–195, Athens, Greece, 1997.

M. K. Warmuth, K. A. Glocer, and S. V. Vishwanathan. Entropy regularized LPBoost. In *Proceedings of the 19th International Conference on Algorithmic Learning Theory*, pages 256–271, Budapest, Hungary, 2008.

S. Watanabe. Information theoretical analysis of multivariate correlation. *IBM Journal of Research and Development*, 4(1):66–82, 1960.

S. Waterhouse, D. Mackay, and T. Robinson. Bayesian methods for mixtures of experts. In D. S. Touretzky, M. Mozer, and M. E. Hasselmo, editors, *Advances in Neural Information Processing Systems 8*, pages 351–357. MIT Press, Cambridge, MA, 1996.

S. R. Waterhouse and A. J. Robinson. Constructive algorithms for hierarchical mixtures of experts. In D. S. Touretzky, M. Mozer, and M. E. Hasselmo, editors, *Advances in Neural Information Processing Systems 8*, pages 584–590. MIT Press, Cambridge, MA, 1996.

C. Watkins and P. Dayan. Q-learning. *Machine Learning*, 8(3):279–292, 1992.

G. I. Webb and Z. Zheng. Multistrategy ensemble learning: Reducing error by combining ensemble learning techniques. *IEEE Transactions on Knowledge and Data Engineering*, 16(8):980–991, 2004.

G. I. Webb, J. R. Boughton, and Z. Wang. Not so naïve Bayes: Aggregating one-dependence estimators. *Machine Learning*, 58(1):5–24, 2005.

P. Werbos. *Beyond regression: New tools for prediction and analysis in the behavior science.* PhD thesis, Harvard University, Cambridge, MA, 1974.

D. West, S. Dellana, and J. Qian. Neural network ensemble strategies for financial decision applications. *Computers & Operations Research*, 32(10): 2543–2559, 2005.

T. Windeatt and R. Ghaderi. Coding and decoding strategies for multi-class learning problems. *Information Fusion*, 4(1):11–21, 2003.

D. H. Wolpert. Stacked generalization. *Neural Networks*, 5(2):241–260, 1992.

D. H. Wolpert. The lack of a priori distinctions between learning algorithms. *Neural Computation*, 8(7):1341–1390, 1996.

D. H. Wolpert and W. G. Macready. No free lunch theorems for optimization. *IEEE Transactions on Evolutionary Computation*, 1(1):67–82, 1997.

D. H. Wolpert and W. G. Macready. An efficient method to estimate bagging's generalization error. *Machine Learning*, 35(1):41–55, 1999.

K. Woods, W. P. Kegelmeyer, and K. Bowyer. Combination of multiple classifiers using local accuracy estimates. *IEEE Transactions on Pattern Analysis and Machine Intelligence*, 19(4):405–410, 1997.

J. Wu, S. C. Brubaker, M. D. Mullin, and J. M. Rehg. Fast asymmetric learning for cascade face detection. *IEEE Transactions on Pattern Analysis and Machine Intelligence*, 30(3):369–382, 2008.

L. Xu and S. Amari. Combining classifiers and learning mixture-of-experts. In J. R. R. Dopico, J. Dorado, and A. Pazos, editors, *Encyclopedia of Artificial Intelligence*, pages 318–326. IGI, Berlin, 2009.

L. Xu and M. I. Jordan. On convergence properties of the EM algorithm for Gaussian mixtures. *Neural Computation*, 8(1):129–151, 1996.

L. Xu, A. Krzyzak, and C. Y. Suen. Methods of combining multiple classifiers and their applications to handwriting recognition. *IEEE Transactions on Systems Man and Cybernetics*, 22(3):418–435, 1992.

L. Xu, M. I. Jordan, and G. E. Hinton. An alternative model for mixtures of experts. In G. Tesauro, D. S. Touretzky, and T. K. Leen, editors, *Advances in Neural Information Processing Systems 7*, pages 633–640. MIT Press, Cambridge, MA, 1995.

L. Yan, R. H. Dodier, M. Mozer, and R. H. Wolniewicz. Optimizing classifier performance via an approximation to the Wilcoxon-Mann-Whitney statistic. In *Proceedings of the 20th International Conference on Machine Learning*, pages 848–855, Washington, DC, 2003.

References

W. Yan and F. Xue. Jet engine gas path fault diagnosis using dynamic fusion of multiple classifiers. In *Proceedings of the International Joint Conference on Neural Networks*, pages 1585–1591, Hong Kong, China, 2008.

Y. Yu, Y.-F. Li, and Z.-H. Zhou. Diversity regularized machine. In *Proceedings of the 22nd International Joint Conference on Artificial Intelligence*, pages 1603–1608, Barcelona, Spain, 2011.

Z. Yu and H.-S. Wong. Class discovery from gene expression data based on perturbation and cluster ensemble. *IEEE Transactions on NanoBioscience*, 18(2):147–160, 2009.

G. Yule. On the association of attributes in statistics. *Philosophical Transactions of the Royal Society of London*, 194:257–319, 1900.

B. Zadrozny and C. Elkan. Learning and making decisions when costs and probabilities are both unknown. In *Proceedings of the 7th ACM SIGKDD International Conference on Knowledge Discovery and Data Mining*, pages 204–213, San Francisco, CA, 2001a.

B. Zadrozny and C. Elkan. Obtaining calibrated probability estimates from decision trees and naive Bayesian classifiers. In *Proceedings of the 18th International Conference on Machine Learning*, pages 609–616, Williamstown, MA, 2001b.

B. Zadrozny, J. Langford, and N. Abe. Cost-sensitive learning by cost-proportionate example weighting. In *Proceedings of the 3rd IEEE International Conference on Data Mining*, pages 435–442, Melbourne, FL, 2003.

M.-L. Zhang and Z.-H. Zhou. Exploiting unlabeled data to enhance ensemble diversity. In *Proceedings of the 9th IEEE International Conference on Data Mining*, pages 609–618, Sydney, Australia, 2010.

T. Zhang. Analysis of regularized linear functions for classification problems. Technical Report RC-21572, IBM, 1999.

T. Zhang, R. Ramakrishnan, and M. Livny. BIRCH: An efficient data clustering method for very large databases. In *Proceedings of the ACM SIGMOD International Conference on Management of Data*, pages 103–114, Montreal, Canada, 1996.

X. Zhang, S. Wang, T. Shan, and L. Jiao. Selective SVMs ensemble driven by immune clonal algorithm. In *Proceedings of the EvoWorkshops*, pages 325–333, Lausanne, Switzerland, 2005.

X. Zhang, L. Jiao, F. Liu, L. Bo, and M. Gong. Spectral clustering ensemble applied to SAR image segmentation. *IEEE Transactions on Geoscience and Remote Sensing*, 46(7):2126–2136, 2008.

Y. Zhang, S. Burer, and W. N. Street. Ensemble pruning via semi-definite programming. *Journal of Machine Learning Research*, 7:1315–1338, 2006.

Z. Zheng and G. I. Webb. Laze learning of Bayesian rules. *Machine Learning*, 41(1):53–84, 2000.

D. Zhou, O. Bousquet, T. N. Lal, J. Weston, and B. Schölkopf. Learning with local and global consistency. In S. Thrun, L. Saul, and B. Schölkopf, editors, *Advances in Neural Information Processing Systems 16*. MIT Press, Cambridge, MA, 2004.

Z.-H. Zhou. Rule extraction: Using neural networks or for neural networks? *Journal of Computer Science and Technology*, 19(2):249–253, 2004.

Z.-H. Zhou. Comprehensibility of data mining algorithms. In J. Wang, editor, *Encyclopedia of Data Warehousing and Mining*, pages 190–195. IGI, Hershey, PA, 2005.

Z.-H. Zhou. When semi-supervised learning meets ensemble learning. In *Proceedings of the 8th International Workshop on Multiple Classifier Systems*, pages 529–538, Reykjavik, Iceland, 2009.

Z.-H. Zhou. When semi-supervised learning meets ensemble learning. *Frontiers of Electrical and Electronic Engineering in China*, 6(1):6–16, 2011.

Z.-H. Zhou and Y. Jiang. Medical diagnosis with C4.5 rule preceded by artificial neural network ensemble. *IEEE Transactions on Information Technology in Biomedicine*, 7(1):37–42, 2003.

Z.-H. Zhou and Y. Jiang. NeC4.5: Neural ensemble based C4.5. *IEEE Transactions on Knowledge and Data Engineering*, 16(6):770–773, 2004.

Z.-H. Zhou and M. Li. Tri-training: Exploiting unlabeled data using three classifiers. *IEEE Transactions on Knowledge and Data Engineering*, 17 (11):1529–1541, 2005.

Z.-H. Zhou and M. Li. Semi-supervised regression with co-training style algorithms. *IEEE Transactions on Knowledge and Data Engineering*, 19 (11):1479–1493, 2007.

Z.-H. Zhou and M. Li. Semi-supervised learning by disagreement. *Knowledge and Information Systems*, 24(3):415–439, 2010a.

Z.-H. Zhou and N. Li. Multi-information ensemble diversity. In *Proceedings of the 9th International Workshop on Multiple Classifier Systems*, pages 134–144, Cairo, Egypt, 2010b.

Z.-H. Zhou and X.-Y. Liu. Training cost-sensitive neural networks with methods addressing the class imbalance problem. *IEEE Transactions on Knowledge and Data Engineering*, 18(1):63–77, 2006.

Z.-H. Zhou and X.-Y. Liu. On multi-class cost-sensitive learning. *Computational Intelligence*, 26(3):232–257, 2010.

Z.-H. Zhou and W. Tang. Selective ensemble of decision trees. In *Proceedings of the 9th International Conference on Rough Sets, Fuzzy Sets, Data Mining and Granular Computing*, pages 476–483, Chongqing, China, 2003.

Z.-H. Zhou and W. Tang. Clusterer ensemble. *Knowledge-Based Systems*, 19 (1):77–83, 2006.

Z.-H. Zhou and Y. Yu. Ensembling local learners through multimodal perturbation. *IEEE Transactions on Systems, Man, and Cybernetics - Part B: Cybernetics*, 35(4):725–735, 2005.

Z.-H. Zhou, Y. Jiang, Y.-B. Yang, and S.-F. Chen. Lung cancer cell identification based on artificial neural network ensembles. *Artificial Intelligence in Medicine*, 24(1):25–36, 2002a.

Z.-H. Zhou, J. Wu, and W. Tang. Ensembling neural networks: Many could be better than all. *Artificial Intelligence*, 137(1-2):239–263, 2002b.

Z.-H. Zhou, Y. Jiang, and S.-F. Chen. Extracting symbolic rules from trained neural network ensembles. *AI Communications*, 16(1):3–15, 2003.

Z.-H. Zhou, K.-J. Chen, and H.-B. Dai. Enhancing relevance feedback in image retrieval using unlabeled data. *ACM Transactions on Information Systems*, 24(2):219–244, 2006.

J. Zhu, S. Rosset, H. Zou, and T. Hastie. Multi-class AdaBoost. Technical report, Department of Statistics, University of Michigan, Ann Arbor, MI, 2006.

X. Zhu. Semi-supervised learning literature survey. Technical Report 1530, Department of Computer Sciences, University of Wisconsin at Madison, Madison, WI, 2006. http://www.cs.wisc.edu/~jerryzhu/pub/ ssl_survey.pdf.

X. Zhu, Z. Ghahramani, and J. Lafferty. Semi-supervised learning using Gaussian fields and harmonic functions. In *Proceedings of the 20th International Conference on Machine Learning*, pages 912–919, Washington, DC, 2003.

X. Zhu, X. Wu, and Y. Yang. Dynamic classifier selection for effective mining from noisy data streams. In *Proceedings of the 14th IEEE International Conference on Data Mining*, pages 305–312, Brighton, UK, 2004.

Index